ALFRED FRIENDLY

—

The Dreadful Day

The Battle of Manzikert, 1071

HUTCHINSON

London Melbourne Sydney Auckland Johannesburg

Hutchinson & Co. (Publishers) Ltd
An imprint of the Hutchinson Publishing Group
3 Fitzroy Square, London w1p 6jd

Hutchinson Group (Australia) Pty Ltd
30–32 Cremorne Street, Richmond South, Victoria 3121
PO Box 151, Broadway, New South Wales 2007

Hutchinson Group (NZ) Ltd
32–34 View Road, PO Box 40–086, Glenfield, Auckland 10

Hutchinson Group (SA) Pty Ltd
PO Box 337, Bergvlei 2012, South Africa

First published 1981
© Alfred Friendly 1981

Set in Monotype Garamond

The coins on pages 15 and 16 were
redrawn by Sally de Wilde

The author and publishers gratefully acknowledge
the Cambridge Medieval History, which provided sources
for some of the maps herein.

Printed in Great Britain by The Anchor Press Ltd
and bound by Wm Brendon & Son Ltd
both of Tiptree, Essex

British Library Cataloguing in Publication Data
Friendly, Alfred
  The dreadful day.
  1. Malazgirt, Battle of, 1071
  I. Title
  956.1′01   DS27

ISBN 0 09 143570 6

*For my children
and theirs*

Contents

Maps

Maps

Acknowledgements

A writer beset from time to time with doubts about the worth-whileness of his efforts owes more than a little thanks to those who, hearing what he was about, urged him on. I hope that a multitude of friends, too many to name, will recognize themselves as members of a valued cheering section and will know my appreciation.

Abundant help in a more learned form came from such authorities in Turkey as Professors Mehmet Altay Köymen and Yavuz Ercan, and from Güner Gürdil, who accompanied me during four hot, dust-blown and tiring days through the regions of historical Armenia where the climactic events of this history took place. In Britain and the United States, authorities such as Professors Carl Max Kortepeter, George Y. Dennis s j, and Geoffrey Lewis read parts or all of my text and gave me as many constructive suggestions as they saved me from a multitude of errors. I hasten, however, to exonerate all of those scholars from any charges that they necessarily endorse my treatment of the material or subscribe to my views and judgements on the events. The mistakes remaining in the book are exclusively home-made; criticisms about them and the substance must run to me, not them.

Unfortunately, I read no Greek, Turkish or Arabic. For necessary source material not translated into modern European languages, I am a most grateful debtor to Father Dennis and David Kovacs for translations from the Greek and to JoAnne Noonan Gümüş, Armağan Tranter and Zeyneb Uşakligil for those from Turkish.

For help of a dozen different varieties my thanks run to a scurry of diplomats: Evan Fotos, Erol Suner, Amet Ersoy; an encyclopedia of scholars: Sir Steven Runciman, Dr Esin Atil, Helen Hill Miller, Lieutenant Commander Andrew David RN; and an excellency of ambassadors: William B. Macomber, Ronald I. Spiers, Martin Herz, Raymond L. Garthoff.

The usual kindnesses were forthcoming from the staffs of the British Library, the London Library and that of B. C. Bloomfield, erstwhile director of the library of the London University School of African and Oriental Studies. My largest debt is to the Dumbarton Oaks Library in Washington and its director, Dr Giles Constable, Susan Boyd and, in particular, its librarian, Irene Vaslev who, with her unfailingly genial staff, showed me far more goodwill than I deserved.

I trust that Sally deWilde already knows my gratitude for the illustrative material she prepared and that the same is true for typing, as endless as it was cheerful, by Caroline E. Cotterell and Maureen L. Rogers.

Throughout the preparation of this book my wife's passion for Turkey and things Turkish gave the word 'helpmeet' deeper meanings than I ever had realized.

ALFRED FRIENDLY
Washington, April 1980

Note on
Names and Spelling

As far as I can determine, no one who has attempted to present to English-speaking readers names of persons and places originally written in Arabic, Armenian, Persian or Turkish has solved the problem of transliteration without violating one or more of the desiderata: reproduction of the original pronunciation, fidelity to the original orthography, consistency and ease of comprehension and identification by the reader. Succeeding no better than anyone else, I have concentrated on the last-mentioned purpose, often at the cost of neglecting the others.

With place names I have attempted at first mention and occasionally thereafter to give the most common medieval use followed by the modern designation, e.g. Melitene/Malatya. With some exceptions where a different rendition seems to me more readily recognizable, I have followed the spelling of the *Cambridge Medieval History*, itself inconsistent, with both Greek and Latin renderings for names and places, but without diacritical marks. Only with modern Turkish names do I oblige the reader to accept a few letters and pronunciations not common in English usage, in order to reproduce the Turkish spelling in modern maps and documents. These are:

c = j

ç = ch

ğ itself silent, but serving to lengthen the vowel that precedes it

1 (undotted) = the shortest vowel in English, as in m*u*rd*e*r, cous*i*n or sail*o*r

j = zh

ö pronounced as in German

ş = sh

ü pronounced as in German

Alp Arslan

Romanus IV and Eudocia

Christ crowning Romanus IV and Eudocia

INTRODUCTION

Plunging Point

Battles should not be called decisive unless they alter history in a durable way, and few of them do so. . . . Yet the aim of all art is to lead to a climax, and the art of war, which is no exception, sometimes brings fate to its plunging point.

Freya Stark
Rome on the Euphrates

By Dame Freya's definition – by any definition – the Battle of Manzikert (modern Turkish: Malazgirt) in August 1071 was decisive. It was the plunging point from which recovery for the Byzantine Empire proved to be impossible. Byzantium, incomparably the world's greatest power for seven centuries, lost at one blow the richest part of its domain, its heartland, leaving the rest to be plucked at and torn away piecemeal by predatory neighbours until, after the longest death-rattle in history, its last remnant, the city of Constantinople, fell to the enemy's sword. At Manzikert a Byzantine emperor was captured for the first time in history. Thereupon the way was opened for the swift Turkish conquest of most of Asia Minor where, some centuries later, a new empire, the Ottoman, was to acquire the dominance and territory that once were Byzantium's.

In a little more than a single generation the victors, unlettered nomadic herdsmen, had moved from the Eurasian steppes to subjugate what is now Iran and Irak; in the next generation, less than twenty years later, their victory in a one-day battle on the steppes of Armenia was to transform Greek Christian Asia Minor into the homeland of a new nation, Moslem Turkey.

The consequences of that sudden victory of the army of Sultan Alp Arslan over that of Emperor Romanus IV Diogenes were not confined to the combatant nations, one ancient, the other in the process of being born; they spread to the entire medieval western world. A balance of power that had endured since the great days of Rome was shattered. A new force appeared to face Europe, utterly different in its culture, its religion and its values. Europe spent the next eight centuries struggling to beat it back.

The most immediate result of Manzikert beyond the borders of Asia Minor was its provocation of the Crusades. Had there been no Turkish triumph, 'no western Crusade would have been possible at all'.[1] There would have been no cause for that convulsive movement with its immense revolutionary aftermath.

It is curious, almost inexplicable, therefore, that a battle that was so profoundly 'to alter history in a durable way' remains so unknown to non-Islamic peoples. Hailed of course by Turks today as a momentous, creative event in their history, its very name goes unrecognized – not even heard of – by most educated laymen in Europe and America. That unawareness has led me to write this book. I believe that the story of the beginning of Byzantium's plunge to extinction, of the Turkification of once-Greek Asia Minor, and of the repercussions on the western world deserves to be better known. The events and conditions leading to the defeat of the Eastern Roman Empire also seem to me to invoke speculation about political matters that concern us today, although I do not suggest that the Near East in the eleventh century presents precise parallels to the world of the twentieth nor that it provides concrete precepts for our own behaviour. Nevertheless, I see matters of timeless relevance in the sour fruits of greed, of unbridled lust for power, of fanatical religious intolerance, of indifference to decency and of the lack – to use an unfashionable word – of patriotism.

It is impossible to imagine a hypothetical national collapse in today's world that would be comparable to the fall of the

Byzantine Empire. No single modern power or people holds such a monopoly of learning and skills, of military strength and cultural superiority, as did the heritor in Constantinople of the Graeco–Roman world. Its Empire did not stretch as far as Rome's at its peak, from the border of Scotland to Mesopotamia, but its territory was large enough: from the top of the Adriatic, through Sicily and Crete, from the Danube to the borders of Persia and into Syria. More important, it had stamped its character more deeply in the lands it held than had Rome. Its territory was Christianized, its military power unrivalled, its political and commercial institutions and its cultural achievements were not merely far superior to those of the rest of the world (China perhaps excepted), but in all important respects these simply did not exist elsewhere.

In assessing the importance of the Battle of Manzikert on the collapse of that mighty organization, a question arises which, although unanswerable, is worth a moment's consideration. Had the decay of the Byzantine Empire by then reached such a point that its doom was inescapable? Was the military defeat only the headsman's blow to a body already sentenced to execution? Or, conversely, if the engagement had ended in a victory for the Emperor Romanus – entirely possible had his strategy during the preliminary stages and his tactics on the day itself been different – could the Empire have survived for many more years of power and glory and would the invaders have been held beyond the borders of Asia Minor? Would not a defeat of the sultan and the destruction of *his* army have relieved Byzantium of its greatest military threat and have granted it a substantial period of recovery and reconstruction under the reign that could have been expected from a triumphant and defence-oriented general?

Most historians take a negative view, convinced that the Empire was doomed and that, had it not been Manzikert, there would have been an equally fatal defeat somewhere else, sooner rather than later. Yet there is room for argument.

For our purposes, however, we can move from speculation to certainty: whatever might have been, the reality is that Manzikert, entailing the annihilation of the Byzantine army and the loss of Asia Minor, was profoundly decisive. It was a giant stride on the road to collapse. 'The Byzantines themselves had no illusions about it,' Steven Runciman notes in *A History of the Crusades*. 'Again and again their historians refer to that dreadful day.'

Since the climactic event was a military one, this book focuses on the developments in the two contesting powers that, in combination, led to a victory for the Seljuk Turks and the greatest battlefield defeat of the Byzantines in their history. Its relatively sudden result – in from two to ten years – was the stripping from Constantinople of its rule over more than half of its territory, that which was the richest producer of food, revenue, commerce and the finest soldiery. Its writ in Asia Minor came to run, if at all, only here and there, sporadically and uncertainly.

Amazingly, no one in Europe at the time appears to have appreciated the consequences that were implicit in the dreadful day of Manzikert. No one seemed to grasp that the bastion that for more than seven hundred years had withstood pagan and Moslem invasion of Europe had fallen. Even the Popes, notably Gregory VII and Urban II, saw need for action only for essentially religious objectives in Asia Minor and the Holy Land alone. Quickest to see in the collapse of the old balance of power a self-serving opportunity – although not any menace to Europe – were the Italian trading states. They set out to strip commercial advantage from the broken victim. Ultimately the Crusaders came to see what the Venetians and Genoese and Pisans saw, and in the end acted even more greedily and ruthlessly.

I remarked above that Manzikert as an event and even as a name remains almost unknown to the western world. I must add at once, however, that it has been thoroughly studied by European and Near Eastern historians of Byzantium and Turkey. Their work, intense for more than a century, has disclosed most of what there is likely to be known about Manzikert and its immediate period – barring some wonder like the discovery of the Dead Sea Scrolls. Their books and monographs fill libraries; Byzantine and Turkish historical research, long neglected, now thrives as it deserves.

Those scholars, therefore, will find nothing new in this book. At best, they will discover some small fraction of their own exhaustive labours repeated in these pages. My debt to them is total, as will be apparent. The bibliography and references show those from whom I have drawn in stepping into what was for me *terra incognita*.

The justification I make for writing this book is to present a distillation of the major work of those specialists about one crucial event in Turko–Byzantine history in terms that I hope will serve the general reader.

1   *Asia Minor, Armenia, Syria, Northern Mesopotamia*

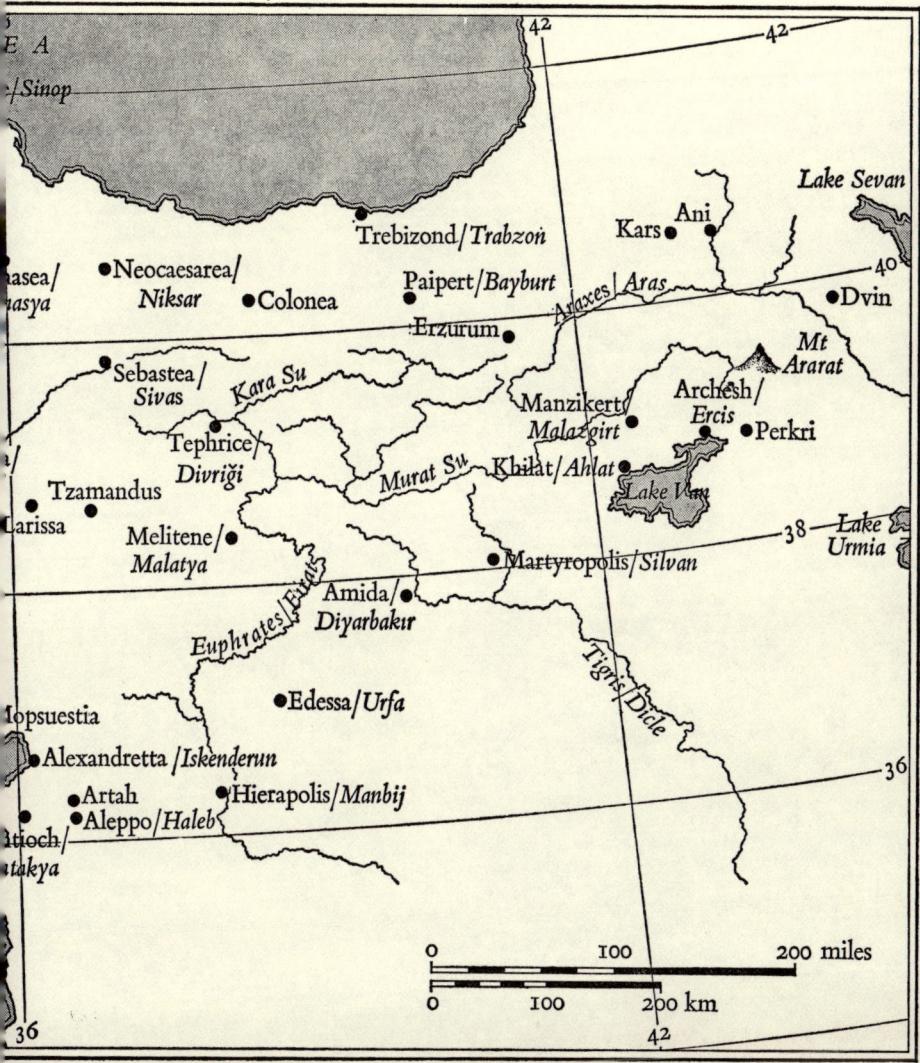

E A

/Sinop

asea/
asya

Trebizond/*Trabzon*

Kars Ani

Lake Sevan

42

42

●Neocaesarea/
Niksar

●Colonea

Paipert/*Bayburt*

Dvin

40

●Erzurum

Araxes / Aras

●Sebastea/
Sivas

Kara Su

Manzikert/
Malazgirt

Archesh/
Ercis

Mt
Ararat

●Tephrice/
Divriği

Tzamandus

Murat Su

Khilat/*Ahlat*

Perkri

Larissa

●Melitene/
Malatya

Martyropolis/*Silvan*

Lake Van

Lake
Urmia

38

Amida/
Diyarbakır

Euphrates/Furat

●Edessa/*Urfa*

Tigris/Dicle

1opsuestia

●Alexandretta /*Iskenderun*

●Artah

Hierapolis/*Manbij*

●Aleppo/*Haleb*

36

tioch/
takya

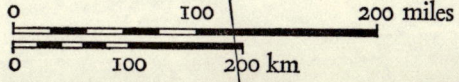

0   100   200 miles

0   100   200 km

36

42

I

The Wolves of the Steppes

Armed with a huge bow and long arrows, the Hun
never misses his mark. Woe to him at whom he aims, for
his arrows bring death!

Sidonius Apollinaris[1]

From a beam of light came a great dog-wolf with a grey
coat and mane.

Oghuz-name
(Medieval Turkoman epic)

For the Seljuks, as for the Oghuz Turks (Arabic: *Ghuzz*;
Byzantine: *Ouzoi* or *Uzes*) of whom they were a part, fighting
was a way of life. From their first appearance toward the end
of the tenth century until they were no longer discernible as
an entity some three hundred years later, the history of the
Seljuks was one of warfare – against Iranians, Arabs, Armenians, Byzantines, European Crusaders and not least against
their own Turkish cousins.

By origin they were nomads, and great bodies of them
remained so to the end. As such, their economic imperatives
allowed scant regard for the niceties of legal ownership or for
the sanctity of their settled neighbours' posessions and
borders. In Owen Lattimore's often-quoted epigram: 'A pure
nomad is a poor nomad is a hungry and daring nomad.' They
were, as well, people of the horse, animals which not only
permit but seem also to impel those who own them to dominate
those who do not. And finally, at the beginning of their history

or soon thereafter, they became Moslems at a time and place where ardour for holy war against infidel and dissident was flaming; the Seljuks seized the torch with the zeal of the convert.

For them and their neighbours, then, there was no peace. The truces to which they occasionally agreed carried little expectation of durability and their formal treaties were almost as fragile. If they entered an alliance with a stronger power, they committed themselves to supply troops in inevitable future battles with other enemies; if they were victors, they imposed an equivalent obligation on the vanquished.

Although the Seljuks wrote no contemporary accounts of their early history, their story is well enough documented by Persian, Arab and Christian chroniclers to be followed with some clarity. Much less is known of their ancestors, but something must be said of them nevertheless (although a 'probably' or 'perhaps' must be implicit in many statements about them) if the deeds and nature of their descendants are to be understood.

The earliest peoples, generally identified as Turks, although not so named, were the Huns, known to the Chinese as early as the third century BC and to the late Roman and Germanic worlds towards the end of the fourth century AD. Something of the terror which their incursions into Europe engendered, even before Attila, can be seen in the account of Ammianus Marcellinus, last of the great Roman historians, writing towards the close of the fourth century.

The Huns exceed anything that can be imagined in ferocity and barbarism. They gash their children's cheeks to prevent their beards growing. Their stocky body, huge arms, and disproportionately large head give them a monstrous appearance. They live like beasts. They neither cook nor season their food; they live on wild roots and on meat pounded tender under the saddle. They are ignorant of the use of the plow and of fixed habitations, whether houses or huts. Being perpetually nomadic, they are inured from childhood to cold, hunger, and thirst. Their herds follow them on their migrations, with some of the animals being used to draw the covered wagons in which their families live. Here it is that their women spin and make clothes, bear children, and rear them until puberty. If you inquire of these men whence they come and where they were born, they cannot tell you. Their dress consists of a linen tunic and a coat of ratskins sewn together. The tunic, which is of a dark color, is worn until it rots away on their bodies. They never change it until it drops off. A helmet or cap pushed back on their heads and goatskins rolled about their hairy legs complete their attire. Their shoes, cut without shape or measure, do not allow them to walk in ease: thus they are quite unsuited to fight as infantry. Yet mounted they seem riveted to their ugly little horses, which are tireless and swift as lightning. They spend their lives on horseback, sometimes astride, sometimes sideways, like women. They hold their meetings thus; they buy and sell, drink and eat – even sleep, lying on the neck of their mounts. In battle, they swoop upon the enemy, uttering frightful yells. When opposed they disperse, only to return with the same speed, smashing and overturning everything in their path. They have no notion of how to take a fortified position or an entrenched camp. Yet there is nothing to equal the skill with which – from prodigious distances – they discharge their arrows, which are tipped with sharpened bone as hard and murderous as iron.[2]

The passage is quoted at length because it remained valid for more than a thousand years with only insignificant variations in detail, not merely for the Huns, soon to disappear from history, but for all Turkic peoples in their nomad state, including the Seljuks with whom we are directly concerned.

The first references to elements of this vast ethnic aggregation as Turks were made by the Chinese and the Byzantines in the sixth century. Almost certainly sharing a common ancestry with the Huns, the Turks appeared initially in Mongolia and soon expanded south and west.* But, inasmuch as their earlier history is non-existent, they came on the scene as if out of nowhere, proprietors and constituents of a Turkish 'empire', embracing in the sixth century most of what is now Russian Turkestan, stretching from the Volga and Caspian Sea east and north to the Altai Mountains and the borders of Siberia, that is, in the political terms of the time, from the Persian and Byzantine territories to China. It was the largest nomad realm up to that time[4] and second only to that of the Mongols some seven hundred years later. 'Empire' it

*The Chinese name for a major tribe, since become the term for a whole group of peoples sharing a common language, was T'u-chüeh, probably a Mongol plural form Türküt, from the singular Türk.[3]

was called in early chronicles and as an 'empire' it was remembered by Turks and others for centuries to come. In actuality, it was doubtless a loose confederation of various tribal groups, each retaining and asserting its autonomy when it chose: an amalgam 'which might pass within a few days from a vast creation to utter disintegration or vice versa, one day following and the next disavowing a chieftain who . . . was no more than a leader of military operations'.[5] The original 'empire', then, was anything but stable; at one stage it split in two, with parts being subjected to Chinese rulers; at another short moment it was reunited, and finally it was completely fragmented.[6]

Depending on the geographical areas into which the several tribal segments dispersed, they were inescapably influenced by the different civilizations they encountered – principally the Chinese, Persian and Byzantine – but, as with many other primitive peoples, they clung conservatively to their fundamental tribal political systems, their pastoral economy and their nomad way of life – characteristics that survive today in many areas of Central Asia and among a not inconsiderable number of family groups or clans in Turkey itself. Above all, and of enormous future consequence in terms of solidarity and ultimately of nationhood, their language survived triumphantly, resisting, displacing and supplanting others. Centuries later, knowledge of Turkish was the entry requirement to real power and social status for Albanian, Greek, Slav, Kurd and Arab constituents of the Ottoman Empire.[7]

Their economy was based on their flocks of sheep, driven over long distances to and from summer and winter pastures as the seasons dictated and on the two-humped Bactrian camel, resistant to cold but not to excessive heat.[8] But if mutton and milk were the means of their survival, the horse was the means of their conquests. The steppe, Grousset observes, is the land of the horse and the man of the steppe is the horseman born. 'The horseman of the lightning raids was a mounted archer who brought down his adversary from a distance, shot by retreating . . . and waged war as he pursued game or mares: with the arrow and lasso.' So mounted and with that weapon, he was invincible for a millennium wherever he chose to attack. For the Middle Ages, he was the master of a weapon 'almost as effective and demoralizing in its time as that of the gunners of our time'.[9] His superiority was ended only in the sixteenth century, and then of a sudden, when he was met by artillery. Small wonder that in his folklore, such little of it as has survived, the horse stands as the status symbol of the warrior and leader, the object of pride and satisfaction and the sacred sacrifice in the funeral ritual.[10]

As his history and folklore make clear, the steppe-dwelling Turk rejoiced in the act of war; fighting, *per se*, was a gladsome thing, a means of attaining a glorious death, much to be preferred to perishing by accident or illness. But it requires no deep analysis to realize that a philosophy in which battle is the ultimate good must derive from an existence in which battle is a necessity for survival.

As a herdsman on the semi-desert, confined to its meagre resources, the nomad lived a life of terrible privation: '. . . one year in ten the watering places dried up, grass withered, and livestock perished, and with them the nomad himself'. But on his borders, east and west and south, he could glimpse what seemed to him unimaginable riches.

The poor Turko-Mongol herdsman who in years of drought ventured across the meagre grazing of the steppe from one dried-up waterhole to another, to the very fringe of cultivation . . . gazed thunderstruck at the miracle of sedentary civilization: luxuriant crops, villages crammed with grain, and the luxury of the towns. This miracle, or rather its secret – the patient toil required to maintain these human lives – was beyond [his] comprehension. . . . If he was fascinated, it was like the wolf – his totem – when in snowy weather it draws near to the farms and spies its prey within the wattled fence. He too had the age-old impulse to break in, plunder and escape with his booty.[11]

The time came when the rude herdsman of the steppe saw that that wealth which he beheld from a distance could be his for the taking.

What is surprising is not so much that these poor herdsmen became the military superiors of their neighbours but that even while still on the steppes they possessed no small skill in the art of governance. They were talented in tribal administration and knowledgeable in the diplomacy and policy of the nation states on their borders.[12] But if they were no innocents in political affairs, judged by their material possessions they were an astonishing barbarian anachronism. Except for the metal in their weapons and utensils (and the goods plundered from across their frontiers), their material culture was a relic, surviving into the late Middle Ages, of societies that ante-dated the civilizations of ancient Egypt and Mesopotamia. From the Indies, across China, southwards through Persia, westward to Byzantium and on to Europe, there was in the tenth and eleventh centuries A D an almost uniform level of agricultural and manufacturing achievement; in those terms, however, the steppe 'remained a preserve of bar-barism'.[13]

In such circumstances, Grousset argues, the periodic, bloodthirsty raids of the nomads into cultivated areas 'amoun-ted almost to a physical law, dictated by conditions prevailing in their native steppes'. The lure was not booty alone, but territory itself, land for the flocks. As noted above, the nomad did not understand how to perpetuate the agriculture of his sedentary neighbours once he overran them, nor did he care to; the result of his early conquests, accordingly, was the reversion of ploughed fields to pastures. The nomad's demand for a pastoral life was inborn and remained dominant. In the course of expansion, Owen Lattimore points out, 'a society may move into a gradually changing terrain; but if so, it is not to seek a different terrain, but one that is as like as possible to the terrain that it already knows how to use.'[14] It was precisely thus with the Oghuz Turk and with its tribe which became dominant, the Seljuks: Transoxania, where their first major assaults began, Northern Persia, Azerbaijan and Armen-ia, where the conquests continued, and the Anatolian plateau, where they approached their climax, are all extensions of the Central Asian steppe.

One of the most illuminating descriptions of the Oghuz in the first quarter of the tenth century, when the spread of Islam was in its early stages, was written by Ahmad Ibn Fadlan, sent by the Caliph of Baghdad in 921 to the King of the Bulgars, then on the Volga. The prince had asked for an engineer to design fortifications and for a scholar capable of instructing him in the Islamic religion.[15]

Leading what was apparently a large party, Ibn Fadlan set out for the Volga by way of Turkestan, then a better and safer route than via the Caucasus, and soon found himself in the middle of Oghuz territory. He kept a journal, in effect a report to the Caliph, portions of which have come down to us in various manuscripts. It is, Cahen observes, 'a document of the highest importance on the subject of the customs, which he observed excellently, of peoples about whom, but for him, we should know almost nothing'. As distinct from the journals of travellers before and after him, retailing fanciful nonsense about incredible monsters and non-existent marvels, Ibn Fadlan reported with a dispassionate accuracy.

A translation of an early section of his account provides a portrayal of the Oghuz almost on the eve of their conversion to Islam:

The Oghuz are nomads and have houses of felt. They stay for a time in one place and then travel on. One sees their dwellings placed here and there according to nomadic custom. Although they lead a hard existence they are like asses gone astray. They have no religious bonds, nor do they have recourse to reason. They never pray, rather do they call their headmen lords. . . .

The Oghuz do not wash themselves either after defecation or urination, nor do they bathe after ejaculation or on other occasions. They have nothing whatever to do with water, especially in winter.

Their women veil themselves neither in the presence of their own men nor of others, nor does the woman cover any of her bodily parts in the presence of any person. One day we stopped off with one of them and were seated there. The man's wife was present. As we conversed, the woman uncovered her pudenda and scratched it, and we saw her doing it. Then we veiled our faces and said, 'I beg God's pardon.' Her husband laughed and said to the interpreter, 'Tell them we uncover it in your presence so that you may see it and be abashed, but it is not to be attained. This, however, is better than when you cover it up and yet it is reachable.' Adultery is unknown among them; but whomsoever they find by his conduct that he is an adulterer, they tear him in two: they bring together the branches of two trees, tie him to them and then let both trees go, so that he is torn in two. . . .

Their marriage customs are as follows: One of them asks for the hand of a female member of another's family, whether his daughter or his sister or any other one of those over whom he has authority, against so and so many garments from Khwarizm [Moslem principality south of Lake Aral]. When he pays it, he brings her home. The marriage price often consists of camels, pack-animals or other things; and no one can take a wife until he has fulfilled the obligation. If, however, he has met it, then he comes without any ado, enters the abode where she is, takes her in the presence of her father, mother and brothers; these do not prevent him. If a man dies who has a wife and children, then the eldest of his sons takes her to wife if she is not his mother.

None of the merchants or other Moslems may perform in their presence the ablution after seminal emission, except in the night when they do not see it, for they get angry and say, 'This man wishes to put a spell on us for he is immersing himself in water,' and they compel him to pay a fine.

No Moslem can enter their country until one of the Turks has become his host, with whom he stays and for whom he brings garments from the land of Islam and for his wife a kerchief and some pepper, millet, raisins and nuts. When the Moslem comes to his friend, the latter pitches a tent for him and brings him sheep in accordance with his (the Turk's) wealth, so that the Moslem himself may slaughter the sheep, for the Turks do not slaughter, but one of them beats the sheep on the head until it is dead. . . .

[A certain Turk declared that] 'if any of the Turks becomes sick and has female and male slaves, these look after him and no one of his family comes near him. They pitch a tent for him apart from the house and he does not depart from it until he dies or gets well. If, however, he is a slave or a poor man, they leave him in the desert and go their way.'

When one of their prominent men dies, they dig for him a great pit in the form of a house and they go to him, dress him in a *qurtaq* with his belt and bow . . . , put a drinking cup of wood in his hand with intoxicating drink in it and come with his entire possessions and put them with him in this house. Then they set him down in it also. Then they build a house over him and make a kind of cupola out of mud. Then they go at his horses in accordance with their number. They slaughter one to two hundred at the grave down to the last one. Then they eat their flesh down to the head, the hooves, the hide and the tail, for they hang these up on wooden poles and say, 'These are his steeds on which he rides to paradise.' If he has killed anyone and has been a hero, then they carve statues out of wood in the number of those whom he has slain, place them upon his grave and say, 'These are his pages who serve him in paradise.' . . .

We stopped with their army commander [and gave him presents of money], musk, red leather, two suits from Merv out of which we cut two *qurtaqs* for him, then a pair of boots of red leather, a coat of brocade and five coats of silk. . . . Then he took off the coat of brocade which he wore to don the garment of honor we have mentioned. Then I saw that the *qurtaq* which he had on underneath was fraying apart from dirt, for it is their custom that no one shall take off the garment which he wears on his body until it disintegrates. . . .

The Turks speak of him as their best horseman; and I in very truth saw one day when he raced with us on his horse and as a goose flew over us how he strung his bow and then, guiding his horse under it, shot at it and brought it down.[16]

Ibn Fadlan's report shows, if nothing else, how little manners and customs had changed among the Turkic nomads in the six centuries since Ammianus first described the Huns.

In the raids of the Oghuz southwards and south-westwards towards the Persian Empire, just as in their kinsmen's raids centuries earlier northwards, and eastwards, against China, the nations that were attacked disposed of vastly greater military forces than were at the nomads' command. How, then, were the latter so successful?

The principal explanation has already been stated: an incredibly mobile cavalry of expert bowmen. But there were also other contributing factors. The nomads were habitually armed, always under the discipline of tribal military leaders and ready for the word of command. They were trained from childhood in hunting, the techniques of which – the ruses, the patient stalking, the driving of deer for miles across the plain – were almost identical to those employed against human prey.

Moreover, the horse nomads could mobilize for war not only swiftly but at little economic cost to themselves and with few changes in their customary way of life. Striking tents, loading possessions and equipment on their camels and carts, moving quickly and in an organized, long-accustomed system over large distances were the fundamental rhythms of their lives; 'mobility in fact was the key to successful grazing of animals'.[17] The routine for purposes of conquest and booty was little different from and not much more difficult than that followed in periods of peace. But, in contrast, for a people and a society based on settled agriculture the cost of conversion to a war footing was high and the difficulties were considerably greater. The nomads could concentrate for surprise assaults, pillage quickly and then disappear; the conventional forces of the peoples who were attacked could respond only slowly and by cumbersome marches to the scene. If the marauders were pursued, they could turn, harry the pursuer, weary him and, if they failed to bring him down through feints and ambushes, they could simply melt away.

Speaking of Turko–Mongol attacks at an earlier period on China, but in a pronouncement valid in every respect for the later Oghuz raids, Lattimore writes:

Only rarely and when they were lucky could expeditions from China [read, equally well, Persia or Byzantium] inflict real damage on the nomads by capturing their camps and herds; normally, there was time to move out of the way. When the nomads attacked, on the other hand, they attacked fixed targets; they could raid the farm-lands in the harvest season and carry away grain, and when they succeeded in cutting the communications of a city and capturing it, the plunder was immense. Moreover they could often, by the mere threat of attack, collect a kind of blackmail or Danegeld.[18]

It is worth remembering – as the Seljuks themselves always remembered – that those military advantages were always theirs to exploit, and were in fact continuously exploited with disastrous results for the much more advanced peoples whom they attacked. The nomad tactics ended only with their con-quest of most of what is present-day Turkey, when and where they established settled principalities of their own. If the Battle of Waterloo was won on the playing-fields of Eton, so also that great Seljuk triumph, the battle for Anatolia, was won on the steppes of Central Asia.

2

From Pagan to Moslem

> Of counting the nobles of the Oghuz there could be no
> end; ... without more ado they charged at the infidel,
> they wielded their swords. The thunderous drums were
> beaten, the brazen horns, gold-curlicued, were blown.
> On that day the manly warriors showed their mettle. On
> that day the unmanly spied out roads by which to slink
> away. On that day there was a battle like doomsday and
> the field was full of heads. Heads were cut off like balls.
> Falcon-swift horses galloped until they lost their shoes,
> pure black swords were wielded until they lost their
> edges, the three-feathered beech-wood arrows were shot
> until they lost their points.[1]
>
> *The Book of Dede Korkut*

The Turks who were to overrun Asia Minor in the last quarter
of the eleventh century were inspired not only by prospects of
pillage and pasture but also by the holy purpose of extending
the faith of Islam and crushing the infidel. Yet barely a century
earlier their religion was shamanism (as it no doubt had been
for some millennia) and however ardently they embraced the
new doctrine a sizable residue of the old customs, practices
and religious concepts remained deeply embedded.* That

*A good bit of shamanist inheritance in the form of popular supersti-
tions and folk stories of the supernatural, replete with ogres, benign
spirits, seers and workers of prodigious miracles, remains even among
many of today's Turks, not to mention those of Ottoman times. For
interesting and amusing evidence see *Everyday Life in Ottoman Turkey*, by
Raphaela Lewis, London, 1971, Chapter 3, and *Tales Alive in Turkey* by
Warren S. Walker and Ahmet E. Uysal, Harvard, 1966, Part I.[2]

heritage, coupled not as incongruously as it might at first appear with the fervour of Islamic dogma, helps explain the ferocity with which the Seljuk raiders fell upon Byzantine territory. Both shamanism and primitive Islam were the religions of warriors.

Shamanism, attributing to deities or transcendental beings – some beneficent, some malign – the ability to control natural and supernatural forces and who therefore must be dealt with by conjuration, would appear to have been the 'natural' or earliest of all religions; one form of it or another appears among a large number of primitive peoples. The cave-paintings, engravings and carvings of paleolithic populations attest to its antiquity. The agent by which the powers of the world beyond are to be influenced, or by whom their intent is to be determined, is the shaman, a member of the tribe who is in some way extraordinary, often physically or psychologically aberrant (one Turkish scholar, Fuat Küprülü, notes that all shamans sported handlebar moustaches), who is able to communicate directly with those occult majesties while in a trance or ecstatic state. Shamanism has been investigated more extensively among Ural–Altaic peoples than among others, doubtless because it lingered longer with them than elsewhere – well into this century – and to some extent still continues among peoples in the Altai Mountains, Manchuria and Siberia.

The observed rites and beliefs are thought to be strikingly similar to those of the medieval Turks on the eve of their conversion to Islam.[3] They need not be described, nor the hierarchy of the spirits, nor the manner, often coercive, of enlisting the shaman to his calling, nor the methods of his divinations and conjuries. All that is important for our purpose are two aspects of shamanism that must have had some survival value to the society and seem themselves to have survived even after its members embraced the Koran.

In performing the vital role of communicating directly with the gods above the earth and the evil spirits below it, the shaman

gave to his tribal members what has been termed 'psychic integrity', the assurance that a member of their own tribe could intercede for them in critical circumstances produced by inhabitants of the unseen world. Thus, in matters of birth, death, marriage, warfare and tragedy, the shaman was called upon to speak a good word. . . .

Perhaps most important in terms of the Turkic authority structure, every head of a family was recognized as the head of the domestic cult. . . . The implication here is fundamental: the family patriarch could communicate with the spirits to reinforce family discipline and his authority. Symbolically, the weapons of the warriors served as a defense against evil spirits in the struggle for life, health, fertility and the world of 'light' against death, disease, sterility, disaster and darkness.[4]

Shamanism among the Oghuz, if not elsewhere, was remarkably devoid of the moral content or ethical bases that underlie Judaism, Christianity and Islam. There was to be a sure faith in the hereafter, but there was little if any emphasis on the notions of judgement by a higher authority and punishment for transgressions. Indeed, it *was* no transgression to pillage and destroy as long as the injury was done to an extratribal enemy; as for slaughtering such enemies, the more the better, inasmuch as those killed would be servitors of the killer in the hereafter, in token of which statues of those who had fallen to the victor's sword or arrow were erected near his grave,[5] as noted by Ibn Fadlan.

Mohammed's warrior-followers, bent on conquest and converting, made Iraq and Western Persia their own within only two or three decades after the Prophet's death. The expansion continued rapidly in the next few years to Eastern Persia as well. Besides the Arab colonists themselves, the body of the faithful came to include the Persian aristocracy who ruled the Khurasan.[6] All were staunch adherents to the orthodox Sunni persuasion. It was from this group – established in Persia well before the end of the seventh century – that Islam was carried to the Turkic peoples on the steppes to the north.

When the Oghuz and other Turkic peoples were ultimately converted, it is significant that their successful proselytizers were not the Moslem lawyers or scholars preaching a doctrinaire theology replete with sectarian controversy. That was something which the nomads always found unsuited to their needs. Rather, they embraced 'the universal, primitive Islam at war with its infidel neighbours', which was brought to them

by itinerant monks and Moslem mystics, particularly the
Sufis, by frontier soldiers and by Arab merchants venturing
northwards from Persia on the trade routes leading eastwards
across Central Asia towards China, or in the other direction,
towards the Bulgars and Khazars north of the Black Sea.[7]
Although the Oghuz princes who were soon to rise to military
and political power in the Moslem states took on the role of
the most dedicated defenders of Sunnite orthodoxy, the mass
of their followers, while no less Moslem, 'professed a folk-
Islam very different from the orthodoxy'.[8]

The change from shamanism to Islam, even folk-Islam,
may have been revolutionary in terms of theology but it
probably did not greatly affect the age-old values and patterns
of the nomads' daily lives. If anything, Moslem authoritarian-
ism reinforced the leaders' tribal and family discipline. And
if taking lives and ravaging the lands of the infidel were the
means by which the ends of expanding Islam were served, then
the new converts' traditional pleasures were now happily
endowed with a pious rationale. No substantial change was
demanded in the virtues they had cherished: loyalty to the
family and the group and their leaders, reckless and romantic
courage, military prowess, lavish and ostentatious largesse
to their companions and generosity to the poor among them.

One sees those values illustrated best – and, since not much
else of the Oghuz' pre-Islamic literature has survived, almost
uniquely – in *The Book of Dede Korkut*. It is a series of a dozen
stories from the heroic age of the Oghuz; although it was not
put in written form until sometime between the thirteenth and
fifteenth centuries, and accordingly appears as if in an Islamic
setting, 'there is no possible doubt that the basic material of
the stories is far older'.[9] In the society that the document
glorifies, the members eat horsemeat, a practice not forbidden
by the Koran but nevertheless not often encountered among
Moslems; wine and fermented milk are drunk at their feasts;
on the death of a hero, his horse is slaughtered and an elaborate
funeral feast is held; a dying hero demands that his horse's
tail be severed; a boy is not given his lifetime name until he
has lopped off heads in battle.

The narrator is Dede ('Grandfather') Korkut, who may or
may not have been a real person. He appears as soothsayer,

priest, bard and occasional wonder-worker. He celebrates an aristocratic society; the heroes are almost exclusively of noble blood; their treasured possessions are horses – above all, horses – camels, flocks, falcons, hordes of slaves of both sexes, gold-decorated felt tents, ornate robes, gold and silver jewellery and a variety of weapons: mighty bows, maces, swords and 'sixty-span' lances. Warriors of fearsome mien (one could knot his moustache six times behind his neck before going into battle), they slaughtered their enemies by the hundred. Monsters, demons and miracle-workers abounded in their plains and forests. A typical pre-battle boast – invariably fulfilled by the end of the story – was, 'I shall raid the bloody infidels' land,* I shall cut off heads and spill blood, I shall make the infidel vomit blood, I shall bring back slaves and slavegirls. I shall show my cleverness.'

One senses here a nomad society with faint and distorted Arthurian overtones: high-born, boon companion knights wage the wars of their king, undertake deeds of derring-do, rescue captured princes (and occasionally princesses) against insurmountable odds, but with only an occasional act of chivalry and totally without any notion of purification through the quest for the Holy Grail and, principally, without the near-pathological reverence for chaste and gentle maidens.† There are no Lily Maids of Astolat among the Oghuz. The ideal heroine-princess of *Dede Korkut* could wrestle her noble suitor to the ground, out-ride him, out-shoot him and, as often was necessary, rescue him from peril by slaughtering as many of the enemy as he could.‡

*'Infidel', used in an Islamic context in the written work, is almost surely a latter-day substitution for 'enemy', devoid of any religious connotation.

†There may be another parallel: *The Book of Dede Korkut* was probably composed under the patronage of certain fourteenth-century Turkish sultans seeking to demonstrate their descent from the Oghuz heroes – and thus the legitimacy of their reign. So also the post-Conquest British sovereigns: Norman dukes – whose allegiance could be rightfully claimed by the French kings – were understandably eager to assert an independent royal succession in their new realm. Geoffrey of Monmouth's twelfth-century *History of the Kings of England* supplied such a record, featuring their Arthurian heritage. Later dynasties, even down to the Tudors and Stuarts, continued to brandish the book for similar purposes.

‡The profoundly non-Islamic role of women as muscular warriors and

One exception must be noted to the proposition that conversion to Islam entailed little change in values for the erstwhile shamanist: the role of women. It must have been rather a large wrench to switch from the idealization of the Amazon to the veiling and seclusion of a humbly subservient, docile tent-mistress and bedfellow. One wonders why the nomads accepted the change. Perhaps, as Professor Kortepeter asks, 'were the Turkic women becoming too powerful or else less attractive to their men [when they began to enter Islamic lands] as they began to take as wives and concubines the more sophisticated and [submissive] Muslim women?'[10]

The process of conversion of the Oghuz began in the ninth century and was largely completed by the end of the tenth. The inducements were almost entirely non-theological. Vasily V. Barthold, the Russian anthropologist who wrote extensively earlier this century on Central Asian peoples, noted that proselytizers' promises of celestial felicity to those who died fighting the infidel had little effect. Nor, contrary to the conclusions of contemporary chroniclers, was the threat of inferno for worldly sins persuasive. The nomads had heard the same talk of hell-fire or its equivalent from Buddhist, Manichean and Nestorian Christian preachers who preceded the Moslems, and it had fallen on deaf ears.[11] The decisive factors were economic imperatives and politico-military developments.

After the disintegration of their sixth-century Empire, the constituent tribes of the Oghuz, recorded originally as twenty-four in all (in numbers unknown but certainly in the tens of thousands), moved progressively westward and southward over the next two to three hundred years. Pushed in that direction under the pressure of other newly dominant peoples, principally the Mongols, the Oghuz came to occupy a region to the north of the Caspian and Aral Seas between the Irtysh River on the north-east and the Ural or Volga Rivers on the

---

aggressive instigators of action nevertheless remains in current Turkish folk-tales, surely an inheritance from the pagan past. See for example 'The Son of the Fisherman' and 'The Sultan's Forty Sons' in *Tales Alive in Turkey*.

west: in short, today's Kazakhstan.[12] As early as the end of the seventh century, in the southern part of that vast expanse, they made their first contacts with their new neighbours, the Moslem Arabs who had conquered Persia and Afghanistan. The Arabs' northern boundary, spiritual and temporal, was roughly the ethnographic frontier of the Persians and the cultural dividing line between agricultural land to the south and the pastoral steppes to the north.[13]

The consequences of those early contacts, to be played out in a complicated military and political game over the next several centuries, were ironic; the Turks became Islamized and the Moslem lands fell to Turkish rule. But that is to get ahead of the story.

At first and for some time to come, the relations were hostile: as was their custom, the Turks raided more or less settled Islamic territory and the Moslems were obliged to continue the old Iranian tradition of a frontier defence along the Jaxartes/Syr Darya, the northern boundary of Transoxania [Arabic: *Mā warā' al-nahr*, 'what is beyond the river', i.e., the Oxus/Amu Darya]. It was carried out by a special military organization which, as its opponents were at that point infidels, tended to attract the fraternity of *ghazis*, soldiers of fortune whose interests were booty and combating infidel and heretic. Wandering bands of *ghazis* operated in Transoxania and Khurasan (today's north-east Iran) as early as the Samanid period, living off plunder won in the *ghazwa* – expeditions, raids or incursions. For them, war was an economic necessity; lack of opportunity transformed them easily into brigands. Their bands also became the refuge of political and religious dissidents and provided an occupation for those adventurers of all races attracted by the lure of plunder. From the ninth century onwards they were heavily Turkish in composition. Once converted to Islam, Turks were inspired by the idea of *jihad*, or holy war, but did not attempt territorial conquest, busying themselves instead with defence and counter-raids.

Paradoxically, even as the *ghazis* carried out their razzias, and to some degree even because of them, closer relations developed between Faithful and infidel, as they negotiated over exchanges of prisoners and booty. There may well have been an instinctive recognition on both sides of elements common in their ways of life and warfare. Most of them spoke the same language, which made communication easy.

About the same time, and in addition to the proselytizing effects of the mystics and merchants, another powerful influence was at work: peaceful trading by the Turks (presumably between raids) with their new neighbours on the frontier. Nomads, it has often been pointed out, must almost of necessity maintain a symbiotic relationship with settled peoples. The Oghuz needed certain products, especially textiles and clothing, which they obtained by bartering their own produce of pasture and war – meat, furs and slaves. At various times and places they were so needful or eager that they did not wait for the Moslem traders' appearance in their camps, but brought their own trade goods down to the Moslem borders. As time passed, it became increasingly clear to the nomads that the best and obvious way to augment that beneficial commerce was to embrace their Faith.[14] (The welcome given by the Moslems to the new converts was evilly repaid as it opened the gates of the Moslem world to the Turks. In the mind of more than one Turkic chieftain, this prospect was the sole motivation for his conversion.[15])

Also, in the ninth century, still another process of Islamization began to operate, with the most profound political and military consequences for all of the Near and Middle East. Although the overwhelming proportion of the Central Asian peoples were nomads, here and there along the borders of Transoxania a few small but settled Turkish communities were established. They became sufficiently Islamized – from proximity if nothing else – for some of their members to join the armies of the Abbasid Caliphate, where they were quickly recognized as good soldiers, especially as mounted archers. The Caliphate, in Baghdad, soon began to prefer them to its Arab soldiers, whose constant political and religious infighting made them of doubtful loyalty, and to the troops of the Khurasanians who were free men and thus unreliable in the caliph's cause. But recruitment of Turks from their little settlements was only on a small scale; a new method, involving much larger numbers, was needed. It took the form of the impressment of Turkish slaves. They were acquired by capture, tribute or outright purchase, and were brought up in the caliph's realm as Moslems, with a status far superior to that of privately owned domestic slaves. These were the *gulams* or Mamluks; their rise was meteoric. 'From the second half of the ninth century,' Cahen declares, 'the majority of the military commands, and hence, soon afterwards, of the political offices too, were held by Turks of slave origin who had been rapidly promoted.'

The result could be guessed even if the extensive history of it did not exist. It provides a cautionary tale for any nation foolish enough to import foreign troops in the fond notion that they will help preserve its independence. The slaves became the masters. They were enrolled in the armies of the potentates by their tens of thousands. 'One after another, the dynasties and principalities of western Asia during the tenth and eleventh centuries suffered from and eventually succumbed to the violence of their Turkish troops.'[16] The Turks had a knack for turning the tables on their employers: not only did they extirpate the political power of the Iranian and Arab rulers, but also during the same period made many a Byzantine emperor who called on them for help as mercenaries in Asia Minor regret what he had done.

3

The Seljuks

In the words of God Himself: 'I have an army, composed of people whom I have named Turks and whom I have installed in the East. When a people arouses my anger, I give to them the power to subjugate it.'

Pronouncement attributed to Mohammed by Mahmud al-Kashghari[1]

Knowledge of the cultural level of the various Turkic peoples not long before they entered the Moslem world is relatively meagre, but it clearly differed from place to place and group to group. One tribe was reported by an Arab traveller as still in the neolithic age, without metal for its weapons and using only stone points on its arrows. Another Arab chronicler of the first half of the eighth century tells of a community, which he unfortunately does not identify by tribe or location, whose leader paraded his forces before Moslem envoys sent to convert them to Islam. Among the band there was not a single artisan – no barber, smith or tailor. How, asked the chief, were they to make a living if, in obedience to Islamic tenets, they were obliged to give up plunder-bent forays on their neighbours?[2]

Some Oghuz were undoubtedly at a more advanced state of development, but even so they were culturally much inferior to certain other Turks such as the Karluks, Moslem since about 960, who founded the Karakhanid Empire in Transoxania and to the east of it.[3] By the same token, however, they more truly preserved the traits of their pre-Islamic life.[4]

How much of their political inheritance from the days of their
sixth-century Empire they retained and whether they operated
still as a loose confederation or, alternately, whether the tribes
incessantly fought each other, are matters of scholarly dispute.

Wherever the truth may lie, and however primitive were
their conditions and possessions under their felt tents, it is
clear, as noted earlier, that they were not innocents in the
realm of politics. On the contrary, their forebears on the eastern
reaches of the Central Asian steppe were intensely involved,
diplomatically as well as militarily, with the highly sophisticated Chinese of the day. Their trade with the Chinese had
been substantial and visitations of envoys between them were
commonplace.[5] Similarly, in the last third of the sixth century
the western T'u-chüeh kingdom made an alliance with Byzantium, under Justin II, to act jointly against the Persian Sassa-
nids; for several years the two powers dispatched a series of
envoys, the Turks to Constantinople, the Byzantines to the
Turkic king's headquarters in the T'ien Shan foothills. The
fact that the alliance was soon broken testifies in itself to
political shrewdness in understanding what constituted
trickery: on discovering that Justin had also made an alliance
with other tribal groups whom the T'u-chüeh considered
their enemies, they not only renounced their agreement but
set about punishing Byzantium by raiding its territories as far
as Cherson, at the southern tip of Crimea.[6]

Nor were the Oghuz merely 'simple herdsmen', with all the
stereotypes those words imply. Indeed, that phrase was a
contradiction in terms. There was nothing simple in assigning
summer and winter pastures, in co-ordinating the movement
to and from them in transit, and negotiating with other groups
and territorial proprietors encountered *en route*. There could
be nothing haphazard about such operations; planning and
careful control were essential, from such individual matters as
breeding and rearing of horses (a relatively slow process) and
maintaining the family hierarchical system, to the complex
relations of the even more hierarchical intra- and inter-tribal
organization of a community as a whole.[7]

With their growing involvement with Islamic lands, the
political sophistication of the nomads increased apace. With
it came the beginnings of Turkish sovereignty over organized

PATZINAKS

Danube

BYZANTINE

CRIMEA

Cherson

BLACK SEA

Constantinople

Nicaea

Halys

Ancyra

Sebastea

Caesarea

Trebizond

Kara Su

CAU

Tifli

GEOR

Araxes

ANATOLIA

EMPIRE

ARMENIA

Murat Su

Manzike

Iconium

Lake
Van

Hierapolis

AEGEAN SEA

CRETE

Taurus Mtns

Antioch

Aleppo

Mosul

MEDITERRANEAN
SEA

CYPRUS

SYRIA

MESOPOTAMIA

AZE

PALESTINE

Damascas

Caesarea

Euphrates/Firat

Jerusalem

Baghda

Cairo

FATIMID
EGYPT

RED SEA

2 *The Near East, eleventh century*

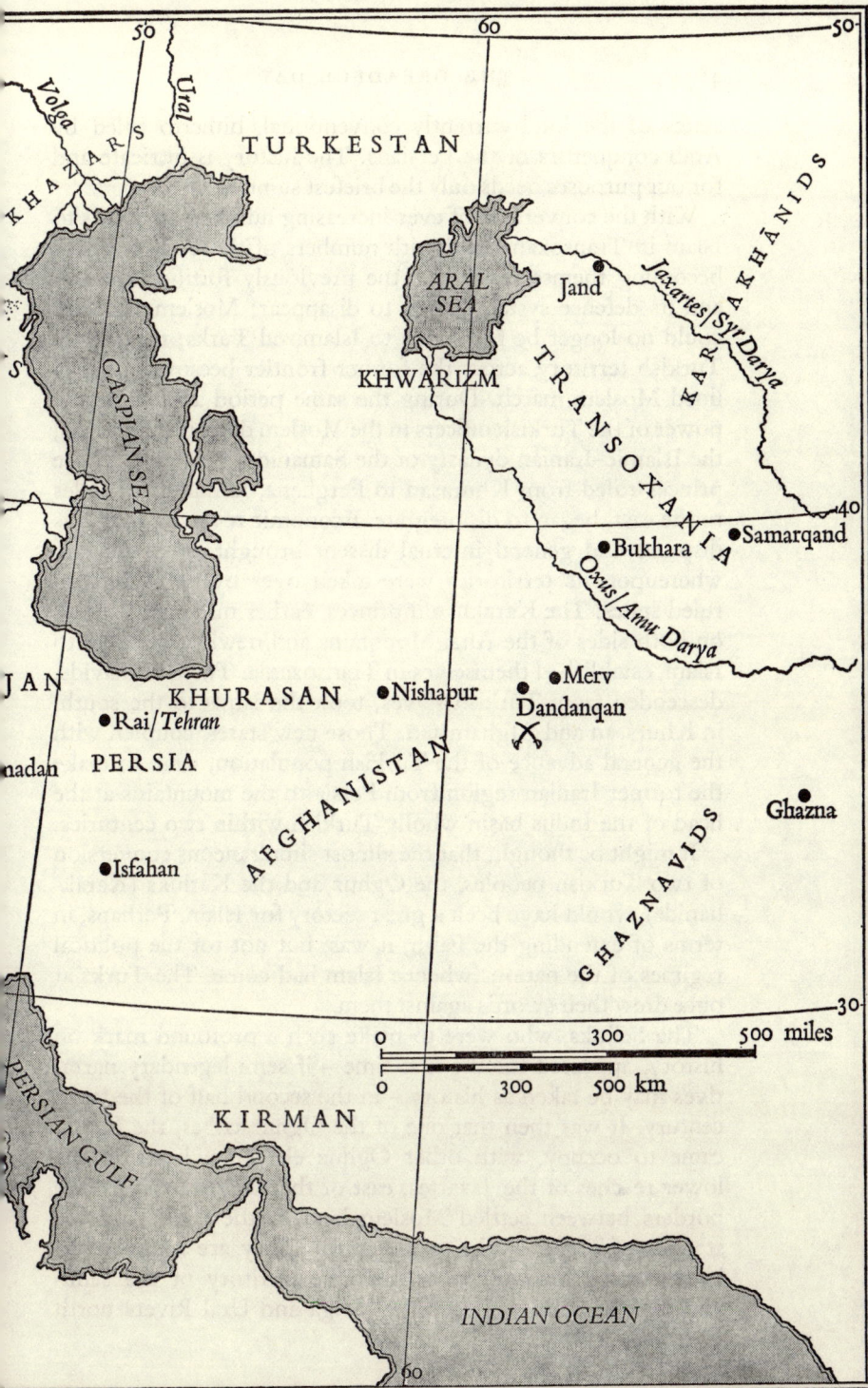

states of the kind currently conventional, hitherto ruled by
Arab conquerors of the Persians. The history is intricate and
for our purposes needs only the briefest summary.[8]

With the conversion of ever-increasing numbers of Turks to
Islam in Transoxania and with numbers of those same Turks
becoming themselves *ghazis*, the previously fortified frontier
and its defence system began to disappear; Moslem territory
could no longer be forbidden to Islamized Turks; meanwhile
Turkish territory across the former frontier became an unde-
fined Moslem march. During the same period and while the
power of the Turkish officers in the Moslem domains increased,
the Islamic–Iranian dynasty of the Samanids (819–999), whose
princes ruled from Khurasan to Ferghana, hundreds of miles
to the east, began to disintegrate. Economic reverses, religious
disputes and general internal dissent brought about its fall,
whereupon its territories were taken over by two Turkish-
ruled states. The Karakhanid princes, earlier masters of a state
on both sides of the Altai Mountains and newly converted to
Islam, established themselves in Transoxania. The Ghaznavids,
descended from Turkish slaves, took the lands to the south,
in Khurasan and Afghanistan. Those new states, coupled with
the general advance of the Turkish population, were to make
the former Iranian region from Persia to the mountains at the
head of the Indus basin wholly Turkish within two centuries.

It might be thought that the almost simultaneous conversion
of two Turkish peoples, the Oghuz and the Karluks (Karakhanids), would have been a great victory for Islam. Perhaps, in
terms of extending the Faith, it was, but not for the political
regimes of the nations whence Islam had come. The Turks at
once drew their swords against them.

The Seljuks, who were to make such a profound mark on
history, appeared for the first time – if semi-legendary narra-
tives may be taken as history – in the second half of the tenth
century. It was then that one of the Oghuz tribes, the Kınık,
came to occupy, with other Oghuz elements, lands in the
lower reaches of the Jaxartes, east of the Aral Sea and on the
borders between settled Moslem land to the south and the
steppes of pagan Turks to the north. They are supposed to
have come from within or near the territory of the semi-
Judaized Khazars, between the Volga and Ural Rivers north

of the Aral Sea. Their legendary leader was a certain Dokak (or Dodak or Dukak or Tukak or Duqaq, depending on the transliterator.)

Ibn al-Athir, an Arab historian writing more than two hundred years after the event, had this to say about him:

He was leader of the (Oghuz); they had implicit faith in him and they never contradicted him in a speech or neglected a command of his. Then it happened one day the king of the Turks named Baighu collected his army and wanted to march against the lands of Islam. Dukak then gave him a box on the ear and wounded him in the head. Then the king's servants surrounded him and tried to seize him, he defended himself and fought with them; his people gathered round him and separated him from (the king). The dispute between them was settled and Dukak remained with him.[9]

Another version of the story is that Dokak left the Khazar khan after the quarrel* and led his people to Islamic lands. Still another, more likely, makes the leader the son of Dokak, Seljuk, from whom the dynasty and its people took their name. The intent of all such legends would seem to have been a pious one, demonstrating the appeal of Islam to the revered founding father(s).

Some of the legendary material made its way into a work, the *Malik-name*, commissioned by Seljuk's great-grandson, Alp Arslan, to record the family history. The book is now lost, but its contents are fairly well known from its use by medieval writers. It was drawn on by the Syrian monk, Gregory Abu'l-Faraj, better known as Bar Hebraeus, writing in the thirteenth century. He provided in addition a different account still, told to him by 'a great Amir, and an old man, very far advanced in days'. It amounts to an opportunistic, politico-economic explanation of the Seljuk conversion, as suggested in the preceding chapter:

When the Khakan [King or prince] of the Khazars burst forth, he had with him in his service a certain warrior whose name was Tutak [Dokak], who, because of his strength, was called Temuriyalig, that is to say 'Iron Bow' [modern Turkish: *Demiryayli*]. There was a son born to this man and he was called by the name of Saljuk, and he

*Gibbon would have it that he daringly intruded into the harem of his prince.[10]

was reared in the palace and he loved him greatly. And one day when he was in the presence of the Khakan according to his custom, the queen was scandalised and made a sign to the king, saying 'If this (young man), though still a child, possesseth such freedom of speech (or behaviour) toward us now, when he groweth up how will he behave (toward us)? Then the Amir Saljuk, having been secretly informed of this, went out and took with him fellow tribesmen secretly, and they marched away with horses, and camels and sheep, and oxen in large numbers.

And he went forth from the land of Turan, that is to say of the Turkaye [Turks] to the land of Iran, that is to say of the Persians, under the pretence that they were shepherds. And when they saw that Persia was flourishing with Islam, they took counsel together and said: 'If we do not enter the Faith of the people in the country in which we desire (to live) and make a pact with them (or conform to their customs), no man will cleave to us, and we shall be a small and solitary people.' And they all agreed . . . [and were converted to Islam] and they remained there (for) years, and they prospered exceedingly and increased greatly in number.[11]

According to legend, Seljuk lived to the ripe age of 107 and was converted to Islam late in life along with his sons, Isra'il, Musa (Moses) and Mikha'il. (The name Isra'il, otherwise unknown in Islamic dynasties, raises, although it certainly does not confirm, the speculation that in the land of the Khazars the family had been under Jewish or possible Nestorian Christian influence.)

Once ensconced in the north-eastern part of Transoxania, probably in the late tenth century, the Seljuks and other Oghuz soon began to become accustomed to Moslem ways of life, even to the point of some of them becoming *ghazis* themselves, defending the frontier and fighting the pagan nomad Turks to the north. They also began to form ties with the orthodox Moslem leaders. Although some of the new arrivals took up a settled way of life, the larger proportion retained their nomad ways, raiding and plundering the older settled and agricultural regions. It was at this point that the settled peoples and the chroniclers began to use a new term for them: Turkomans (Turkish: *Türkmenler*; Arabic: *Turkuman*). It designated the Islamized nomads, distinguishing them on one hand from the heathen nomads and on the other from Moslem Turks who had settled on the land. A great deal was to be heard of them in the troubled centuries to come. Their locus changed, their ways did not. Above all others, it was the Turkomans who were the heritors and preservers of the customs and attitudes of their militant wild past on the Central Asian steppes.

Ultimately to be the conquerors of Greek, Armenian and Georgian Asia Minor, the Turkomans were naturally feared and disliked by their victims. But Islamic society, and even their fellow Turks, once they acquired a degree of more sophisticated civilization from their Persian and Arab neighbours, also developed a considerable distaste for the Turkomans. An Arab source was to say of them:

Without any doubt, what is fine in the Turks is present [in the Turkomans] in a superlative degree, but so also is what is ugly in them. Their faults in general are that they are blunt-witted, ignorant, boastful, turbulent, discontented and without a sense of justice. Without any excuse they will create trouble and utter foul language, and at night they are poor-hearted. Their merit is that they are brave, free from pretence, open in enmity and zealous in any task allotted them.[12]

The Seljuk leaders had large forces under their military command, always ready for fighting and pillaging. Their services were accordingly solicited by warring princes during the period of the Samanid Empire's decline and were as readily supplied. The loyalty of these quasi-mercenaries ran less to the policies of their employers than to their purses, or at least to the prospects of gain held out to them, and were subject to easy shifts.

On Seljuk's death, the family was divided into two principal branches. One was led by his oldest son, Isra'il, by now bearing the Turkish name of Arslan (Lion), the other by grandsons of Seljuk (sons of Mikha'il, who met an early death in battle), Chaghri Bey and Tughril Bey. For a time the two groups were divided, with Arslan fighting for the embattled and moribund Samanids and coming to live for a term on the steppe near Bukhara. His nephews, driven from the lower Jaxartes by hostile Oghuz, lived with a Karakhanid clan further north. In 1025, however, they came together again in the service of the Karakhanic ruler of Bukhara and shared in his defeat by Mahmud of Ghazna.

According to a well-known story,[13] during one of his campaigns Mahmud inquired about the strength of the Seljuks, apparently with an eye to their future. When the question was put to Isra'il/Arslan, he produced two arrows and declared that if he sent them around to his people 100,000 of them could be mobilized, but if he added his bow, as many as one could wish would turn out. Mahmud foresaw trouble with such a force in his future dominions and asked a counsellor what might be done with those pugnacious people. The adviser suggested that each man's thumb should be cut off so that he could no longer draw a bow,* or, according to the version of Ibn al-Athir, that they all should be drowned in the Oxus. Finding those proposals either inhumane or impracticable, Mahmud let them cross the Oxus and settled them here and there in Khurasan, where an eye might be kept on them.

He soon had reason to regret not having opted for a policy of genocide. The Turkomans' habits were not subject to change: they were unwilling or, by the very nature of their means of existence, incapable of respecting the property and lands of their new neighbours; they persisted in their raiding, destroying harvests and thus cutting down revenues. Soon they found themselves masters of a land before they even had the idea of conquering it.

In 1029 Mahmud tried to drive them back, but they escaped to the west, crossing Iran to Azerbaijan. It was a natural direction for them, an extension of the steppe, with prospects of new pastures, booty and holy war against the infidels still further west, and one which waves of Turkomans were to follow again and again in the future (with the result that Azerbaijan remains predominantly Turkic today). Once arrived there they were employed by local princes as a means of preventing raids in their own lands, to fight rivals or to work their depredations on the Armeno-Byzantine frontier. There and then the Turkomans began for the first time the

*From historical beginnings of archery and continuing today with Zen archers in Japan, Oriental and Central Asian bowmen draw the string with the thumb, bending the first two fingers of the hand over it to hold it before release, as distinct from Western archers, generally using three fingers for drawing the string and the thumb only for holding the arrow in place. See Chapter 7.

pursuit or pastime of harrying the Christians of Asia Minor, a process they were to continue for the next half-century, to the battle of Manzikert and beyond.

In 1035 the other branch of the Seljuks, those led by Chagri Bey and Tughril Bey who had taken refuge with a vassal of Mahmud on the steppes south of the Aral Sea, were threatened by other Oghuz. Attracted by the land in central Khurasan vacated by their cousins six years earlier, they sought leave of Mahmud to settle there. Consent was denied, but they moved in nevertheless and behaved exactly as the first Turkoman group had, raiding and plundering. This time, however, their leaders had a new and clear objective in mind – sovereignty for themselves – and a clear idea how to obtain it – by harassing the indigenous population to the point where to submit was the easiest way out.

The Khurasanians succumbed, taking such comfort as they could from the fact that the invaders, although alien, at least professed the most severe orthodoxy, more Sunnite, as it were, than the caliph. Thus the larger cities, including Merv and Nishapur, the capital of Khurasan, submitted in hopes that the Seljuk depredations would be turned elsewhere.

Chaghri and Tughril procured for themselves recognition by the caliph of Baghdad as 'clients of the Commander of the Faithful' and with that new sanction claimed an authority they had not possessed before. Hitherto, they had been acknowledged by the Turkomans merely as military leaders, to be followed or deserted at will. Now, charged with the mission to carry the Sunnite black banner ever further, they asserted themselves as not merely warrior chieftains but territorial rulers.

Mas'ud, son and successor of Mahmud as ruler of the Ghaznavids, recognized the danger too late. With campaigns on his eastern front, he had virtually denuded Khurasan of his army, a circumstance that had greatly facilitated the Seljuk successes in the west of his realm. Now, in an attempt to recover, he called his army back from the east and gave battle at Dandanqan, in the province of Merv, in 1040. The Turkomans, their thumbs still very much intact, utterly routed Mas'ud, who fled to India. Khurasan and, beyond it, the entire Iranian plateau, lay open to Seljuk's grandsons.

*

The half-century that followed Dandanqan saw the rise of the Empire of the Great Seljuks to its apogee under Chaghri Bey, Tughril Bey and their successors. Their conquests were thorough and systematic and extended beyond Persia to Mesopotamia, Syria and Palestine. The history of an empire of such vast domain is complicated and event-filled but need not be recited here at length. It is necessary only to mention some of its aspects that were to have such momentous consequences for Asia Minor and on the initiation of the Crusades. They developed mainly from the campaigns of the oldest brother, Tughril, recognized by the family according to tribal tradition as entitled to dominance.

In a division of territory, Chaghri ruled over Khurasan, adding to it the land south of the Aral Sea and keeping the Ghaznavids and Karakhanids in a position of respectful non-interference. Tughril turned west.

He was in no doubt about his goals: political suzerainty over the lands of Islam – first, those acknowledging the Sunnite caliph at Baghdad, and second, those under the, to him heretical, Fatimid caliph in Cairo. He and his successors, with the same objectives, accomplished the first and failed in the second.

By 1044 Tughril had occupied Persia south of the Caspian, taking Rai (near modern Tehran) and Hamadan, controlling Isfahan through a relation and commanding the Iranian plateau and the crucial routes across it, one leading to Azerbaijan, the Caucasus and Armenia to the west, and the other the pilgrimage road to Baghdad in the south-west. Eleven years later came the climax of his career: his peaceful entry into Baghdad whence he had ejected the Shi'ite Buwayhids of Irak, who had until then exercised oppressive power over the caliph. Tughril was proclaimed vizier to the caliph, Sultan and 'King of the East and West'.

The conquest was made possible in good part by the prowess of his Turkoman bands. In addition, his occupation of Persia won him also the support of the Iranian nobles and their forces. The leaders had little choice in any event but they also correctly foresaw influential roles for themselves as administrators of the lands Tughril was to conquer; the illiterate Seljuks, inexperienced in the governing of established states, would need them to manage their political affairs. With them came the traditional *gulam* or Mamluk (Turkic slave) armies (see Chapter 7), supplied with weapons for taking cities, which the Turkomans never possessed. Ultimately, it was those troops who maintained Seljuk power in Mesopotamia.

The Turkomans, however, disliked its hot climate; moreover, they were forbidden by Tughril to bring their women with them and, worst of all, they were of course not allowed to pillage in what was actual or prospective Seljuk domain. Yet to them pillaging was the principal, if not the exclusive, purpose of war. The result was that well before Tughril completed his campaign for Baghdad, the Turkomans became a major problem for him. It took adroit handling to solve it.

New pastures had to be found for them, but those suitable were in Western Iran and Azerbaijan, in which direction the Turkomans tended to congregate anyway, lured by infidel frontiers where *ghazi* activity could be resumed – more satisfying than conquering lands already Moslem – and by the prospect of booty. Yet that area was far from the scene of Tughril's prospective operations, where he needed Turkoman support.

To be sure, their location on his northern flank would be a useful protection against any trouble from the Armenians and Byzantines who had already begun to respond politically and militarily as early as 1029 or even a decade earlier to the hostile activity of the first Turkomans on their borders.* Their pillaging and forays, moreover, would be useful to Tughril in scouting out roads and preparing the way for any attacks on that front that might become necessary. Yet, in such a remote location, the Turkomans were difficult to control and their capacity for mischief was high. Unruly at best and still extremely primitive, they accepted the Seljuks only in the role of military commanders and not as rulers with kingly authority, in the Persian and Arab pattern. They could desert them for better prospects from other employers; they

*The dates of the earliest razzias are a matter of dispute. The forays may have begun in 1016–17 and resumed in 1021, but the Turks involved were probably not Seljuks but rather tribesmen who had moved westwards in some numbers and were then taken into the military forces of local chieftains in Azerbaijan.[14] See footnote 4, Chapter 6.

could provide help or asylum beyond the Seljuk reach to adventurous rebels and enemies, and they might even take it into their heads to set up a state of their own. Many, in fact, were themselves rebels, fugitive from Tughril's decrees. But Tughril needed them too much to repudiate them; they had to be controlled, not diminished.

His solution, which his successor Alp Arslan was also to adopt, was to summon them to his side when he needed them in Irak, but to keep them happy at other times by allowing them to raid Asia Minor, usually but not always under his direction, supervision and control. He participated in their razzias himself, or through lieutenants, even at the cost of being diverted from his principal goals of beating the Buway-hid rulers of Irak and the Fatimids.

Those raids were the preliminaries to the ultimate conquest of Asia Minor, achieved in less than half a century. But before those devastating forays, the prelude to Manzikert, are detailed, it is necessary first to turn attention to their target, the Byzantine Empire.

4

From Zenith . . .

Pendant mille ans, Byzance a vécu, et pas seulement par
l'effet de quelque hasard heureux: elle a vécu glorieuse-
ment . . . elle a accompli une grande œuvre dans le monde.
Elle a été, avant les croisades, et avec plus de persévérance
peut-être, le champion de la chrétienté en Orient, contre
les infidèles; elle a été, en face de la barbarie, le centre
d'une civilisation admirable, la plus rafinée, la plus
élégante, qu'ait longtemps connue le moyen âge

Charles Diehl[1]

Never in the seven centuries since its founding by Constantine
had the Eastern Roman Empire reached such a pinnacle of
power as it attained in 1025, at the end of the reign of Basil II,
that grim man of steel known to history as the Bulgar-Slayer.[2]
Its territories extended a thousand miles from west to east,
from the foot of Italy across the Balkans, Greece and Asia
Minor to the borders of present-day Iran and the Soviet
Union, and north to south from the top of the Adriatic to
Crete, Cyprus and Syria. Its armies were peerless, the strongest
in the Western world. Its citizens, governed by a tyranny and
often badly governed, were nevertheless better governed and
more prosperous and contented by far than any others on
earth,[3] and the most civilized.[4] Its capital, Constantinople,
the 'Great City', was impregnable, its riches, elegance and
cultivation the wonders of the age.

Less than fifty years later the Empire was reduced to a
fraction of its former extent. The Normans had wrested

away the last of its territory in southern Italy. For three decades after the climactic disaster at Manzikert, Turkic and Slavic tribes rampaged periodically south of the Danube. Seljuks denied Byzantine governance in what had been its heartland since the inception of the Empire. Anatolia, backbone of its strength, major source of its food, trade goods and tax revenues, one time supplier of its best and largest military force, its free peasant-soldiers, was overrun by illiterate plunderers of alien race and religion. The area left under effective Byzantine control was bounded by Adrianople on the west and the Bosphorus on the east.

At Manzikert, Byzantium suffered the most overwhelming battlefield defeat in its history, its huge army completely destroyed. The governmental chaos that ensued was such that another military force of its size could not be fielded for more than a century (only to be similarly annihilated by the same enemy).

To be sure, the amputations suffered at Manzikert and in the years immediately following were not immediately lethal. Besides parts of Greece, various areas and cities on the coasts of Asia Minor and even in Anatolia held out for longer or shorter periods: parts of Armenia – officially or nominally – remained loyal too (but with the local authorities largely operating on their own, controlled if at all only tenuously by the capital, with which their communications and liaison were more often than not disrupted). And, beginning a decade or two later and continuing for almost two centuries, Byzantine authority was reasserted through the western third of Asia Minor. That, of course, was the result of Crusader conquest and the military and diplomatic skills of a number of Byzantine Emperors able to take advantage of the changed situation wrought by the European knights. During that time there was indeed a revival of the Empire in the realm of arts and letters, and a restoration of some of its riches and former glory. Judged by standards of 'civilized' society, Byzantium, even though shrunken and constantly besieged, not least by the Crusaders themselves, remained splendid and fruitful. But long before the famous point of termination of the history books, the fall of Constantinople in 1453, almost four hundred years after Manzikert, the political and military power of what was once the greatest Empire in the known world had been whittled down to insignificance through progressive diminution and disintegration. Without its hinterland, Constantinople was deprived of a body to sustain it.

Thus, in the long view, it cannot be denied that Manzikert was a wound that could not be – or at least was not – healed. As such, it 'marks one of the greatest turning points in world history', opening the way for Turkish conquest and settlement of Asia Minor and it was therefore 'the basic factor in the transition from the Byzantine to the Ottoman empire'.[5]

However, we are not concerned here with Byzantium's four centuries of progressive collapse but rather with the half-century of precipitous decline in its health and strength preceding Manzikert, i.e. from 1025 to 1071. History provides no other example until our own century of such a swift and cataclysmic plunge.

The depth of the fall of Byzantium is best measured by the altitude of the peak on which it previously stood. By the standards of the times – indeed, if today's moral criteria are set aside, by most cold-blooded standards used to judge how effectively a state functions – that peak was astonishingly high.

Despite the corrective work of historians writing since the turn of this century, the impression still persists here and there that the Byzantine Empire was a deplorable if not downright wicked institution. The tone was set by such writers as Voltaire, Montesquieu, Charles Lebeau and, principally for the English-speaking world, by Edward Gibbon. They saw little but a succession of unmitigated evils in the Lower Empire and viewed it more as a poisonous infection than as a beacon of civilization. So also, for another hundred years, did their successors. The venerated moralist-historian William E. H. Lecky, writing at the end of the nineteenth century, declared that Byzantium shaped itself into the most base and deplorable form that civilization ever assumed, a judgement which Charles Oman said was like a 'cheap echo of second-hand historians of fifty years ago, whose staple commodity was Gibbon-and-water'.[6] Gibbon himself had found in his subject the happiest of fields in which to scatter his florid invective: '. . . the subjects of the Byzantine Empire, who assume and dishonour the names of both Greeks and Romans, present a dread uniformity of abject vices, which are neither softened by the weakness of humanity nor animated by the vigour of memorable crimes'.[7]

It is not difficult to understand why the generation for which he wrote, numerous historians who followed him and – for conventional wisdom dies hard – many otherwise well-inform-ed people of our own times still accept the verdict. Moral preceptors of the last century and their dutiful flocks lived in an age that attributed to itself the discovery of virtue, if not indeed its invention, and so reacted with horror to the accounts of infi-nite corruption, of 'Byzantine' duplicity and, Gibbon notwith-standing, of exceedingly memorable crimes committed in the course of a not unusual method of gaining the throne: accession by assassination. To Protestant Britain and America a century ago, the elaborate and extravagant rituals of the Greek Orthodox Church seemed more offensive than those of 'Papism' itself; the obsessive concern of the Byzantines with the most abstruse points of theology was deemed absurd when not in fact totally incomprehensible.* Byzantine extravagance and ostentation in festivals, pageants and other entertainment were affronts to the Victorian ethos of frugality and restraint; the importance and often dominant role of eunuchs in affairs of state and even as patriarchs of the Church seemed scandalous, while an Imperial policy that considered political victories won by deception better than those won by fighting and that paying an enemy tribute was better than going to war with him was the antithesis of the gospel of manliness.

There is, of course, no denying the degree of tyranny, greed, corruption, deceit and brutality in Byzantine history. The prevailing methods of punishment – scourging, immola-ting, lopping off hands and feet and tongues, slitting noses and, in particular, blinding (also used, along with castration,

*'All places, lanes, markets, squares, streets, the clothes' merchants, money changers, and grocers are filled with people discussing unintelli-gible questions', wrote St Gregory of Nyssa, hardly a man to denigrate theology. 'If you ask someone how many obols you have to pay, he philosophises about the begotten and unbegotten; if I wish to know the price of bread, the salesman answers that the Father is greater than the Son; and when you inquire whether the bath is ready, you are told that the Son is made out of nothing.'[8]

as a preventive measure against real or imagined political enemies) – were, in a word, horrible. Yet one is entitled to ask where else, during the millennium of the Eastern Roman Empire's existence, conditions of life and standards of personal and governmental morality were gentler or purer. It can hardly be supposed that the Slavic and Turkic hordes pushing from the east, the Arabs from the south, the Normans from the west, and the tribes of Huns, Goths, Lombards, Vandals and Vikings beating down from the north and still turbulently consolidating their conquests in Western Europe and Russia were notably more tender-hearted in their political affairs, more restrained in the manner of making material acquisitions, more punctilious in observing their pledges and more delicate in their regard for human life or limb. Their histories are written in as bloody an ink as the Byzantine's. Saladin's chivalry came later and in any event walked hand in hand with massacre; that of Tristan and the Round Table, warbled by minnesingers and troubadours in ladies' bowers in a later day, suggests *ex post facto* embroidering.

But whether or not the vices of Byzantium exceeded those of its contemporaries elsewhere in the world, what is beyond doubt is the other side of its coin: from the fourth to almost the end of the eleventh century the great military, political, administrative and cultural accomplishments of the Empire were not even remotely approached by any other contemporary society in the Western world. For five centuries Byzantium was the treasury of Western learning. From the patriarchate of Constantinople came the missions, such as those of Cyril and Methodius and their disciples, that did so much to establish Christianity in Slavic and later in Russian lands; from the palace itself came the politics that held them under Christian influence, with its incalculable consequences. Byzantium's civil administration never deviated from the principle of autarchy, but within that framework it was remarkably resilient and flexible, adapting efficiently to new conditions as they arose; its civil service was not approached in competence and effectiveness by any other (China again perhaps excepted) until well into the Renaissance.

Except for some Arab mathematicians and scientists and some European monasteries, it was the Byzantines who kept classical learning alive when it was lost to the West. It was Byzantine builders, artists and craftsmen who embellished the Aegean, Mediterranean and Adriatic lands with enduring beauty. In no small part, the flames that enlightened a Europe emerging from medievalism flared from fire kept alive in Byzantium, even during its long decline.

But, lest the notion arise that Constantinople's major service was to have constituted a precursor of the best of Bloomsbury, Boston and the Left Bank, it must be emphasized that during its millennium of splendour it was also the rampart that defended Europe. The barbarian hordes of Slavs and Turks were held at the Danube and the Saracens were prevented from crossing the Dardanelles by the blood of the Empire's soldiers.

The Empire's greatness was the product of a multitude of strengths exercised in its military, administrative, religious, agricultural and commercial systems. So too was its collapse brought about by ultimate failures and decay in those same systems. But the great disaster that those failures and decay engendered began with a sudden, gigantic, military catastrophe. It is on the military system, therefore, that the examination is here focused.

In its administration, composition, recruiting, equipment, strategy and tactics, the army remained until 1025 essentially unchanged from the forms instituted by major reorganizations made in the late sixth and mid-seventh centuries. By the tenth century, 'it was the only [military] system of real merit existing in the world',[9] 'incomparably superior to that of any of its neighbours',[10] and 'without parallel until modern times'.[11]

The heart and power of that great fighting machine were the 'theme' (province) armies of free peasant-soldiers, provincial militia, subject to call-up when need arose, under the command of the *strategos* of the theme. Appointed by the central administration in Constantinople, he was in effect a viceroy, civil governor of the province and commanding general rolled into one. In major campaigns when several theme armies took the field in combined action, a high imperial officer or the emperor himself took overall command.

In the earliest centuries of the Eastern Roman Empire the system had been different: the army, largely mercenary, was under central imperial control and a separation between civil and military authority was maintained. However much that division reduced the temptation to rebellion by regional potentates, it also led to a certain paralysis of action; it was accordingly abandoned in the sixth and seventh centuries when barbarian invasions pressed from all corners of the Empire, and militarization of the provincial administrations under a unified authority became the rule.

With the change came the settlement of bands of professional soldiers in the various themes. They were granted land-holdings sufficient to support themselves and their families and to provide their fighting equipment (including a horse for the cavalryman), in return for a hereditary obligation of military service whenever the *strategos* called them up. The land grant and the military obligation went together. As the system took root, dependence on mercenaries was greatly reduced, their place being taken by what was in essence a yeoman militia, much more deeply motivated to defend their own hearths and homes and, indeed, to fight for a country of which whatever their ancestors' origins, they came to feel themselves loyal citizens.*

The system of using yeomen or at least locally mustered soldiers was considerably short of universal conscription for military service – the obligation rested on the oldest in the family of military age – but it came closer to a national army than any other in existence. (As will be seen, by the time of decline centuries later the wheel had turned full circle, with the theme armies virtually disappearing and mercenaries replacing them, with disastrous results.)

The strength of a theme army is believed to have ranged from 4000 to 15,000, depending on the population of the province and its military importance. Its officers were mainly members of aristocratic families with large estates for whom such service was traditional.

---

*Scholarship in recent years has rendered some of the details of the system uncertain. The possibility has been raised that the farmer himself did not do the fighting but used his income to hire locally recruited fighters or, alternatively, if he took arms himself, he hired others to look after his farm. It is conceivable that the system operated differently in different parts of the Empire.

The importance of the military and social role of the peasant smallholder cannot be over-emphasized, both when they throve during the days of Byzantine conquest and when they were virtually extinguished as a class during the Empire's swift decay. 'The thematic system served as a vital impetus to and support of the existence of the free peasant society, which in turn not only served as a balance to the landed aristocracy, but fought the Arabs and was a major contributor to the imperial tax collectors.'[12]

Besides the theme armies, there were a considerable number of troops under the semi-independent command of local potentates on the frontiers with the special function of guarding the passes, mostly in the Taurus Mountains, to block Arab invasions and raids and to trap booty-laden intruders on their withdrawal. Also, on the Armeno–Cappadocian frontiers there were traces of semi-feudal military organizations, distinct from the theme armies and accustomed to take care of their own defence. Among them were the *akritai*, celebrated in Byzantine poetry, dare-devil riders, counterparts in warlike and religious zeal and in their methods to the *ghazis* on the Moslem side. They functioned as border raiders and defenders, serving as the armed retainers of castle-dwelling chieftains.

In addition, beginning in the ninth century, there were groups of Turks, freebooters looking for a living as they were pushed westwards by population pressure in Central Asia, who served as mercenaries (and enjoyed the reputation of formidable pillagers).[13]

Finally, there were the *tagmata* or guards regiments, professional soldiers all and increasingly foreign in composition in later centuries. They constituted, in effect, the standing army, stationed in or near Constantinople, which accompanied the emperor when he led campaigns or, if he did not take the field himself, the commanding general in the capital, the Domestic of the Schools.*

Reliable figures of the size of Byzantium's armies do not exist; only estimates, themselves much disputed, are possible. An Arab author of the ninth century put the theme levies at

---

*The Byzantine navy, the engine of brilliant conquests in the Mediterranean and so often Byzantium's saviour from Saracen and Russian attacks, does not play a significant role in the history considered here.

70,000; whatever the true figure was then, the total would have been larger a century or so later. A historian's consensus is about 100,000. Runciman suggests 120,000, including thematic armies and the imperial regiments,[14] although Hans Delbrück[15] and Ferdinand Lot[16] feel any such totals to be greatly overstated. Obviously, the forces were never assembled into a single campaign army; defensive battles on the frontiers were waged with much smaller armies and even grand campaigns such as those of Basil II would not have denuded every region of all its troops. An officer of the great general and later emperor, Nichephorus Phocas, writing in the later half of the tenth century, in a work titled *Skirmishing Warfare*, declared that a force of 6000 picked men was adequate to repel any frontier attack.[17]

He was speaking of a body of heavy cavalry, heart and sinew of the Byzantine army, defensive or offensive. At least until the end of the eleventh century the major assault in the majority of battles was that of the cataphracts, horsemen heavily armoured, the term deriving from the Greek word meaning 'clad in full armour'.

The well-trained individual trooper wore a steel cap, a long mail shirt reaching from neck to thighs, gauntlets and steel-clad shoes.[18] He covered his armour with a light linen surcoat and for cold weather carried a large woollen cloak strapped to his solid, well-stuffed, iron-stirruped saddle. The horses of the officers and the frontline riders were also armoured with steel frontlets and breastplates. The cataphract's weapons were a broadsword, a dagger, a horseman's bow and quiver and a long lance fitted with a thong near the butt end. Some troopers also apparently carried an axe slung from the saddle. The tuft of the helmet, the pennon of the lance and the surcoat were of a distinctive colour for each regiment, thus constituting a kind of uniform, something not adopted by any Western army until the sixteenth century.

The cataphract tended to be a man of some substance, less than a country squire but rather more than a simple yeoman, possessed of a landholding sizable enough to afford him his own horse and often a servant to accompany him on campaign. Leo VI the Wise, whose *Tactica* was the military bible of the ninth century, wrote in his chapter on recruiting troops:

C

The *strategos* must pick from the inhabitants of his theme men who are neither too young nor too old, but are robust, courageous and provided with means, so that, whether they are on garrison or on expedition, they may be free from care as to their homes, having left those behind who may till their fields for them. And in order that the household may not suffer from the master being on service, we decree that the farms of soldiers shall be free of all exactions except the land-tax. For we are determined that our comrades (for so we call every man who serves bravely in behalf of our own Imperial authority and the Holy Roman Empire) shall never be ruined by fiscal oppression in their absence.[19]

The infantry played a much inferior role. When a *strategos* set out on a campaign some infantry would be left behind for garrison duty and protection of towns, passes and fortresses in the home territory. Those taken into the field could be used in mountainous terrain not feasible for cavalry warfare, or elsewhere as supporting troops for the cataphracts (most major battles, however, especially those against opposing horsemen, were carried out by the cavalry alone). The infantry was divided into light- and heavy-armed units, the former apparently operating principally as archers, a category, however, which was increasingly neglected or reduced in numbers over the centuries (a diminution that contributed to the defeat of the emperor at Manzikert). The heavy-armed foot soldier, the *scutatus*, wore a steel helmet, a mailed shirt and sometimes gauntlets and greaves. He carried a large round shield, a lance, a sword and a dual-purpose axe, one side of the head a cutting edge, the other a spike. As with the cavalryman, decorations of different colours on his arms and garb designated his unit.

A campaign force would also include a corps of engineers, usually in the van, to entrench each night's camp or more permanent positions. There was also an 'ambulance corps' with surgeons and bearers, and an artillery force to drag and operate siege machinery – catapults and ballistas – some extremely large and heavy.* In addition, there would be a large body of camp-followers, men and boys, bondsmen or hired, functioning as servants or performers of menial tasks. Leo recommended that even the poorest troopers be encour-

---

*One, used by Basil II, required 400 men to set it in position.[20]

aged to keep one attendant for every four or five of them and if possible a packhorse to transport baggage that they could not sling to their individual saddles. The camp-followers and pack trains considerably delayed the movement of a cavalry corps but were thought to justify their existence by sparing the fighting men some of the non-combatant tasks and keeping them supplied with food and fodder in barren areas where living directly off the land was difficult or impossible.

It was enough for the enemies of Byzantium – the Slavs, Arabs and even the Normans – to see to it that their men could sit their saddles and handle their weapons, and to trust to dash and courage for victory. Not so for the Byzantines; they developed warfare to a fine art if not a science. Leo's *Tactica*, the earlier sixth-century *Strategicon* of the Emperor Maurice, the manual of Phocas's officer and other writings, now lost, provided detailed instructions in theory and practice tailored to the various strategies and tactics of the several different opponents whom they fought. 'It is no exaggeration', General Fuller wrote, 'to say that not until well into the nineteenth century were military manuals of such excellence produced in Europe.'[21] And in training, Oman declared, no Western nation could match Byzantine armies until the sixteenth or seventeenth centuries.[22]

On what could be called the Byzantine philosophy of war, Oman is worth quoting at some length:

Of the spirit of chivalry there was not a spark in the Byzantine, though there was a great deal of professional pride, and a not inconsiderable infusion of religious enthusiasm. The East-Roman officer was proud of his courage, strength and skill but he was . . . remote from the haughty contempt for sleights and tricks which had inspired the ancient Romans. . . . Courage was considered at Constantinople as one of the requisites necessary for obtaining success, not as the sole and paramount virtue of the warrior. The generals of the East considered a campaign brought to successful issue without a great battle as the cheapest and most satisfactory consummation in war. They considered it absurd to expend stores, money and valuable lives of veteran soldiers in achieving by force an end that could equally well be obtained by skill. . . . They had no respect for the warlike ardour which makes men eager to plunge into the fray: it was to them rather the characteristic of the brainless

barbarian, and an attribute fatal to anyone who made pretensions to
generalship. They had a strong predilection for stratagems, ambushes and simulated retreats.* For the officer who fought without
having first secured all the advantages for his own side they had the
greatest contempt . . . the East Romans felt no proper sense of
shame for some of their over-ingenious stratagems in war. It is
with a kind of intellectual pride that [Leo] advises that if negotiations
with a neighbour are going on, and it is intended to break them off,
the softest words should be reserved to the last day but one, and
then a sudden expedition be launched against the enemy, who has
been lulled into a belief of the certainty of peace. He is quite ready to
send bribes into the hostile camp. He recommends two ancient
tricks that were already a thousand years old in his own day. The
first is that of addressing treasonable letters to officers in the enemy's
camp, and contriving that they shall fall into the hands of the
commander-in-chief, in order that he may be made suspicious of his
lieutenants. The second is that of letting intelligence ooze out to the
effect that some important person in the hostile country is secretly
friendly, and adding plausibility to the rumour by sparing his
houses and estates when raids are going on. . . . A trick too well
known in later as well as in Byzantine times is that of sending
parlementaires to the enemy on some trivial excuse, without any real
object except that of spying out the numbers and intentions of the
hostile forces. . . . [But] it is only fair to say [the *Tactica* declares]
that no plighted treaty or armistice must be broken, no ambassador
or *parlementaire* harmed, no female captive mishandled, no slaughter
of non-combatants allowed, no cruel or ignominious terms imposed
on a brave enemy.[23]

Even as fighting was a way of life for the Seljuks, so was
constant warfare a condition of life for the Byzantine Empire.
From its beginnings until its fifteenth-century extinction it
knew no prolonged periods of peace; its armies were almost
continually battling one or another enemy across or within its
borders, or – such was its fate – it was often obliged to fight
concurrently on two fronts: against Persians, Arabs, Saracens
or Turks to the east and south, against Turkic and Slavic
hordes in the north and, later, Normans in the west and
Crusaders within.

To survive, therefore, the paramount purpose of its national
policy had to be the maintenance of its defensive military

*Yet, as will be seen, they also had a weakness, fatal at Manzikert, for
becoming victims of just such devices.

strength. Until Byzantium fell into the hands of fools and weaklings on Basil II's death, it was a rare emperor who ever forgot that imperative for survival.

For its first five centuries since Constantine set up his capital on the Bosphorus, the Empire's posture, with a few heroic exceptions, was basically defensive, as could be inferred from the army organization outlined above. The problem was to preserve the inheritance of the Roman Empire, pressed on the Rhine and the Danube by Germanic tribes and forever menaced on the south-eastern front by Persia. By the fifth century the Empire of the West was battered down by the barbarians; the line of Western emperors became extinct; what was left in the East became the Orthodox Empire, to be torn internally by religious disputes and diminished externally by conquests and defections around its eastern, southern and western rim from Armenia to Spain.

Glory came again in a climax of achievement during the reign of Justinian (527–65). The Persian front was held, Africa and parts of Spain were recovered and the resistance of the Ostrogoths in Italy was broken down, thanks to the genius of Justinian's generals, Belisarius and Narses; Constantinople was beautified as never before; Saint Sophia, the finest man-made enclosure of space ever created, rose to its present majesty.

But on Justinian's death the tide turned again disastrously: most of Italy was lost to the Lombards, Spain to the Visigoths; the Avars triumphed on the Danube and the Slavs poured in around them; the Persian wars continued unabated with victories first to one side, then the other. When again, in the seventh century, Heraclius (610–41) brought Byzantium to a second great resurgence, at last smashing the Persian Sassanid dynasty and establishing his sovereignty over the Slavs in the Balkans, those achievements were only the prelude to the darkest days ever suffered until then. A new enemy had arisen to dwarf the prowess of those known earlier: in the first flush of religious zeal, the followers of Mohammed swept the Near East and North Africa before them. All Byzantium's strength was needed to keep them from seizing land inside the Taurus and even that was insufficient to prevent them from periodically crossing the mountains and raiding again and again deep into the Empire's heartland. By the end of the century the entire Mediterranean coast of Africa and part of Spain was in their hands; their navy was established in the Sea of Marmara and the walls of the capital itself were under their attack every year from 673 to 677. To the north, the Slavs repeatedly ravaged Thrace and threatened the Empire's second city, Thessalonica. New chaos was created when the Hunnish tribe of Bulgars crossed the Danube and settled areas to the south of it.

The Empire was saved by the Isaurian dynasty, founded by Leo III (717-40) who, with his successors, perfected its military apparatus into 'the best defensive organization that Christendom has known'.[24] Leo's son, Constantine V (740-75), dubbed by his enemies with the miserable sobriquet of Copronymus,* beat the Arabs back beyond the Taurus, temporarily crushed the Bulgars and magnificently reorganized both the military and civil administration. Saviours they were, but he and his father went down in Byzantine history as its arch-villains, the promulgators of Iconoclasm – rejection of the use or veneration of religious images – a dogma more politically divisive even than the earlier Christological disputes that one ecumenical council after another strove vainly to resolve.

It was a century and a half before the restoration of the veneration of images brought religious peace under a new dynasty, the Macedonian. It was destined as well to lead the Empire to its peak of power and greatest territorial expanse since the reign of Justinian. Under the Macedonians the corner was turned: Byzantium went on the offensive. A Byzantine *reconquista* took place.

Basil I (867-86), the first of the line, was a peasant's son turned general and a favourite of the preceding sovereign, Michael III, the Drunkard. Michael and his favourite seem to have set up some sort of *ménage à quatre*. Michael's mistress was Eudocia Ingerina, who was much disliked by his mother. She forced Michael to marry Eudocia Decapolita but, to keep his former mistress handy to his needs, the emperor had her married to Basil, with whom presumably he had made an arrangement. Whatever its terms, Basil ultimately cuckolded

---

*Literally, 'Named-from-Dung'; Gibbon implies that he defecated in his baptismal font.

his patron; the two men seem to have traded Eudocias. Whether the matter grew too complicated or for other reasons, Basil murdered Michael and made his liaison with the Empress Eudocia Decapolita legal by marrying her. In the end, by which time he appears to have become completely insane, he seems to have switched his affections to a young man. But whatever his moral qualities, Basil was a capable military commander, driving the Arab fleets from the Adriatic, bringing southern Italy again under Byzantine rule. Furthermore, he considerably strengthened the Empire's authority in the Balkans, held the Bulgar kingdom firmly within the influence of the Orthodox Church and, most important, began offensive operations in the east, pushing as far as the Euphrates.

Ironically, his son, Leo VI the Wise (886–912), for all of his fame as author of the *Tactica*, failed to continue his father's successes in arms. But perhaps more important than the military aspects of the reigns of Basil and Leo were their performances as law-givers and codifiers, returning to old Roman principles and gathering total powers to the emperor. However autocratic the result, it was greatly to strengthen and unify the state's power and its effective execution. Leo's legislation consolidated authority in the hands of the imperial bureaucracy.

The next Emperor of note, Romanus I Lecapenus* (914–44), one of the greatest,† was confronted with the massive force of the powerful Bulgar monarch, Symeon, who had earlier invaded as far into the Empire as the walls of Constantinople. By military strength, patient timing and skilful diplomacy, Romanus gained the upper hand and effected a satisfactory peace.

Once the Bulgar danger had been eased, brilliant campaigns were carried out by Romanus's great general John Curcuas on the Empire's perpetual and ineradicable second front, significantly expanding Byzantine territory in the east. For a time

---

*His father, an officer under Basil I and reputed saviour of his imperial master's life in battle, bore one of the most intriguing names in Byzantine history, Theophylact the Unbearable (Abestactus).

†Not as widely acknowledged as such as he deserves to be. Gibbon gave him a bad name, declaring that 'in his licentious pleasures he forgot the safety both of the republic and of his family', a profoundly mistaken judgement.[25]

3 *The Byzantine Empire, mid-eleventh century*

Themes thus: *ANATOLIKON*
Regions thus: THRACE
— — — Extent *c.* 1025
········· Acquisitions after 1025

Cherson

BLACK   SEA

Trebizond

Kars Ani Dvin
1045

IBERIA   Erzurum   ARMENIA   *Araxes*

AMENIAKON   Colonea   TARAUN   Manzikert

Sebastea   MESOPO-   VASPURAKAN
TAMIA

Aneyra   Amida   Martyropolis

CAPPADOCIA   Melitene

Halys   1032
Edessa   Mosul

OLIKON   Adana
CILICIA   Antioch   Aleppo   *Euphrates*   *Tigris*

Cyprus

Emessa

Baalbek

Damascus

Tiberias

Nazareth

Jerusalem

the war against Arab forces in Armenia and northern Mesopotamia gave victories alternately to one side and then the other, but in the end the Byzantines captured what had been a long-sought objective, the city of Melitene/Malatya, and in addition Amida/Diyarbakir, Martyropolis (Mayyafariqin)/Silvan, Nisibis and, as the pearl in the crown, Edessa/Urfa, with its intensely venerated miracle-working picture of Christ. The victories paved the way for even greater territorial expansion in the east under succeeding emperors. And in between those eastern campaigns, Byzantine forces smashed a surprise Russian invasion on the Asiatic shore of the Black Sea – proving that Byzantium had indeed a *third* front to defend – and demolished the enemy fleet. In all, the victories demonstrated the awesome increase in the Empire's military strength since the dark days of the earlier centuries.

But internally, Romanus confronted an enemy more lethal to the Empire than the Bulgars, Arabs and Russians combined, and was the first to recognize it. This was the increasing – and increasingly malign – power of the landed military aristocracy. Ever since the third century, even before Byzantine history as such began, large quasi-feudal estates had been a feature of the Roman 'Establishment'. The development of the soldier-peasantry in the seventh century lessened the power of the large landholder, but by the ninth century both the number and size of the estates of the 'powerful', the *dunatoi*, began to increase, as did their efforts to acquire the land of the 'poor', the *penites*. Holding important administrative positions, the magnates used their vantage points to absorb the smallholdings, often by dubious means, and began to behave more and more as if they were almost autonomous princes in the areas under their dominance. Romanus and his successors fought this development for more than a century, recognizing that as long as 'immense and growing influence was wielded by military magnates jealous of and hostile to the crown, the legitimate Emperor could never be the master of his own soldiers and his own revenues'.[26]

In the end, the battle was lost by the Crown. The history of the struggle and of the ultimate – and fatal – extinction of the free peasantry, foundation of the Empire's military power over the centuries, is outlined in the following chapter.

Next after Romanus came Constantine VII (944–59), more of a scholar than a warrior, and after him his son, Romanus II (959–63), a political incompetent. But under their generals Curcuas and, later, Nicephorus Phocas and John Tzimisces, victories continued over the Arabs, who had been weakened by a prolonged period of political chaos and anarchy. Crete, key to control in the Mediterranean and in Moslem hands for almost a century and a half, was taken by Nicephorus; at the other end of the Empire he took, and for a time held, Aleppo/ Haleb, eradicating the power of the Hamdanids after a thirty-year struggle and extinguishing the most dangerous centre of Arab strength in the Near East.

On the death of Romanus II, Nicephorus's reward was the throne, by the acclamation of his troops, and the hand of his predecessor's widow, the beautiful, immoral and supremely ambitious Theophano. Of a great aristocratic family, but austere, rough and sullen in his manners, Nicephorus Phocas was a religious zealot who saw a holy mission in fighting the infidel. His conquests included the recovery of Cilicia and Cyprus and, by a siege he initiated and that was continued by one of his generals, the capture of the great city of Antioch/ Antakya, under Moslem rule for three centuries and deemed lost forever to the Empire.

The fate of Nicephorus, 'Bearer of Victory', was epitomized by lines in a poetic epitaph:

'O Nicephorus, well-named indeed, since thou wast Conqueror of all thine enemies, except thy wife.'[27]

Six weeks after the fall of Antioch, Theophano and Nicephorus's cousin, a leading general and erstwhile best friend, John Tzimisces, murdered him in his bed. Theophano had fallen in love with her husband's dashing young officer and became his mistress; he, in turn, had boiled with resentment at the emperor, who had denied him the recognition and position of leadership he deserved.

Like the man he had murdered, the new emperor (969–76) was a brilliant general. He conquered half of the kingdom of the Bulgars, beating them and their Russian allies in a campaign that ranks among the most splendid military accomplishments in Byzantine history, and promptly annexed it. Tzimisces then turned almost at once to renew the war in the east against attempts of the newly established Fatimid Caliphate in Egypt to extend its power in the Levant. From Antioch, Tzimisces pushed south, took Emessa/Homs and Baalbek and accepted the surrender of Damascus. Thence he invaded the Holy Land, captured Tiberias, Nazareth and finally Caesarea, the Arabs' principal stronghold. He stopped short of Jerusalem, recognizing the dangers of over-extension. But his conquest, almost to the suburbs of the Holy City and of Damascus, took Byzantine rule further into Arab territory than at any time since the Moslem banners first streamed out of Arabia three centuries before.

Byzantium's dominance being established in the Near East – for a time – Tzimisces returned in triumph to Constantinople, there to die suddenly, either of typhus, typhoid or poisoning, depending on which historian's conclusion one chooses to accept.[28]

The legitimate heirs to the throne in the Macedonian line were the two sons of Romanus II, Basil, aged eighteen, and Constantine, aged sixteen – Nicephorus and Tzimisces were interlopers married successively to Romanus's widow – but it was taken for granted that the imperial power would be exercised on Tzimisces's death by their great-uncle, the eunuch Basil, the *parakoimomenus*, or first minister.* He set about removing from power officials from the previous regime who might threaten his position. Taking unkindly to their enforced demotions, the aristocrats who were affected launched two distinct civil wars. These, one separated from the other by some years, were of truly 'Byzantine' complexity, replete with intrigue and characterized by the phenomenon of the leaders switching allegiance as opportunity afforded. The turmoil extended, with interruptions, for thirteen years until the throne finally came safely to rest in the hands of the legitimate Macedonian co-emperors. The younger, Constantine, was as frivolous as his father, Romanus II. By contrast the elder, Basil II (976–1025), learned from the revolts of the aristocrats to despise them and to trust no one. Putting behind him the pleasures to which he was devoted in his youth, he made

*If Tzimisces did indeed die by poisoning, the eunuch Basil almost certainly had a hand in it.

himself into a man of pure muscle and iron determination. He dismissed his great-uncle from office and became a loner, taking advice and counsel from none and apparently never marrying. Austere, rough and dour, rejecting the luxuries, ceremonies, spectacles and panoply of court life, contemptuous of the rhetoric that Constantinopolitans so much admired, Basil spurned the capital and took his troops into the field to stay with them years on end, campaigning in winter as well as summer.

His wars *within* the borders of the Empire were political: the enemy was the powerful aristocratic land-owning magnates. He held them subjugated until his death at the age of seventy.

Abroad, Basil's wars were primarily against the Bulgars, risen in revolt on the death of their conqueror Tzimisces. Under a skilful and valiant new leader, the Tzar Samuel, they were determined to recover their former lands and kingdom. In all, Basil fought them for thirty years. Initially, Samuel was all too successful, thrusting forward from his Macedonian mountain strongholds. He re-created the Bulgar kingdom from the Black Sea to the Adriatic and ravaged Thessaly and Thrace and even Greece as far as the Peloponnesus. In the end, however, Basil's military genius, his determination, organization and patient timing won out. In the summer of 1014 he surrounded Samuel's army in Macedonia. Although the tzar escaped, a large number of his soldiers were killed and even more were captured – some fourteen or fifteen thousand according to contemporary accounts (probably exaggerated). Basil blinded the lot, sparing one eye to one captive of each hundred, so that he could guide the rest back to Samuel. At the sight of his men, the tzar fell senseless to the ground and died two days later. The surname that his grateful subjects bestowed on Basil, Bulgaroctonus, the Bulgar-Slayer, is not endearing but it was dreadfully accurate.

The conquered Balkan region was made a component part of the Empire, and in contrast with his brutal conduct in war, Basil treated its peoples with moderation and good sense. For the first time in centuries the Bulgar menace was liquidated and once again the Empire extended from the Black Sea to the Adriatic, as far north as Aquileia.

Basil II was not a man to forget the punishment that befell an emperor who, however deeply enmeshed in fighting on one front, forgot about the other. In the midst of his early warfare in the Balkans, reverses were threatened in Syria by the encroaching power of the Fatimid Caliphate. His generals on the scene failing to respond adequately, the emperor himself gathered some levies and, by forced marches, crossed the Empire from west to east in twenty-six days (an average of about twenty-five miles a day), securing Antioch and relieving a threat to Aleppo. Four years later, in 999, he was recalled to the Syrian frontier to deal with a similar Moslem foray. On returning, but still in winter quarters in Tarsus, he heard of deeply unsettling political developments in Armenia and, not one to neglect an opportunity, pushed north-eastwards to make arrangements consolidating control of various principalities in that region.

Finally, after the conclusion of the Bulgar wars, Basil turned a third time to the east. The events are sketched in Chapter 6, but the result may be summarized as being the acquisition of almost all of Armenia, Iberia and Vaspurakan, up to the mountain ramparts which are today approximately the border between Turkey and Iran. As will be suggested later, Basil's annexation of those lands and their incorporation in the Empire may have been the only great mistake in his otherwise brilliant forty-year career.*

Basil died in 1025, still unsatisfied and seeking further territorial acquisitions, in the midst of planning a campaign to conquer Sicily. Within the Empire, the landed aristocracy were embittered but helpless in the iron trap in which he held them. The peasant communes and the soldiers' smallholdings, freed from oppressive taxation, enjoyed a hitherto unexperienced prosperity. The army was invincible and, despite the emperor's enormous expenses in maintaining it at war for four decades, the treasury had been so enriched by his booty and his austere and shrewd fiscal policy – with the rich paying the exactions – that taxes on the poor were left uncollected for the last two years of his reign. Contemporary historians relate that Basil

*The date of its inception is taken as 985, when Basil assumed real power with the expulsion from office of his great-uncle, the *parakoimom-enus*.

was obliged to build huge underground chambers to store the excess in the treasury.[29]

Of all the Emperors in Byzantium, [wrote R. J. H. Jenkins] Basil II, in his own person, came nearest to the imperial ideal of boundless power and boundless providence. . . . The unity of the world under the elect of Christ, which the sovereigns of the ninth and tenth centuries had postulated, was finally consummated in the person of their prodigious offspring.[30]

Never had the Empire's borders seemed so secure. A ten-year truce (which lasted fifty) was concluded with the Fatimid Caliphate. As for any danger from the east, as long before as Nicephorus Phocas's time, the manual on the conduct of skirmishing war contained an apology for including a passage that the author felt was not of current utility but rather of purely historical interest:

. . . To write a treatise on frontier operations may seem at the present day no longer very necessary, at least for the east, since Christ, the one true God, has in our day broken and blunted the power of the sons of Ishmael.[31]

His complacency is understandable: the Abbasid Caliphate of Baghdad was growing progressively weaker and a Central Asian tribe of nomads, the Seljuks, only beginning to enter Transoxania, had hardly been heard of in Constantinople. There was still no insistently evident cause half a century or so later, on Basil's death, for the ordinary citizen to be disturbed. Emperor or commoner, bureaucrat, churchman or peasant

might very well have felt that no external power could disturb the internal security and peace of the empire. For the first time in its long existence Byzantium had no well organized and powerful states on its borders. . . . Basil II transmitted to his successors an empire whose prestige, power and territorial extent had never been greater than since the day Heraclius triumphantly entered the Persian capital.[32]

But what Basil and his contemporaries did not see is evident in hindsight: his conquests were 'purely military: he ravaged, fought and won, and left behind him vast depopulated areas – mere vacuums of victory'.[33] With weak foundations, the newly aggrandized territorial structure he left as his monument could not be solidified.

Internally, too, the appearances were deceptive. Byzantium gave the impression of being the most robust political body on earth. Basil and his predecessors in the Macedonian dynasty had seen the cancer within and had prevented its spread, but they had not excised it. Their successors either saw no need to continue applying the medicine or found it too distasteful to insist upon.

5

. . . to Nadir

It is not through hatred and envy of the rich that we take these measures, but for the protection of the small and the safety of the empire as a whole. . . . The extension of the power of the strong . . . will bring about the irreparable loss of the public good. . . . For it is the many, settled on the land, who provide for the general needs, who pay the taxes and furnish the army with its recruits. Everything falls when the many are wanting.

Romanus I Lecapenus[1]

Cut down the governors who become over-proud. Let no generals on campaign have too many resources. Exhaust them with unjust exactions, to keep them busied with their own affairs. Admit no women to the imperial councils.

Bardas Sclerus's advice to Basil II[2]

The reasons adduced for Byzantium's plunge appear at times to be as many and varied as the historians who have recorded it. The spectrum ranges from philosophical conclusions drawn from the long historical perspective to those taken from concrete contemporary occurrences.

A few – by no means all – of the first category are as follows:

In a world on the threshold of change, Byzantium stood rigid, unable to adapt or understand. Its claim to divine sanction for earthly imperium obliged it to view all pluralism as being, by definition, heretical. What was foreign was barbarous, contemptible, iniquitous. Its dogma could tolerate no other religion or culture; Western

Christianity was as abhorrent as Islam. The Empire could make no common cause with Christians in the western world who might have joined with it against a common enemy. In consequence it appeared to the world outside it as an enemy, hated and feared.[3]

The clash of races inside its borders was a bomb that could not fail to explode.

The superhuman efforts during its centuries of defending itself against foreign enemies followed by its centuries of conquest drained it of strength for the future. It shot its bolt and fell back exhausted.

Age-old population pressures in Central Asia came to a climax, propelling predatory Slavs and Turks to Byzantium's northern and eastern borders at exactly the time that equally aggressive Normans set out to batter it from their Mediterranean bases.

Its own financial and moral corruption brought inescapable punishment; its iniquity withered its sinews, leaving it to rot to death.

Basil's conquests had been all too successful; vigilance was abandoned and, to use that most tedious of cliches, the nation was lulled into a false sense of security.

The second family of explanations of the collapse focuses, as mentioned, on actual contemporary events. Again, a few of those that have been offered:

In less than half a century a succession of ten Emperors came to the throne, eight of them miserably incompetent, weaklings, wastrels and fools, as unmanly as the women and the eunuchs and as self-serving as the court politicians who dominated them.

Greed for power by the clergy, the politicians and the generals, of a virulence theretofore not experienced, plunged the Empire into 32 years of civil war, a new one arising on the average of almost one a year. The intestine battles were so much a matter of normal expectation that the general Catacolon Cecaumenus included in his *Strategicon* a chapter on how a prudent man should behave during a period of insurrection.[4]

Doctrinal passion plus territorial greed effected the extinction of Armenia, either as a buffer state or a defensive bulwark. It was annexed but left undefended.

An intractable battle to the death arose between the civil bureaucracy and the aristocratic military magnates.

An intolerable and therefore self-defeating taxation system destroyed the nation's finances.

The aristocrats' and the bureaucrats' avarice and lust for land and power accomplished the destruction of the free peasant-soldiers, backbone of the loyal army.

The military establishment was deliberately starved of funds to destroy its power – so successfully that the means for national defence collapsed.

All or almost all of these propositions, those stemming from the long view and those arising from immediate events, have a degree of validity, some being more readily measurable than others, but none by itself bringing the Eastern Empire to the decline of its last centuries.[5] The great collapse of the balance of power that had existed for centuries in the eastern Mediterranean and the Near East evolved, like almost all other changes of similar magnitude, not from one cause alone but from the conditions and circumstances of the place and times.

It is also obvious that most of the suggested reasons listed above for the Eastern Empire's amputation are themselves interrelated, presenting an analytical chicken-and-egg problem. Did a succession of playboy (and playgirl) monarchs invite their subservience to the civil service, or did the power-hungry officials see to it that the monarchs they selected or maintained were milksops *ab initio*? Did the civil wars reduce the throne to ineffectuality, or did the ineffectual throne tempt the rebels? Were those same civil wars brought about by civilian politicians' resisting the domination of the military, or was the military attempting to fight off its projected extinction at the hands of the bureaucrats? Was it unceasing attacks from abroad that reduced the army's ability to resist, or was the army's weakness such as to tempt relatively riskless invasions? Was it the tax system that destroyed the peasantry, or did the rape of their lands force a suicidal alternative set of fiscal exactions? Was Armenia's inability to repulse Seljuk raids the reason why Byzantium was forced to annex it in its own defence, or did Byzantium so abuse the Armenians as to destroy their will to fight for the Empire?

The elements, of course, were combined. The individual eggs that went into the omelette can be considered separately, but once having been mixed, no one of them can be identified as *the* most active ingredient in the poisoned dish.

But since the proximate cause of the almost instant loss of Asia Minor after Manzikert was a battlefield defeat, this chapter approaches the analytical dilemma by concentrating on those factors bearing most directly on the Empire's defensive military capability, rather than speculating on the several diseases at the root of the whole society.

Three developments in the years 1025 to 1071 seem to have been the most significant in rendering the Empire incapable of beating back the Seljuks. One, to be considered in the following chapter, was the loss of Armenia as a military bastion. The second and third were the unremitting civil-military strife and the loss of the peasant-soldiery, ineffectively replaced by mercenaries.

As early as the sixth century, Justinian felt compelled to oppose the acquisition of peasant-held land by men of wealth,[6] but it was not until the ninth and tenth centuries that the process swelled to proportions profoundly dangerous to the Empire's social, fiscal and military structures; nor was the threat recognized by any subsequent emperor until Romanus I Lecapenus. In 922, two years after his accession, he reversed earlier permissive policy by a celebrated edict. A concluding passage explained his rationale:

The small landed proprietor is immensely valuable, since his existence implies that the state military taxes will be paid and the obligations of military service observed [in the theme armies]: both of these things would completely founder if the number of small proprietors were diminished.

His reasoning was entirely correct. In a demonstration of notable non-wisdom, Leo the Wise, one of Romanus's predecessors, believing men of wealth should be the ones to hold high positions, abolished an ancient ruling prohibiting office holders from purchasing estates or acquiring them by gift or legacy. Worse, he revoked a former right of the neighbours of land that came on the market to pre-empt them; that right, of course, had performed the wholesome service of helping to keep agricultural property in the hands of the small farmers and to block its capture by the big estates.

Convinced that powerful proprietors must be forestalled at all costs, Romanus determined to turn matters around. His edict restored the right of local pre-emption and increased the categories of neighbours, small cultivators and kinsmen entitled to exercise it, thus fending off acquisition by wealthy strangers.

The emperor was forced to continue his battle by a series of further decrees aimed at restoring to the smallholders without indemnity fields cozened from them in the past at less than a fair price. In an edict of 934 he denounced the great land engrossers as 'more merciless than famine or want' and declared:

When we have done so much to repel the attacks of external enemies, how could we fail to extirpate also our domestic enemy, as one might describe him, the enemy from within, the enemy of nature, of creation and of all the beneficence of the rule of law? Our just intention is to let liberty reign, our keen-edged weapon this present liberating legislation, rooting out the insatiable passion for engrossment with wrath and loathing.

The trouble was that that passion was indeed insatiable. Every major emperor from Romanus to Basil II found it necessary to continue to do battle against those enemies by decrees and legislation. Compounding the difficulty was the fact that all too frequently the smallholders connived at their own destruction: even when they were not the victims of fraud and coercion they often voluntarily gave up their land to the magnates to escape the burden of taxation and military service or to survive the poverty to which famine and crop-failure reduced them; they thus became *coloni* – dependants or serfs – settled on the big estates that became increasingly feudal in structure.

Promulgating laws to suppress the corrosive process that Romanus Lecapenus had recognized before him, Constantine VII Porphyrogenitus declared that the army was to the state as the head is to the body, and that his decrees against engrossment were a work 'for the welfare of all'. Nicephorus II Phocas fought on the same battlefield against 'the enemy from within' as did his successor, John Tzimisces. The latter issued decrees expressly forbidding peasants to change their status into dependants on the great estates, whether lay or ecclesiastical, to escape taxes and their hereditary military obligation. Grégoire, convinced that Tzimisces was in fact a victim of murder rather than disease, suggests that the motive of the presumed poisoners stemmed directly from the emperor's efforts to keep the soldier-peasants from the clutches of the *dunatoi*.

Despite the 'socially conscious' rhetoric of the emperors' decrees, all professing zeal for the welfare of the *penites* and concern for the downtrodden, their underlying purpose was not purely or even principally compassionate. The battle was not between the rich and the defenders of the poor so much as it was a contest between two rival powers, the Crown and the landed aristocracy, for the services and control of the tillers of the soil. But if honours were even in the lack of charitable sentiments of both factions, at least the position of the emperors was at one with the defence imperatives of the state: its purpose was to maintain a body of rural citizenry subject to conscription in the theme armies and liable for payment of the land-tax. Peasants formerly under obligation to the state who had lost their land and settled on the estates of the magnates were in fact not greatly 'liberated' by the decrees returning their old farms; they were merely relieved of one master to be delivered to another, the Crown: they became *paroikoi*, colonists of the state, deprived not only of the right to dispose of their land as they chose but also of their freedom of movement.[7]

Imperial decrees and denunciations slowed the process of land alienation but did not stop it. Basil II was obliged to carry on his predecessor's struggle, but did so, as was his habit, with an iron hand. His edict of 996 ordered retroactive correction even more extensive than the decrees of Romanus on divestiture. As the law stood before Basil's decree,

forty years of undisputed tenure were required to establish rights of ownership and disposal. But it was easy enough for a powerful proprietor, whether by bribery or brute force, to suppress any claims for restitution during the period of suspense. The provision was openly derided; and estates held by no legal title whatever were handed on from father to son as though they had been real property of the testators. This provision was now repealed [by Basil]. Estates which had been held, and could by properly authenticated documents be shown to have been held, during seventy-five years or more, were confirmed on the possessors. The rest were to be handed back, without compensation, to the original proprietors. But for crown lands seized and held through bribery of government inspectors, no time limit less than one thousand years was to be valid. Documents emanating from the Treasury and purporting to make grants of such land in the imperial name were revoked.[8]

Basil's enforcement was brutal. Some nobles were evicted from their property, some were humbled even to the status of peasants and others were beggared; one huge and wealthy land-grabber was imprisoned for life. All this, said the emperor 'so that the powerful may take note of it, and not leave this sort of inheritance to their children'.

For thirty years the law was rigidly enforced. Military, civil and ecclesiastical holdings were greatly reduced, some to the point of extinction. Yet even that was insufficient. In 1003-4, Basil felt it necessary to issue the most severe decree of all, his famed *allelen gyon*, putting an even more pressing burden on the 'powerful'.

Before its promulgation, the tax due from peasants too impoverished to meet it had to be paid by the neighbours of the insolvent farmers, in accordance with the principle of collective payment of taxes by the village community. Basil's change in the law shifted the burden to the great landowners alone, whether lay or ecclesiastical. Protests and petitions for its abatement, especially from the Church properties hardest hit – Church landholdings were as extensive as those of the Crown itself – were dismissed with contempt.

Had Basil's successors been of his calibre, the existence of both a free peasantry subject to the call to arms and of a supreme power that tolerated no opposition below it from the civil bureaucracy or the military aristocrats might have been sustained, perhaps for a long time. But his younger brother, Constantine VIII, coming to the throne on Basil's death in 1025 after sitting in the wings for fifty years, was devoid of instinct or ability for the function of ruling. He conceived his primary duty to be the enjoyment to the utmost, for his personal pleasure, of the huge wealth Basil had accumulated in the state treasury. He squandered it in three years, putting it – and his time and energy – to use in satisfying his creature comforts and his passion for horse-racing, gambling, and blinding everyone bold or careless enough to cross him. He was, Fuller declares, 'both a pacifist and a despot, and no worse extremes can be met in combination'.⁹ Approaching death after three useless years on the throne, with no sons, he fixed the succession of the Macedonian house on the second of his three daughters, to rule as empress. Her consort emperor was an ageing aristocrat, whom she was obliged to marry at her father's death-bed.

The daughter was Zoë, then fifty years old and still a spinster, but still beautiful, as well as vain and ambitious. She may have discovered the delights of sex at some earlier stage, but whenever it was that she did, she became an enthusiast, a development that clouded whatever judgement she may once have had. Her husband, Romanus III Argyrus, enjoyed a mercifully short reign, but long enough for him to make a fool of himself in a disastrous military foray towards Aleppo in 1030 (revenged two years later by the great general George Maniaces, of whom more will be heard) and to repeal Basil's *allelengyon*. A member of the aristocracy, Romanus III was in no way inclined to resist the hitherto suppressed cravings of the wealthy military nobility. The result was that the peasants were unable to pay their share of the communal taxes and the 'powerful' were unwilling to.

Nicephorus Phocas and John Tzimisces had been also of distinguished aristocratic descent and Constantine VII and Basil II had been nothing if not of military lineage; they knew the breed of military landholders at first hand and knew their menace. Hence their measures against them; they were men enough to stand up to what must have been charges that they were, to use an epithet of a later day, 'traitors to their class'. Not so Romanus III.

The older laws forbidding the powerful to acquire the lands of the peasants or military smallholdings were not, however, officially repealed and conscientious judges at this time regarded them as legally valid. But it was sufficient that the long series of decrees protecting the smallholder came to an abrupt end with the death of Basil II. Even the government regulations of the tenth century with all their severity had not been entirely able to prevent the acquisition of lands from peasant and military holdings, but now the negative attitude of the state meant that it was possible for the wealthy landlords to expand at will. Both in political and economic issues the 'powerful' had won all along the line. . . . The free small-holdings rapidly disappeared without a protest, and the wealthy landlords absorbed the property of peasant and soldier, turning the former owners into dependants. Thus the very foundations on which Byzantium had been built ever since its revival in the seventh century were swept away, with the result that the strength of the armed forces and of the revenue declined, and the consequent impoverishment weakened the military power of the state still further.[10]

Romanus's interest in the person of his empress-wife soon abated, but her taste for tangible male affection did not. Her eye fixed on the young son of a peasant who had been insinuated into the women's quarters by his brother, John the Orphano-trophus (Guardian of the Orphans), an unscrupulous but extremely capable and influential eunuch. He had determined that, as he was disqualified as a castrate, someone from his family should attain the throne. Zoë was enamoured of the young man and in one way or another it happened that the old gentleman, her husband and emperor for six years, turned up dead in his bath, on Good Friday 1034.

That same evening the young lover became Zoë's husband and emperor, Michael IV, the Paphlagonian. His passion for his wife, if it ever existed, soon waned but not his vigilance over a spouse whose solution to the problem of an unsatisfactory husband had just been so clearly demonstrated. He and his uncle John had Zoë carefully guarded and saw to it that no imperial power was shared with her.

Somewhat surprisingly, Michael IV turned out to be an able general, a relatively effective emperor and a ferocious tax-collector. Without any aristocratic background himself, and his uncle a bureaucrat, Michael presided over an administration that served the interests of the capital's huge civil bureaucracy* and tended to oppose those of the provincial military magnates. The fight between the two factions, long germinating, grew apace.

* In relative size – the 'civil list' was enormous – and in the extent of its authority, no other institution of its kind approached it for several centuries. Presiding over what André M. Andréadès termed 'at once a semi-

The emperor was afflicted with epilepsy; the seizures increased in frequency and his general health deteriorated during his seven-year reign. John the Orphanotrophus realized that new action would be necessary to retain the Crown in his family and, not long before Michael IV retired to a monastery, there to die the same day, John had persuaded him and Zoë to adopt as a son another Michael, the eunuch John's nephew.

He took the throne in 1041, as Michael V Calaphates. An ingrate and a fool, he soon exiled his uncle – an act which met with no great adverse reaction in as much as the Orphanotrophus was universally detested – and also banished Zoë to a nunnery.

His own rascality became steadily more manifest to the citizenry. At the same time, although Zoë was no favourite of theirs, they cherished a feeling for the legitimacy of the Macedonian house – into which Romanus III, Michael IV and Michael V were all intruders – and rose up in wrath. Their demand was for the return of Zoë and of her younger sister, Theodora, long since a nun. Riots, almost certainly engineered by other enemies of Michael in the Church and among office-holders, climaxed in the blinding of the Emperor and of his uncle. Michael's rule lasted little more than five months.

Zoë and Theodora ruled for a short time, jointly and incompetently, neither having the slightest conception of their responsibility or of ways of executing it. Zoë, however, still entertained a burning desire for a male companion, even though by now sixty-four, and accordingly arranged another marriage, her third (contrary to Church law), with a prominent senator and member of the civil aristocracy. He took the throne in 1042 along with the two empresses as Constantine IX Monomachus.

His thirteen-year tenure of the Crown was apparently for him an unalloyed delight. He spent money lavishly on his own pleasures, squandering to the point that the *nomisma*, for centuries the stable coin of the realm and indeed of the world around it, was drastically devalued. The Empress Zoë, some-

Oriental absolute monarchy, a Graeco-Christian community and a capitalist state', the bureaucracy operated a state-directed economy, controlling production, labour, consumption, trade, population movement and public welfare.[11]

how grown tolerant, suffered her mate to appear with her and
Theodora at all ceremonial functions with his mistress, the
beautiful Sclerena, thus making an imperial *parti à quatre*. On
Sclerena's death, Constantine replaced her with a new mistress,
a princess from a tribe on the south Russian steppes, giving
her the same public display and honours.

His reign coincided with one of the greatest flowerings in
Byzantine history of art, literature and learning, all recovering
from neglect a generation before under the harsh military
concentration of Basil II. But the bloom was the effort of a
slowly dying plant: the underlying strength of the Empire
was being destroyed by the civil wars and the civil–military
feuding.

The battle between the Crown and the generals grew in
intensity during the regimes of the playboy emperors who
followed Basil II (all of whom were insinuated into Zoë's
graces by the civil bureaucracy). It became all-consuming during the period of Constantine IX (1042–55), a ruler even more
subservient to the capital's politicians than his recent predecessors. The methods used to beat down their enemies were
the obvious ones: starvation of the army of its funds, reduction
of the generals' authority, progressive substitution of mercenaries under central command for the provincial peasant-
soldiers, the systematic hounding out of officers from aristocratic families and the replacement of able commanders with
relatives and creatures of the court and civil service.

The classic example of that last technique was the treatment
accorded to the brilliant general George Maniaces, avenger of
the defeat, in 1030, of the strutting Romanus III near Aleppo.
Two years later he conquered the seemingly impregnable
Edessa/Urfa and went on to beat the Saracens in Sicily in
1037–40, only to be recalled and imprisoned, it appears, for
arousing the jealousy of and giving offence to the brother-in-
law of the then emperor, Michael IV. Released by Michael V,
he returned to Sicily to recover much of what had been lost
by Byzantine incompetents in the interim. His success once
again aroused the suspicion of the power-wielders in the
capital; moreover, a rival military aristocrat, who had attacked
his estates and his wife, sowed antagonism to him in the
fertile soil of the bureaucracy which had always regarded him

as a rough upstart and parvenu; Constantine decided to recall him.[12]

Just as the abuse apportioned to Maniaces was typical of the methods of the civil bureaucracy, so his own reaction was typical of the military faction: revolt and civil war. He allowed his troops to proclaim him emperor and took them across the Adriatic to march on the capital. In panic, Constantine sent all available forces to meet him. The two armies met in Macedonia in a battle that Maniaces had as good as won when a stray arrow killed him, thus preserving an undeserving emperor on his throne. No one can know whether the man denied the Crown by a chance arrow would have been as able a sovereign as he was a general, but it is a safe speculation that Maniaces would not have let the army run down to the sorry state it finally reached.

Along with the resentment of the officers against the anti-militarist civil service in Constantinople, there was also a general opposition in the provinces to the centralization of power in the capital, adding fuel to rebellious impulses. Thus, in 1047, Constantine IX found himself besieged under his own walls by armies assembled by Leo Tornicius, leading a revolt more menacing even than that of Maniaces. Only Tornicius's loss of nerve at a critical moment saved the emperor.

In the end, the great corrosive battle between the bureaucracy and the magnates fought itself into a kind of paradoxical standstill: the ruling class in the capital controlled the throne and the central administration but its supreme power grew steadily weaker and more constrained; the large estate owners continued to expand, disengaged themselves increasingly from former obligations to the state, especially in the matter of taxes, and became almost law unto themselves. Outside the capital, the nation became increasingly feudal. The developments of the struggle over the years were complex and, in terms of the results with which we are here concerned, need not be detailed. What is important to our purposes is the fact stressed by Ostrogorsky:

The principal characteristic of this period is however the decay of the Byzantine army. The civil government so hated the military aristocracy that it had systematically reduced the strength of the armed forces and in its attempt to discover fresh revenue [to replace taxes now being collected by the magnates for themselves] had converted the peasant-soldiers into taxpayers. . . . [M]any of the surviving *stratoitai* [small farmer-soldiers] were induced to buy exemption from military service by paying an agreed sum. The army of the themes ceased to exist, and even the word 'theme' for troops of the provincial army of *stratoitai*, fell out of use in the eleventh century.[13]

In his search for revenue and his indifference to maintaining national defence – or sheer lunacy in the matter – Constantine IX even disbanded native forces crucial for defence in the vulnerable Armenian region (already suffering Seljuk raids) in 1044. The areas had been under obligation to maintain local levies to support the imperial armies in return for exemption from certain taxes. Constantine turned the process upside down, collapsing a militia perhaps 50,000 strong, and ordering payment to the central treasury of the taxes hitherto waived.[14]

The inevitable consequence of the reduction of native troops was increasing reliance by the central authority on mercenaries. They were recruited from a startling diversity of foreign sources; among them were Patzinaks/Pechenegs (of Turkic stock), Khazars, Russians, Scandinavians, Georgians, Slavs, Albanians, other tribes of Turks, Kurds, Arabs, French, Germans and ultimately English.

The Byzantine armies remained incontestably the strongest military power in the world up to the middle of the eleventh century (in fact, the imperial boundaries were somewhat expanded beyond those of Basil II) but their effective and unquestioned deployment in the service of the Crown became increasingly problematical; the loyalty of the mercenary forces extended no further than their pay packets. And as time went on, even the contracts on amount and frequency of wages to the hired soldiers were breached or ignored.

The judgement of the general Cecaumenus was that Constantine IX 'destroyed the Empire and reduced to nothing the Empire of the Romans'.[15] He indulged himself by parading his brilliance as a judge in the courts when he should have been ruling an empire. The historian Psellus would have the initial fatal steps charged to Zoë for having diverted prize-money and other funds allocated to the army. Her squandering 'was the beginning of the utter decline in our national affairs and the cause of our subsequent humiliation'.[16] But in the end even Psellus was forced to agree that Constantine IX, his favourite emperor and the subject of his most lavish panegyrics, was primarily responsible for the evil to come. He wasted the Empire's resources at exactly the moment when they were most needed. His purpose as emperor, his biographer sadly admits, was to enjoy himself and not to exercise his responsibility for government:[17]

. . . two things in particular contribute to the hegemony of the Romans [i.e. Byzantines], namely, our system of honours and our wealth, to which one might add a third: the wise control of the other two, and prudence in their distribution. Unfortunately, Constantine's idea was to exhaust the treasury of its money, so that not a single *obol* was to be left there, and as for the honours, they were conferred indiscriminately on a multitude of persons who had no right to them. . . .[18]

Psellus was telling the truth, but far from the whole truth, particularly about his own responsibility. It was he who was Constantine's principal palace adviser, as he later became that of Constantine X, an even more disastrous ruler, and was the tutor of Michael VII, who performed the difficult feat of compounding the Empire's ruins after Manzikert into further ruination.

Although he was not of an aristocratic family, Psellus became the outstanding figure of his age as orator, scholar, philosopher, educator, rhetorician and littérateur. Courtier nonpareil, he was the champion of the corrupt civil bureaucracy and probably its chief strategist. His *Chronographia*, a history of fourteen Byzantine rulers beginning with Basil II, is relatively impartial in its first half, but thereafter a slavering and tendentious account of the monarchs whom he knew firsthand and whom he counselled. It provides the liveliest and most vivid account of the period, but it is totally mendacious about his own double-dealing and intrigues and is nauseatingly self-glorifying. His responsibility is heavy as one of the principal architects of the disastrous policies that culminated in Manzikert. His life puts one in mind of the famous denunciation said to have been made about a nineteenth-century American political figure: 'How brilliant and how corrupt! Like a mackerel rotting in the moonlight, he shines and stinks.'

With hindsight only, Psellus noted in his *Chronographia* the decline into which the Empire was plunged, but he never fully sensed the totality of the disaster ahead. Neither Constantine nor his advisers gave any evidence that they appreciated at the time the danger of the Seljuk raids, mounting in frequency, extent and success during his reign.

Constantine IX died in 1055 and the throne was once again held – or at least occupied – by the aged Theodora. On her death two years later the Macedonian dynasty at last came to its end after almost two centuries, most of it a time of triumph but its last three decades diseased. The dying empress chose as her successor the nominee of the Constantinople bureaucrats, 'a man most likely to favour themselves' and 'less qualified to rule than to be ruled and led by others', according to Psellus.[19] He was Michael VI the Aged.

His passion was to hand out favours, gifts and promotions to civil servants and senators to a point that, said Psellus, 'surpassed the bounds of propriety', but he greatly underestimated the strength of the military. A deputation of prominent and powerful magnates, generals in command of such crack troops of the Empire as still existed, soon waited upon him, seeking similar bestowals. The old monarch propelled them from his presence with unparalleled rudeness.

Their immediate response was the preparation of a revolt under the command of Isaac Comnenus, member of a family that was to play a prominent role in the Empire's affairs for almost a century to come.

Isaac marshalled a formidable force of troops from the east (thereby denuding those regions of their armies, a circumstance which the Seljuks promptly put to their advantage) and large numbers of supporters from other parts of the Empire flocked to him. He assembled them at Nicaea/Iznik and there trounced the imperial army sent by Michael to oppose him. The population of Constantinople then rose against the emperor, who was thus obliged to send a team to negotiate with the rebel. It was led by Psellus, who, almost certainly with the connivance of his two fellow-delegates, had decided from the start to betray his emperor.[20] He did. Michael had no choice but to abdicate and embrace the safety of a monk's habit. His delegates, backing the right horse, were rewarded with even higher honours and more prominent advisory roles in the court of the new Comnenian emperor.

Isaac reigned a bare two years, the first soldier-emperor since Basil II and the first to take the field with his troops (against the Hungarians and the Patzinaks in the north) since Michael IV. He set to furiously on what he saw as his most pressing problem: the reorganization of the army. But for that he needed money. To find it, he put an end to the previous extravagance of the court and expelled idle hangers-on from their expensive and useless posts; much more important, he annulled many land grants made by his precursors, confiscated properties of the monasteries and embarked energetically on a programme to collect all taxes due.

As could be expected, his reforms aroused intense opposition. He might nevertheless have succeeded had he not entered a power struggle with the Church and in particular with the Patriarch, the renowed and venerated Cerularius, exiling him from his office and thereby arousing the fury of the citizenry. The bureaucratic aristocracy was already determined to break him. Against that dual opposition, and on the occasion of a fit of sickness and depression, he abdicated. He had been urgently advised to do so by Psellus, intent on his lifelong dedication always to position himself on the winning side. Isaac became a Studite monk and died as such two years later.

Speculation about an alternative after a thousand years is futile, but one is nevertheless tempted to wonder what course the Empire would have taken had Isaac approached his problems less precipitously and more diplomatically, and had he not challenged Cerularius in the realm of Church authority. His foreign policy had been astute, his firmness about reforms had been admirable and his conception of rebuilding military strength was entirely correct. Could he have reclaimed the Empire's defensive forces so that they could have held off the attack from north, east and west (whence the Normans had newly begun to threaten), or had the structure by then so far disintegrated that rescue was no longer possible?

On abdicating, Isaac named his successor – again on Psellus's advice and by his handiwork – the president of the senate, Constantine X Ducas. He was the scion of 'probably the oldest and richest family of the Byzantine [military] aristocracy',[21] but he preferred the luxuries and ease of life in Constantinople; he had come under the control of the civil party and he served it as its puppet. That faction had been profoundly alarmed by Tornicius's revolt and Isaac Comnenus's accession to the throne, a victory of the military party, and was therefore doubly determined to reduce it to permanent impotence. Constantine was to be its instrument in that objective.

'If any event can be singled out as particularly disastrous for the Byzantine Empire in the eleventh century', Hussey declared, 'it is the accession of Constantine X.'[22] Isaac's unpopular economies went by the board; the civil service was expanded and, to placate the clamourers, the senate was also expanded until its members were legion. To meet the resulting expenses, to buy peace from foreign powers, to ensure continued Church and civil support, money was raised by selling offices and setting tax-farmers to work in collecting the levies. But in particular, funds were denied the military, and only partly for reasons of economy.

'The bureaucrats, in a sense at the mercy of the generals when it came to military affairs, defended themselves by embarking upon the dismantling of the military apparatus', Vryonis declares. 'This included the dismissal of competent generals, in some cases the dissolution of entire military corps, but above all the cutting off of financial support of the local indigenous troops forming the thematic levies.'[23]

History provides few such vivid examples of the baby being thrown out with the bath water. At the end of the process the civilian party no longer had anything to fear from the military. But then neither had the Seljuks.

The process had been evident in the reign of Constantine IX Monomachus, but with Constantine X the depletion of the local levies and almost total reliance on mercenaries became nearly complete. Even Psellus, whose adulation of the man he made emperor is close to emetic, was forced to concede that the military organization broke down under his hero's period on the throne.

Constantine's appalling slashes in military expenditures, Oman remarks, 'was sheer madness, when there was impending over the Empire the most terrible military danger that had

D

been seen in four centuries. The safety of the realm was entirely in the hands of its well-paid and well-disciplined national army, and anything that impaired the efficiency of the army was fraught with the deadliest peril.'[24]

The denigration of the generals, both in prestige and authority, was such, according to contemporary historians,[25] that soldiers put aside their arms and became lawyers or jurists. The Empire stood in no need of more lawyers: it desperately needed fighting men.

The replacement of native troops by mercenaries was no satisfactory substitute: they were far more expensive and their loyalty was never secure. When financial difficulties delayed or reduced the payment of their salaries, their bonds to the Empire loosened in proportionate degree. An example is that of the Norman mercenary chief Hervé Frankopoulus, who, on being denied a promotion, retired to lands he held in the east and thereupon simply deserted to the Turks who were raiding the borders. Mercenaries ravaged the territories they had been hired to defend.

The policy of the civil bureaucracy, reaching its peak – or, rather, its trough – under Constantine X, had two inevitable consequences.

The first was the obvious defensive counter-measure of the military faction to break into revolt and support rival claimants for the throne, or to link such forces as they commanded to various leaders of ethnic groups trying to set up small autonomous principalities.

The second was that Byzantium's foes – the traditional ones on the Danube, the rather more recent ones, the Normans in Italy, and, most important and dangerous of all, the Seljuks raiding from the east – saw before them what appeared to be a military vacuum in the lands they so much coveted, and acted accordingly.

What remains inexplicable was the complacency of Constantine and his government in the face of those threats and, in the east, their half-hearted, ineffectual military responses to the predators now raiding not only in Armenia but on occasions deep into the heartland of the Empire.

6

Armenia:
Buffer that might have been

Whenever [the Greeks] found an illustrious warrior,
they took away his sight or drowned him in the sea. Their
most constant efforts were ceaselessly to remove from the
East all men of heart and valiant generals of Armenian
origin and to keep them distant by forcing them to live
among them. They transformed young men into
eunuchs, and in place of strong cuirasses, the apparel of
brave men, gave them clothing of vast and billowing
pleats and substituted large neckerchiefs for coats of mail
encircling their shoulders. Like women, they twittered
and spoke slyly; ceaselessly [the Greeks] contrived
the loss of courageous fighters, and it is thanks to them
that the faithful have been led away into slavery among
the Persians.

Matthew of Edessa[1]

The misfortune of Armenia* was its location. No one could
ever leave it alone.[2] It is a barrier *par excellence*, most of it more
than a mile high, girded around three quarters of its circum-
ference by high mountains with a minimum of passes through
them. It was a formidable block to westward invasion of the
Anatolian plateau, whether from the borders of present-day
Russia and Iran on the east or from Azerbaijan on the south.

*The designation, though generally used and unavoidable, is often
more confusing than helpful. The lands considered here are those south
and west of the Caucasus, bounded on the west by the Euphrates, on the
north-west by the Akampsis (Chorokhi)/Coruh River, on the north by the
Kour/Cyrus River, on the east and south-east by the Araxes/Aras, Lake

Armenia also lay athwart the great trade routes, functioning since early times and still operative, running north–south from the Black Sea ports, principally Trebizond/Trabzon, to the Persian Gulf, and east–west from the Mediterranean, via the Black Sea or Constantinople, to Asia.

Inside the mountainous perimeters of the huge three-sided natural fortress the land is broken by a series of lesser ranges, canyons and otherwise rough terrain; only in a semi-circle of about a hundred miles radius north of Lake Van is there relatively level country. Dry and hot in summer, bitterly cold and under deep snow in winter, Armenia would hardly seem to invite farming and animal husbandry. Nevertheless, some of the land is arable and much of it provides what was for medieval times relatively good grazing. Armenia was in fact famed for its produce of fruits, vegetables, wool, hides and meat. Its handicrafts, the work of extraordinarily diligent and skilled craftsmen, were renowned.

The two great empires that persisted under various regimes from classical to medieval times, Roman–Byzantine in the west, Persian–Islamic in the east, assumed that control of Armenian trade routes and produce would be to its master's advantage. But by far the most important reason for the centuries-long struggle for domination of Armenia was that the region served its possessor both as defensive bastion and offensive launching point. Holding Armenia, Parthia could strike against Rome, Rome against Parthia; so also Persian rulers and their Turkish successors could use Armenia to defend against or strike against Byzantium, and vice versa.

The key geographical considerations for any military operation in Armenia were the entrances to it and the routes through it. Access for the Byzantines was simple enough, entailing

---

Urmia and the valley of the Greater Zab, and on the south by the Tigris/Dicle valley and the mountains of Kurdistan north of today's Turco-Syrian border. It was inhabited by Georgian and Armenian peoples. It consisted of two major kingdoms, Georgian Iberia and the kingdom of Armenia itself, the principalities of Kars and Ani, and a welter of smaller entities, occasionally independent but more often subordinated to larger political units, forever shifting allegiance among them, the Saracens and the Byzantines. More conveniently, the area may be thought of as divided in several regions, the principal ones being the two main kingdoms, plus Mesopotamia in the west and Vaspurakan in the south and east.

only a climb by existing roads from the Anatolian plateau's 2000- or 3000-foot level eastwards to Armenia's 5000-foot level along either of the two branches of the Euphrates, from Sebastea/Sivas to Arzen/Erzurum and thence eastward, or from Melitene/Malatya to Manzikert and the Lake Van area. Equally – and thus the principal threat to Byzantium from an enemy in Armenia – a force intending to invade Anatolia had downhill passage by the same routes. Once the Byzantines annexed and garrisoned Armenia, the problem of the Turks was to regain entrance to it from the east and, to establish control, to take its strategic points: Kars and Ani near the bend of the Araxes's headwaters rising near Erzurum and giving on to the upper reaches of the northern branch of the Euphrates; Manzikert at the great westward turn of the lower branch of the Euphrates (the Murat Su), and the key forts nearby at Van and along the northern shore of the lake. The easiest way into Armenia for them, and the one most used, was to follow the Araxes north from their base at Tabriz, proceed westward with its turn either to its headwaters at Erzurum and thence along the northern branch of the Euphrates into Anatolia, or to turn south through Ağri and then Manzikert, taking the southern branch of the Euphrates westward or descending a bit further to Lake Van, crossing the pass above its westernmost point to Balesh/Bitlis and thence to the Euphrates or Tigris by relatively easy routes. Another less convenient route was to turn west from a point further south on the Araxes and move to the plain north of Lake Van via Doğubayazit (the present lorry road).

Thus, as a glance at a contour map will show, the key points to hold or acquire in Armenia, either for defensive or offensive operations, and whether by Byzantine or Turks, were the upper Araxes, the towns on the northern shore of Lake Van and, particularly, Manzikert a few miles north of them on the Euphrates.[3] The Seljuks' successful efforts to wrest those recent Byzantine acquisitions from their control form the principal military history of the third quarter of the eleventh century.

Only on rare occasions – in Alexander's time, for example – was Armenia allowed to serve as it should have served: as a

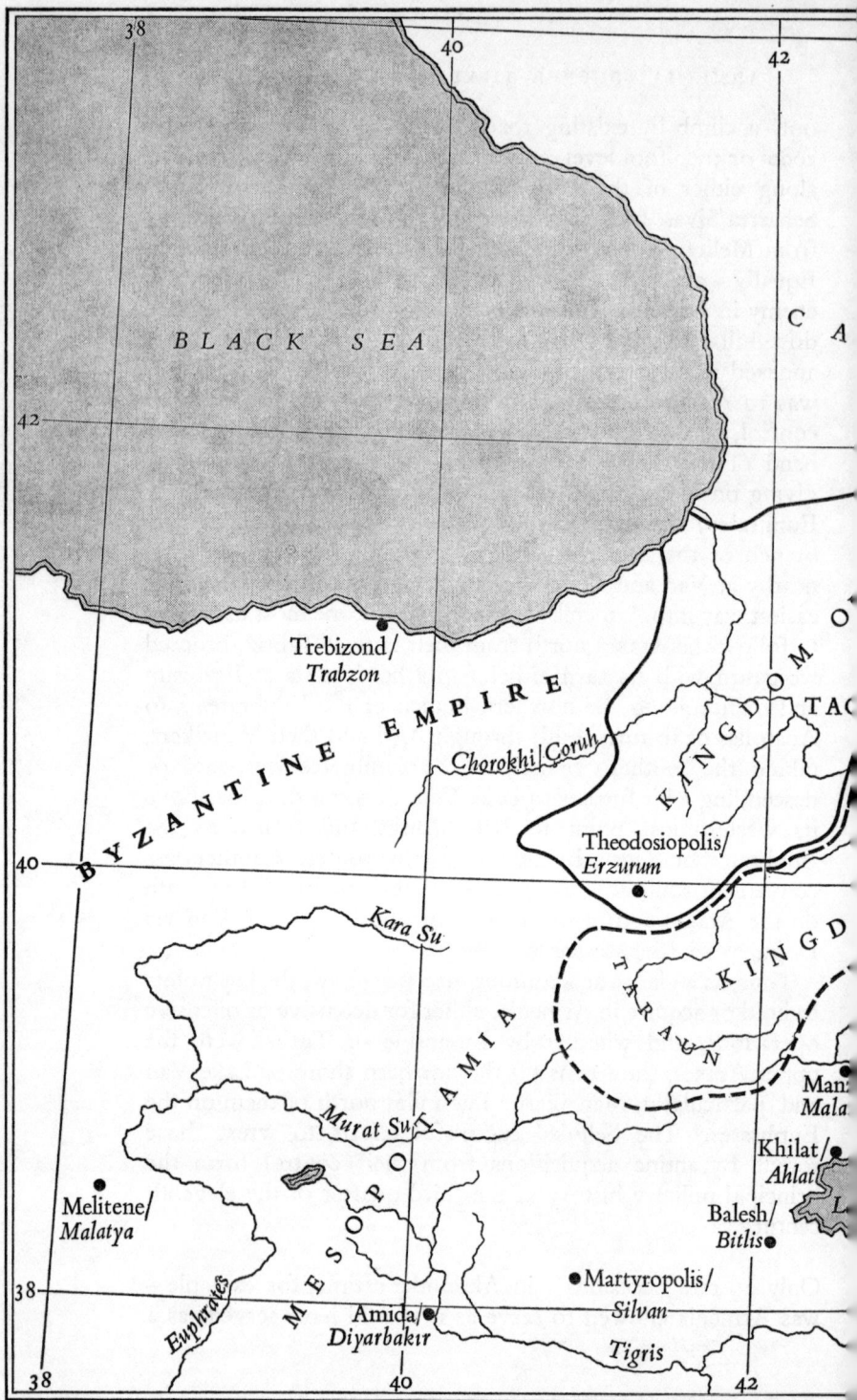

4 *Armenia and environs*

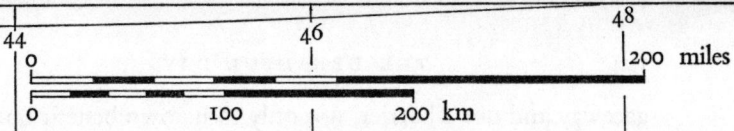

gateway and not a barrier, not only to its own benefit but also to enhance the trade of states on both sides of it. (But Alexander, who took pains to hold it, saw both those sides as part of a single empire, his own.) More frequently and for longer periods, its constituent parts were either incorporated outright into the realms of one or the other of its powerful neighbours, or taken under their suzerainty with varying degrees of autonomy. Even though mere suzerainty fell short of their basic desires, the two sides struggled for it almost ceaselessly for more than a millennium. The ultimate dream of each was to annex the lands and make them integral parts of its own Empire. When, occasionally, either one or the other realized the dream, it turned into a nightmare – always for Armenia itself, usually for the loser and often enough even for the winner.

The wars to dominate the highlands south of the Caucasus can be seen as part of the age-old conflict between East and West; more concretely, they were aspects of the battle between Rome and Parthia. In this account, they form the crucial engagements between Byzantines and Turks – between Christian and Moslem (although the religious element was less important than the political). Had both East and West foresworn political and territorial conquest, Armenia might have been left as the buffer its geographical location dictated for it; its benefit would have been to allow each side to avoid warring with the other as long as that was its wish. But that was almost never the wish; perhaps the East–West conflict lay too deep – or perhaps only its self-perpetuating dynamics rather than any good reason kept the contest alive and malefic.

The struggle for domination of Armenia continued almost ceaselessly through late Hellenistic, Roman and Byzantine times, until the final triumph of the Turks after Manzikert. For most of the long and bloody period when the contestants were not directly at each other's throats, a *modus vivendi* obtained; suzerainty was divided, but the tug-of-war continued, with the presiding Armenian and Georgian princes continually shifting their alliances or subservience and blighting the national consolidation they all dreamed of by waging intestine wars with tedious and murderous persistence.

By the seventh century, however, Byzantium's efforts to

hold the eastern highlands collapsed; the area fell under the direct rule of the Umayyad and Abbasid Caliphates. They set about the devastation of the country, subjecting it to ferocious religious and economic persecution. Through wars and repressions, they decimated the principalities' noble families and aristocracy, forcing a massive exodus of the population, high and low alike, into the Byzantine Empire.

In 885 a respite from external domination of almost a century and a half began when the Abbasid Caliphate, weakened within, could no longer control Armenia; fortuitously, the Byzantines, under constant pressure from other enemies, had neither armies nor interest to turn the situation to their advantage. Although nominally under the caliphs' vassalage, the Armenian Bagratid dynasty established an era of *de facto* independence. Armenia reached the apogee of strength, prosperity and cultural achievement. Its recuperative powers throughout its history were prodigious, now, once again in a position to conduct trade with both the Caspian lands to the east and the Black Sea to the north-west and to market its abundant produce, a happy renaissance ensued.

Yet, always their own worst enemies, the Armenians and Georgians could not or would not make an end to their internal strife. By the end of the tenth century, disintegration had set in. Weakened by their wars, Armenia and Iberia were in no position to withstand a concurrent revival of Byzantine expansion. The Macedonian emperors had at last bested their major enemies and began to look again with longing eyes to the lands beyond the Euphrates.

As early as the 870s Basil I imposed his suzerainty on Taraun, Armenia's westernmost extension, and a century later it was annexed. A few years later Leo VI began recovering parts of Mesopotamia. On the heels of his predecessors' victories in the Balkans, Romanus I determined to regain all the Arab-held Mesopotamian marches that once belonged to the Empire. He set his great general Curcuas – an Armenian – to the task, with notable success. Curcuas occupied Melitene, key to the upper Euphrates, in 931, and a decade or so later captured Martyropolis and Amida, and conquered, although he did not occupy, Edessa.

The reasons for those eastward thrusts were sound: Mesopotamia was a rich and fertile region, much of its population was 'Roman', i.e. Armeno–Greek, and the enemy to be expelled and blocked from potential future assaults was the ancient one, the Arab emirs. In the Tigris–Euphrates valleys their forces were sheltered behind the Taurus, where they could prepare at leisure ravages of the sort that had so devastated Byzantium in past centuries.

In the next decades, however, the Empire moved against peoples who could have no offensive aspirations against it and who were at the time performing the function, willy-nilly, of keeping Saracen troops out of Anatolia. Nevertheless, the Macedonian emperors set out to capture the Armenian lands bit by bit, by warfare, provocation of internal revolts, intimidation and unscrupulous diplomacy. This time their objective was not merely to displace Abbasid suzerainty but to annex the lands outright.

Nicephorus Phocas annexed Bagratid Taraun in 968. Basil II sent a force in 990 against the Georgian Bagratid prince David, ruler of Tao, in south-western Iberia; he had made the mistake of supporting a rebel who, in Basil's early days, had attempted to take the throne from him. Basil's terms to David were in the form of postponed ruthlessness: the prince could retain his homeland and some areas given him in the Empire for earlier services rendered, but only until his death, whereupon the entirety should be ceded to Byzantium.

Ten years later, in the winter of 999–1000, at Tarsus after victories in Syria, Basil heard of David's death and internal Armenian troubles that then ensued (see Chapter 4, p. 78). Basil moved swiftly north-east at the head of his formidable and victory-proud armies. A convocation of Georgian and Iberian leaders, with their troops, came to meet him. Possibly by accident, a battle ensued; the thrashing Basil's army administered did wonders to concentrate the minds of the local potentates on the futility of resistance.

Basil was able to move forward to recovered lands north of Lake Van, to set terms delimiting any further Georgian advance into Iberia and to enforce his old bargain with David to take Tao. After another twenty years, when Georgian princes again stirred up trouble, Basil moved into the area in his third, last and most territorially acquisitive foray. He forced John Sembat, King of Armenia, just as he had forced

David, to cede his kingdom to Byzantium on his death. Turning south, he thereupon annexed the large province of Vaspurakan, of which he had been the nominal protector since the year 1000. Its King, Sennacherib, probably under Byzantine pressure,[4] ceded his possession to the Empire in 1021-2.

Thus all Greater Armenia (except a small area around Ani) beyond the Araxes and almost to Lake Urmia, and as far west as the Euphrates, was now within the Empire or pledged to enter it.

Most historians take it for granted that the primary reason for the acquisition of the Armenian domains was military necessity, for the defence of the Empire's eastern frontiers. But it can be seen that there were also other considerations, less justifiable than apparent defensive need, for a programme that, in the end, helped to defeat its own purpose.

Granted, the formation of an uninterrupted border, an apparent barrier to invasion, along a mountain chain in a great semicircle from the eastern end of the Black Sea around to the plains of Irak and Syria was a goal that would recommend itself to any military power with an enemy on the other side. Furthermore, the constant internal divisions and wars of the Georgian–Armenian potentates had so weakened the land as to undermine its capacity for self-defence.

Yet the question comes to mind, whether in fact, by the end of the tenth century and the first decades of the eleventh, Byzantium faced any considerable menace from enemies east of Greater Armenia. The Seljuks had scarcely been heard of in Constantinople and the Abbasid Caliphate in Baghdad had been growing progressively weaker, puppet of Buwayhid masters. Those latter, meanwhile, were beset by Turkish kingdoms to the north and east of them and were nervously watching the newcomers in Persia, the Seljuks, beginning to accumulate a power that was soon to be turned against them. Byzantine relations with the Fatimid Caliphate in Egypt were essentially untroubled. There was intermittent battling with Arab emirs in Syria but such danger as that entailed was not to be abated by raids into the highlands two to three hundred miles to the north-east. In short, the Moslem world had more military and political turmoil in its own lands than its rulers could handle, without concocting major forays against the Eastern Roman Empire. Arab emirs in Azerbaijan and Caspian lands were congenitally aggressive, but they were hardly in a position to trouble the rulers of Byzantium.

As for the first Turkish raids from Azerbaijan, even if they came as early as 1016 and continued for three or four years after that – and were not, as Cahen believes, begun about 1029 – and even if they were conducted by Seljuks, which is highly improbable, Byzantium's annexations had been made long before, excepting only Vaspurakan in 1021–2.*

If Byzantium's military imperatives were not, therefore, overriding, what other reasons were there for bringing Greater Armenia into the Empire? One was sheer lust for territorial conquest, which has a dynamic all of its own. The Macedonian emperors devoted their lives to gaining territory and not always because it represented a danger to the Empire in enemy hands. The Byzantines' term for themselves was 'Romans' and they thought of themselves as such. Their greatest emperors, it would seem, were dominated by the aspirations that what once was Rome's should be 'Roman' again.

But, to repeat, the annexations and Byzantine policies that followed in Armenia were self-defeating. Basil II, perhaps a better general than diplomat, seemed to have blinkered himself to the political consequences of his actions; his successors were political fools and Constantine IX and X were religious zealots as well, to the point of viewing Armenian calamities as gains for the orthodox Church. Their behaviour as ruthless masters and pig-headed proselytizers made of the Armenians not loyal citizens but oppressed and resentful enemies. The failure of the imperial policy towards the new vassal states was gross enough to be noted by Byzantine writers at the time.[5]

Runciman, who believes that the annexation of Armenia was dictated for military reasons – that no reliance on defence could be placed on the Armenian princes and that the territory was too much of a danger area to remain outside of Byzantine control – nevertheless admits that a grave mistake may have been made:

*See Chapter 3, p. 55. The questions are discussed by Vryonis, *Decline*, fn. p. 81. At the time of writing (1980), the issues of dates and identity of the raiders were still in dispute.

Wise statesmen, less obsessed than the soldier-emperors of Byzantium by the military point of view, would have hesitated to create an Armenian question to destroy the uniformity of the Empire and to add a discordant minority to its subjects.[6]

King John Sembat of Armenia died in 1040 and Byzantium determined to implement the treaty of cession of his country agreed with Basil II twenty-odd years before. Resistance flared, various princes and noble families temporarily united to maintain an Armenian sovereign, ultimately declaring John's nephew, Gagik II, as King. Constantine IX, newly come to the throne, and a man who chose whenever he could to gain his ends by stimulating treachery and internal dissent, applied those tactics vigorously and successfully. In 1045 a traitorous adviser persuaded Gagik to accept an imperial invitation to Constantinople. Once there, without his forces, betrayed and bullied, he had no alternative but to give up his land. The deal was made easier by the grant to him of extensive domains in Cappadocia and a palace in Constantinople itself. The result was that Armenia lost its last king and saw an end to its independence.

Given the quarrelsome nature of the Armenians, a basic religious division together with their own ferocious internal religious conflicts (which the Byzantines took pains to exacerbate), the different language, the national pride and the still burning memory of a once and no longer Armenian Camelot – given all these, a comfortable absorption of the annexed territories would have been inordinately difficult. But even against odds, the Byzantines should have tried. The new masters might have nourished the enduring Armenian dream of a national entity, if not political then at least psychological and spiritual. Instead, exactly the contrary policy was adopted. Every effort was made to extinguish institutions that tended towards native cohesion, in particular, the Armenian Church. Grants of large landholdings within the Empire, similar to that to Gagik, were made to other nobles to lure them into exile. Of those that remained, one was played off against the other. At a lower level the Byzantines extinguished local authority until then exercised by the *nakharars*, hereditary chiefs of cantons; the office was abolished.

Another profoundly weakening process was the continuation of a development that had begun centuries before: the exodus of great numbers of the native population. It had begun as early as the seventh century on orders of the Emperor Maurice for mass deportations of Armenians into far-off areas of the Empire; it was to continue ever since. Some was forced but much was voluntary, with Armenians either seeking to escape the tribulations and cruelty suffered under Saracen dominion or because better opportunities appeared to offer themselves in the west. The emigrations, by the tens of thousands, greatly weakened the homeland, although they infused new strength and vitality into the Empire. Many migrants were organized into the armies of new themes (there were Armenian corps in Sebastea, Tephrice/Divriği, and Melitene); they became some of Byzantium's finest fighting men. Others rose to the throne, still others became its ablest and most famous generals. By their hundreds, luminaries in the cultural, political and commercial annals of the Empire were of Armenian descent.*

With diminished local manpower and the Byzantines' deep distrust of the loyalty of the native military forces still remaining – entirely justified distrust, for the Byzantines had themselves engendered it† – the new rulers installed mercenaries and relied on them almost exclusively for defence of the whole area.‡ Constantine IX's dissolution of the 50,000 strong

*Well before the annexations and continuing thereafter, large numbers of Armenians moved into Cilicia. Just how great a loss that was of staunch warriors is demonstrated by what they did when they hid themselves in their new mountain fastnesses in the Taurus. They became renowned for the invaluable help they gave the Crusaders *en route* to the Holy Land. Under various monarchs the Christian Armenian kingdom in Cilicia held out a century or more against Islam after the Latin kingdom of Jerusalem ceased to exist.

†With evidence culled from a host of contemporary chroniclers, the renowned French Byzantine scholar J. Laurent presents a formidable indictment of the Armenians as traitors when serving in the Byzantine armies, and there and elsewhere as congenital brigands and plunderers, cruel and untrustworthy, ever since the time of Nicephorus Phocas. Laurent's bill of particulars is damning, but he concedes that treason was provoked by the Byzantines' persecution of their eastern vassals in order to force them to abandon their religion and embrace the doctrine and dominion of the Greek Orthodox Church.[7]

‡Cahen notes that after the peasant-soldiery of the themes had been virtually extinguished, Byzantium chose to substitute mercenaries,

Armenian militia has already been mentioned (see Chapter 5, p. 93). Had the mercenaries cared for something more than their pay, or even had Constantinople given them the pay that was due them and supplied them with adequate equipment, they might have been of some use. But, instead, they ravaged and plundered the lands they were contracted to defend.

At first thought, one might suppose that during the seemingly endless centuries of conflict between the Byzantines and the Persians and Saracens, and while the Armenians were suffering indescribably ghastly religious persecutions, first from Zoro-astrian rulers and then from Islamic ones, they would have opted to the last man for the protection and even suzerainty of their fellow-Christians. Furthermore, from almost the beginning the Armenians were western-oriented in custom and outlook. But there are several reasons why such a choice of affiliation was not as automatic as it might seem. Perhaps, most significantly, neither the Armenians nor the Byzantines saw each other as co-religionists.

The theological dispute that began in Christianity's earliest days, and which still exists, grew so divisive and rancorous in the Middle Ages that Byzantines and Armenians viewed each other as heretics, to be feared and despised almost worse than the heathen.

The controversy was over the true nature of Christ. It reached a climax or watershed at the Council of Chalcedon in 451. It was so bedevilled with theological intricacies, verbal ambiguities and implications about matters of faith that today it is close to unintelligible to anyone who has not studied it intensively – which must exclude all but relatively few scholars and ecclesiastics. Indeed, the 'Christological question' is extremely difficult to define in terms relevant to even a devout present-day Christian layman. In grossly over-simplified terms, the 500 to 600 bishops assembled at Chalcedon (slightly south-east of Constantinople on the Sea of Marmara) con-

---

wholly foreign to the country, throughout Anatolia as a whole, not merely in Armenia. It saw the eastern armies as nothing more than private troops enrolled by the great landowners and was properly suspicious of them. Their interest was much more to serve their military masters than the Crown.[8]

firmed the Dyophysite orthodox doctrine (generally accepted by most Christian denominations today) that Christ had two natures, each perfect in itself and distinct from the other, but perfectly united in one person, both God and man. The opposing doctrine of Monophysitism (and several of its near relations, each with further complicating distinctions) held that the nature of Christ was single, one incarnate amalgam of God and Logos, the Word. It and its variations were denounced as heretical, but even though the Armenian Church fathers rejected the words of the principal early proponents of the Monophysite view, the creed to which they clung was deemed by others, then and now, as Monophysite. The Armenian Church proclaimed itself autocephalous. Established as a state religion some years before Constantine the Great decreed Christianity for the Roman Empire, it was not disposed to take instruction on doctrine from pope or patriarch.*

It is difficult for someone in today's tepid theological climate to appreciate the obsessiveness of the dispute – St Gregory of Nyssa's observation (see footnote, Chapter 4, p. 60), though cast in humorous terms, suggests it – or the fury it engendered between Greek and Armenian. Emperors and patriarchs struggled vainly to find reconciliation, or, more often, to force acceptance of their position. Once the break was no longer to be healed, the animus grew worse as the religious conflict came to cloak equally violent political differences.

The bitterness of the Armenians, particularly in the years to come after their conquest by the Seljuks, their despair and their anger at what they considered a betrayal by the Byzantines – and their hatred of them – emerge most shrilly and also most poignantly in the *Chronicles* of Matthew of Edessa, an extract from which appears at the head of this chapter. He was an Armenian monk and head of a monastery in Edessa, whose writings leave something to be desired in historical accuracy. (He probably could not read Greek and Syrian and was ignorant of classical literature and history; moreover, he wrote a century

*Among the explanations easiest for a layman to grasp – and they are difficult enough – are those of Sirarpie Der Nersessian, pp. 29–39, and *E B*, Vol. 4, p. 481.

or so after the events discussed here.) But his work is representative of the feelings of his beaten-down and humiliated countrymen. His account is a long, blood-curdling lament of the woes that befell them, in their own civil wars, and at the hands of the Greeks, Arabs and Turks.

One episode he describes may be suspect as history, but it is nevertheless indicative of Armenian attitudes to the Byzantines and of the relative importance of the religious conflict between the two peoples. It is a piece of gory humour which, apparently, the old monk took delight in relating.

The account purports to tell of an effort by Constantine X to bring the Armenians to see the error of their dogma and to accept that of the Orthodox Church. A debate is held in St Sophia which King Gagik – who had lost his throne and removed to his new lands in Anatolia – attends to dispute with the emperor on the Christological doctrine. So much is fact.

According to Matthew, Gagik wins hands down and departs from Constantinople leaving the monarch as a new convert to the Monophysite persuasion. That, of course, is obvious nonsense, and the story is further clouded by a gross error in Matthew's chronology: the events he goes on to describe almost certainly took place years later, after the Battle of Manzikert, not during Constantine's reign.[9] Whatever the date, though, he tells how Gagik was enraged at the Romans. On arriving at Caesarea/Kayseri on his journey home, 'he ordered his troops to violate the most illustrious Roman women', wishing to outrage Byzantium and intending never to return to Constantinople but to offer his services instead to the Seljuk Sultan, Alp Arslan, then engaged in his ravages.

But, it seems, the ex-king felt there was other work to be done in Caesarea besides systematic rape. The city's Metropolitan, a certain Mark, was a 'schismatic' – no dirtier word existed in Matthew's vocabulary. Mark was a blasphemer, a perverse and impious heretic who hated Armenians to the point that he had named his dog Armen, a deliberate insult implying that dogs were Armenians and Armenians were dogs. But while Gagik was in the city, Mark foreswore his usual denunciation of the Armenians; Gagik sent word that he would like to stay with the Metropolitan. Mark professed delight, Gagik entered his house, taking the precaution of bringing a number of his troops with him, and the two settled down to a fine feast. Both, it would appear, became roaring drunk.

At some point, Gagik told Mark that he understood he had a fine dog and that he would like to see him. Mark still had enough of his wits about him to realize that the request was deliberately provocative and refused it. Gagik persisted, asking the dog's name. The Metroplitan continued to prevaricate for a time but, ultimately, the wine getting the better of him, called out, 'Armen', and the dog came bounding in. 'Aha,' said Gagik, 'the dog is named "Armen"; why?' 'Because he is so gentle,' said Mark, blushing. To which the Gagik replied, 'Now we will see who is more gentle, the Armenian or the Roman.'

The deposed monarch ordered his men to bring in a sack and put the unfortunately named beast inside. Mark, furious, denounced the act. Gagik, smiling in disdain, made a second sign to his men who thereupon surrounded the Metropolitan and stuffed him violently into the sack with the imprisoned dog. 'Now,' Gagik repeated, taking the question from the general to the specific, 'who is the braver of the two, the gentle dog or the Roman Metropolitan?' Gagik then commanded his men to beat the dog severely and in agony, it began to tear at his master.

They continued a good part of the day to beat the dog, which in its rage made the blood flow from the accursed heretic. Mark never ceased to shout horrible cries and lamentations. There was the most violent battle in the sack, from which came the sound of grinding teeth, groans and crying. It was by such a horrible death that the blasphemer perished, as food for dogs.[10]

There is no independent evidence to confirm the episode, but one is probably entitled to accept as accurate the indication of Armenian sentiments.

The historical evidence makes clear that those sentiments were such that, when the Seljuk penetrations began in earnest, the Armenians saw little reason to think that their conquest would place a harsher burden on them than the one they already bore. The ensuing slaughter was too great for the Armenians to have welcomed the Turks as rescuers, but neither did they see much point in joining the Byzantines as defenders.*

*W. H. Ramsay and others profess to find evidence from the historians of the day that the heretics of Armenia (and elsewhere in Anatolia) found the dominion of the Turks a relief from Byzantine fiscal and religious tyranny.[11] That was perhaps the case in later years, especially during the reign of Malik-Shah. But certainly during the time of the raids before Manzikert and for some years thereafter, the Syrian and Armenian chroniclers saw the Turks as the armies of the Antichrist.[12]

7

The Arrows of the Infidels

At the beginning of the year 467 [March 1018] a scourge
manifesting the fulfillment of divine threats of affliction
descended on the Christians, worshippers of the Holy
Cross. The death-breathing dragon appeared accompanied by a destroying fire and struck the believers of
the Holy Trinity. Thereupon the apostolic and prophe-
tic books trembled to their foundations, for winged
serpents came to vomit flames on Christ's faithful. I
mean by these words to make known the first irruption
of the ferocious beasts thirsty for blood. At that period
there assembled the savage nation of infidels known as
Turks. . . .

Until then, the Turkish cavalry had never been seen.
Facing the enemy, the Armenians beheld these men of
strange appearance, armed with bows, and their hair flowing like that of women. They were not accustomed to
protecting themselves against the arrows of those infidels.

Matthew of Edessa[1]

A sagittariis Hunorum, nos defende, Domine.
Prayer in Italian churches at the time of Attila[2]

The first Turkish incursions into Armenian territory, in
Vaspurakan about 1016 (or perhaps some several years later),
which evoked Matthew of Edessa's agonized cry, were almost
certainly not conducted on the orders or with the blessings of
the Great Seljuk military leaders then fighting in Iran; in fact,

they were probably not even the work of Seljuks. More likely, the raiders were other Turkic tribesmen who had drifted westwards some years earlier into Azerbaijan, or Turkish slave-soldiers of local emirs there. Their weapons and tactics, however, were those of the Oghuz of old and the same as those used by the Seljuks then and for fifty-odd years to come in wresting Asia Minor from the Byzantines – and in the succeeding centuries against the Crusaders.

They struck terror into the heart of the King of Vaspurakan, Sennacherib, who, unable to eat or sleep, fell to examining the works of the prophets and saints; he discovered therein that because of his people's iniquity Satan had triumphed and that the end of the world was imminent.[3] Once the Seljuk sultans began to manage the forays two or three decades later and to deploy their own organized forces in the attacks, Sennacherib's conclusion was, for Armenia at least, not far off the mark.

In major respects the composition of the Seljuk forces, their arms and their battle tactics, were very different from those of their opponents; it was in good measure those very distinctions that were decisive.

Indispensable as the Turkomans were on major campaigns, especially those in Armenia, they were only the lesser part of the Great Seljuk Empire's military organization.[4] Once embarked on making for themselves a domain of Iran–Irak and a conquest of Syria and (unsuccessfully) Egypt, the sultans were obviously not content to rely alone on Turkoman nomads, of only sporadic loyalty at best and often downright rebellious. Prudently, they constructed as their principal force a permanent army, similar in composition to those common throughout Moslem lands: a slave (*gulam*, later known as Mamluk) army. The appellation, however, tends to be misleading: the status of the slaves was not that which the word generally brings to mind. The *gulams* were bought and sold – large numbers were purchased in the Empire's slave markets – and could be disposed as gifts from one owner to another or taken over *en bloc* by the victor from the army of the vanquished; they could be punished, to the point of mayhem, at their masters' will. But nevertheless they were paid a wage, and were capable of refusing to fight when their rations or pay fell short; they shared in prize-money and loot.

They were usually recruited from an alien cultural milieu or distant geographical location at an early enough age to be properly trained, moulded and indoctrinated into the new society they were to serve. Transported to an unfamiliar environment, the *gulam* became, in theory at least, 'more obedient to the Sultan his master than were the indigenous Moslem subjects, and because of his spirited and rigorous training became a capable administrator'.[5] Islamic potentates began to rely on these slave-soldiers, principally Turkish, as early as the ninth century. For a long period, the Turkomans on the north-eastern border of the Islamic world were particularly favoured as *gulams* because of their warlike temperament.

The abler ones rose in great numbers to the highest military and administrative ranks, achieving the rank of 'chamberlain'* and 'commanders' (emirs) who were given fiefdoms (*ikta*), some very large and with enormous revenues. After the Seljuk conquest of Asia Minor they played an increasingly important role as major figures in the civil and military administration; the Seljuks' *gulam* army system set the pattern which the Ottoman rulers embraced years later in their military force of Janissaries.

Even in the highest positions, the *gulams* remained slaves in theory, but there was little if any denigratory connotation for them in the word, or even for the common soldier, especially if he was a Turk. Far from feeling abased, the emirs were often of independent minds, deciding for themselves where to bestow their strength and occasionally rebelling and setting up independent regimes of their own.

In addition to the Turks in the sultans' forces, alien volunteers and prisoners of war were often enrolled as *gulams*. Also native troops were pressed into service in distant areas of the Empire when campaigns were being fought there. Finally, especially on the western frontiers, there were the Turkomans, usually and sensibly not left under the leadership of their tribal headmen but put under the orders of the emir in command of a particular operation.

Under their obligation as vassals, the emirs were obliged

*This standard translation of the Turkish *hacib* tends to mislead. The chamberlains were less palace flunkeys than military commanders.

to bring their own *gulams* into the imperial army when ordered. Some commanded only a few – an emir with 500 was considered a substantial person – but some had anywhere from 4000 to 10,000, and the grandest of all supposedly commanded 100,000.

It is impossible to know how many troops the sultans and their commanders disposed of at any given time or in specific campaigns; estimates vary widely and are unreliable at best. Cahen gives the figure of from 46,000 to 70,000 horsemen in the sultan's army.[6] Köymen notes an occasion when Alp Arslan was said to have brought back 50,000 Mamluks from one campaign; he believes that palace guards alone numbered in the hundreds, and cites a figure of 400,000 as given for the army of Alp Arslan's son and successor, Malik-Shah, a total that looks to be much exaggerated. More indicative may be the assertion that on setting out from Persia on the death of his uncle Tughril, Alp Arslan headed a force of 20,000 cavalry and 10,000 infantry. In 1071, turning course from Aleppo back to Armenia to face Emperor Romanus IV, the sultan dispersed the bulk of the troops in his army (presumably local levies) and set off with only 4000 *gulams*. Those, however, probably consisted only of his personal bodyguard.

Contemporary sources mention no army ranks below those of emir and chamberlain except 'head of tent' (of about ten men) and 'head of herd' or 'pavilion' of tents, apparently the leader of a squad and of a company, respectively. In the absence of a more elaborated chain of command, it is remarkable that the Seljuks were able to carry out complex and coordinated operations entailing attacks from one side or the other or the rear, feints, simulated retreats and sudden ambushes, all of which, especially at Manzikert, they performed with great skill and devastating results. They certainly did not evolve the science and art of war into the sophisticated doctrines of the Byzantines but, having once established themselves in Persia, they fielded an organization that was a far remove from that of their wolf-pack assaults on the Central Asian steppes.

As with the Byzantines, the heart of the army was the cavalry. Next in importance was the infantry but there were also individuals or units categorized by the special weapons they employed: archers, slingers, lancers, mace-wielders, axemen, sappers, naphtha-throwers and artillerymen who manned catapults and ballistas once the use and construction of those machines was learned from the Persians. To add ceremony, encourage the horde, panic the enemy, and perhaps give signals, were trumpeters and drummers. It was said to be the glory of the sultans that no craftsman could be found in their armies; all were soldiers. But they were able to repair and maintain their own equipment and could actually manufacture weapons in the field.[7]

But it is to the cavalrymen, the mounted archers, that the main attention must be given. Professor Köymen has summarized the available information. There can be little doubt of his contention: 'Basically, the success of the Turks lay in the unity of man, horse and weapon – the bow and arrow. No other people in history made use of those three elements as harmoniously as did the Turks.'

The value the early Oghuz placed on the horse – indeed, their adoration of it – continued undiminished through Seljuk and Ottoman times. Omar Khayyám, astronomer and poet-laureate of Malik Shah, declared that as the hawk was the king of the carnivores, so was the horse of herbivorous creatures: he relates that a Sassanid ruler held that the emir of man is the sultan and the emir of animals the horse, and that a legendary Turkish ruler said that what the moon is to the heavens, the horse is to kings.

A serviceable steed fetched about the same price, 100 dinars, as a novice *gulam*; a fine one was worth two or three times more; it was the most prized gift that could be bestowed. The animal was relatively small, from its description – small head, extremely small ears, lively eyes, sturdy chest and rump – it would seem to have far more resembled a polo pony (and in fact was much used as such during periods of recreation from fighting) than a Byzantine mount. To carry its heavily armoured rider and often breast armour and frontlet of its own, the cataphract's horse must have been much larger and heavier – and under such a burden was slower and tired more quickly.

The many manuals that existed on the breeding, care and training of Turkish horses showed that they were handled and schooled in a way that would elicit admiration from the most professional of today's trainers. The light-mouthed ponies were broken to the saddle with great tenderness and patience by the time they were two-year-olds; years more of schooling followed in which they learned to turn at the lightest touch to one side or the other and to wheel and reverse course on the spot. They were trained to have no fear of noise, crowds, weapons or the camels and elephants they might meet in battle.* Their speed and stamina, also the result of long training, were proverbial. The average daily distance covered by a horse, presumably on the march in campaign, was said to be forty miles. A swift horse could reportedly travel sixty miles between dawn and dark.

Contemporary Moslem sources give instructions about what colour horses should be used in battles under what conditions of light and darkness, precepts that would seem to be fanciful except perhaps for commanders who had a string of many ponies at their service. But even the humblest cavalryman had two horses at his constant disposal, and perhaps could make some accommodation.

A small mount with the mobility ascribed to it necessarily implies a relatively light burden. Thus, the Seljuk trooper apparently carried no body armour and his shield and weapons – sword, dagger, bow and arrows and occasionally javelin – were much lighter than those of his opponents.

No Seljuk bows or arrows survive today but they almost certainly were much the same, if not quite so finely wrought and embellished, as their Ottoman counterparts, of which an abundance can be seen at the Topkapı and Turkish military museums. Exquisite as works of art, they are equally admirable as instruments of war and the chase, the finest for their purposes ever made. The bows were composite, which is to say built up from a thin, segmented wooden core, itself without propulsive power. Elaborately cooked, shredded and glued fibres from the strongest tendon of an ox or buffalo – the sinew that takes the weight of the beast's cranium from the shoulder – were fixed to the core on the back. Equally ela-

---

*Busbecq, long-suffering ambassador of the Holy Roman Emperor Ferdinand to the court of Sulayman the Magnificent, devoted pages of his letters to his awe and admiration of the care, affection and gentleness bestowed on horses by the Turks, even some five hundred years later.[8]

borately prepared sections of animal horn formed the belly. The bow was also reflexed or recurved; when unstrung its arc was the reverse of what it was when braced and drawn. In the latter position, the tendons were stretched to the point where they almost screamed to resume their former relaxed state, while the horn was subject to a Procrustean compression with the same potential energy.[9]

The bow itself weighed two-thirds of a pound and was only about three feet in length when strung. Yet the draw weight or measure of strength – the weight required on the centre of the bowstring to pull it back the full length of the arrow – of an Ottoman bow is given as 118 pounds (modern target archers use bows of from 20 to 60 pounds strength). Bare fingers would be cut through by such pressure concentrated in little more than an inch; the Turk, therefore, used a ring of bone, stone or ivory around his thumb to hook and hold the string. Although it is impossible today to string such a bow without the aid of a table on which pegs are set in order progressively to lever back the ends a few inches at a time, illustrations indicated that the archer of the time did it unaided, using one leg as a fulcrum; or else, from a sitting position, he used a belt crossed around the midriff, its ends attached to the tips of the bow; with his feet pushing at the centre of the bow and he himself leaning backwards to pull in the end-cords, or 'bastard strings', he could thus reverse the curve and slip the bowstring into its nocks.

The Seljuk cavalryman – and the early Oghuz, as Ibn Fadlan reported (see Chapter 1, p. 33) – was supposedly able to string his bow in the saddle, a feat that suggests that his weapon was not nearly as powerful nor such an unyielding monster as the Ottoman version just described, used mainly for setting long-distance flight records. But there can be no doubt it was reflex and composite, and murderously capable. Arrows were equally well-made, probably heavier than those used for long-distance competitions, probably not armour-piercing (contemporary illustrations of Crusader times, only a few decades later, show Christian soldiers returning from battle, not mortally wounded, with enemy shafts protruding from their chain mail like the bristles of a porcupine).

Köymen declares that the range of a Seljuk arrow was about

one mile but that cannot be true: the later Ottoman bow, designed for distance-shooting, carried at record best between 500 to 600 yards plus, and no one today can shoot that far.*

The Seljuk cavalryman, with from thirty to fifty arrows in his quiver, unopposed by enemy archers in like numbers and of anything like equal skill, would have undoubtedly launched his missiles at much shorter ranges than those cited above. For success, he was not obliged to bring down the cataphract directly with a piercing shot: killing or even wounding his horse, or panicking the beast with pain, would have been enough to reduce the trooper to a clumsy foot-soldier, lumbered with his armour and relatively defenceless against an enemy now wielding his sword instead of his bow, charging him from horseback.

Ample testimony from eye-witness chroniclers of the Crusades makes clear that the Turkish archer was a magnificent marksman. But in hand-to-hand conflict, horseman against horseman, foot-soldier against foot-soldier, the Europeans and Byzantines had the better of the Turks. So also, moving in a phalanx against a foe in equivalent formation, the cataphracts overpowered them. But, especially in the eleventh century, when Byzantine archers were less accomplished and, at Manzikert, insufficient, and the mounted Seljuk archer harried the foe from flanks and rear at a distance, he was himself safe and his enemy was close to defenceless. The bowman's only enemy then was rain: a wet bowstring was useless.

There had been a time, half a millennium earlier, when the Byzantine and not his barbarian opponent in the west was the master bowman. The skill of Justinian's cavalry-archers accounted for the major victories of his great generals, Belisarius and Narses, over the Ostrogoths. Procopius's description of the Romans' skill and technique gives a picture of cavalry

*In 1798, the British Ambassador to the Sublime Porte is reported to have paced off a shot by Sultan Selim III at 972 yards. One suspects that His Excellency minced his steps rather than strode, in order, for some pressing diplomatic reason, to present the Grand Signeur with an egregious piece of flattery.[10]

tactics in most respects the same as the Seljuks were to demonstrate.[11]

But over the years the Byzantines failed to maintain that crucial skill, a fact recognized clearly and morosely three centuries later by Leo VI the Wise. In his *Tactica* he declares: 'Since archery has wholly been neglected and has fallen into disuse among the Romans [Byzantines], the many present reverses are wont to take place.'

By that he probably did not mean that there were no archers at all in the Byzantine forces: his manual offers considerable instructions on manoeuvres involving bowmen. Rather, he seems to imply that their skill with bow and arrow in his day was much inferior to that of Justinian's time.[12]

Michael Attaleiates, serving in effect as judge advocate general in the Byzantine army on many fronts, and the only Byzantine eye-witness to record the Battle of Manzikert,[13] testifies again and again to the superiority in archery of the Turkish enemy, both Patzinaks and Seljuks. The Anatolian soldiers, he reports, were more than a match for the Patzinaks in close combat, but in attacking a camp, they were routed by 'those barbarians who used bows [and thus] panicked the horses of their adversaries by the wounds they inflicted'. On another occasion in the reign of Constantine IX, the Patzinaks, 'planning to deprive the Byzantines of their mounts, shot down their horses with a mass of arrows discharged at a distance. They were unable to engage the Byzantines in hand-to-hand combat for, [the Patzinaks] having made attempts at close fighting, they had, many times, lost a great number of men.' When Constantine's armies were fighting on the Euphrates, Attaleiates describes how 'The barbarians were good at shooting from a distance and still far off, easily wounded many Romans, while remaining untouched themselves. . . . Those who stood on the banks kept shooting at the Romans, causing a great many casualties, and forced them to turn and run.'[14]

In their skill with the bow, their reliance on it as their principal weapon, and in their techniques of warfare, the Seljuks fought in a Central Asian tradition that had originated more than a millennium earlier and was to continue after them until the invention of gunpowder. The feigned retreat of the Parthian horseman and his 'Parthian shot' over his mount's tail were known to Alexander. Three centuries after the Seljuks had passed from the scene, Ottoman cavalry practised the identical art, as Busbecq testifies:

They fix a brazen ball on the top of a very high pole, or mast, erected on level ground, and urge their horses at full speed toward the mast; and then, when they have almost passed it, they suddenly turn round and, leaning back, discharge an arrow at the ball while the horse continues its course. By frequent practice they become able without any difficulty to hit their enemy unawares by shooting backward as they fly.[15]

And Marco Polo, writing of a time two centuries after Manzikert and of a scene a thousand miles to the east, but of a people, the Tartars, who like the Seljuks had Central Asian origins and traditions, gives a classic description of exactly those tactics of warfare used by their Turkic cousins of old in fighting the Byzantines and the Crusaders who followed them:

When those Tartars come to engage in battle, they never mix with the enemy, but keep hovering about him, discharging their arrows first from one side and then from the other, occasionally pretending to fly, and during their flight shooting arrows backward at their pursuers, killing men and horses, as if they were combatting face to face. In this sort of warfare the adversary imagines he has gained a victory, when in fact he has lost the battle; for the Tartars, observing the mischief they have done him, wheel about, and renewing the fight, overpower his remaining troops. . . . Their horses are so well broken-in to quick changes in movement, that upon the signal given, they instantly turn in every direction; and by these rapid manoeuvres many victories have been obtained.[16]

The continuity of the tactics over so many years and their wide diffusion are remarkable.

It was not merely the marksmanship of the Turkic cavalry but their remarkable mobility that dictated their tactics. Except for Attaleiates, we have little description of them from Byzantine sources, but an abundance from the chroniclers of the Crusaders, who found themselves constantly facing them.

The Turks' superior mobility meant not merely being able

to attack with relative safety at will, but to elude counter-thrusts. Together, those abilities led to four distinct, if related, techniques.[17]

The first was the device of keeping at a distance from the enemy until they chose the moment to attack. If the enemy, drawn up in a solid phalanx which they never could vanquish head-on, moved against them, they needed only to retreat. Even if scattered they could always return to the fight.

Second, they adopted the device of the feigned retreat. Incredibly, the Byzantines, who often indulged in precisely that tactic, seemed blind to it when it was employed by their enemies; time after time they were lured like flies into the spider's web. The trick was used to draw the enemy away from their bases: a few Turkish horsemen offered themselves as bait, pretending to invite annihilation in order to provoke attack but, as decoys, drawing the assailants towards their main forces, at the ready for sweeping down on the pursuers. Execution of such a manoeuvre was by no means easy; the issuing of orders and co-ordination of the feigned retreat imply expert and sophisticated central command.

Third, there was the Seljuk preference for attacking on the flanks and rear and compassing the enemy about, putting one Crusader chronicler in mind of Psalm 118: 'They surrounded me like bees.'

Finally, the Turks used their mobility to force the enemy to fight while on the march, a method that is possible only if the attacker can move faster and further than his opponent. This tactic, ordinarily used against the rear of an enemy column, faced the enemy commander with a far more difficult problem than that of an attack on his vanguard, i.e. that of maintaining control. And even when the attack was made against the flanks of a moving phalanx, the continuing losses of horses and men on its fringes, unable to retaliate without breaking up their own formation, was extraordinarily frustrating and demoralizing.

The aim of all those methods was to destroy the cohesion of the enemy, as easily done by bringing down horses as by killing their riders. Always, the manoeuvres were carried out under a hail of arrows, as testified to by the constant use by chroniclers of words like *pluvia* (rain), *imber* (shower), *grando* (hailstorm) and *nubes* (cloud) to indicate the volume of the missiles.

William of Tyre, describing a Crusade encounter, could have been speaking of every Seljuk assault:

At the first onset the Turks shot at us with such rapidity as to darken the heavens as neither rain nor hail could do, so that we suffered many casualties; and when the first had emptied their quivers and shot their bolts the second wave, in which there were yet more horsemen, came after them and began to shoot faster than could be believed.[18]

8

The Seljuk Raids: 1048–69

> The army entered the city, massacred its inhabitants,
> pillaged and burned it, leaving it in ruins, making
> prisoners of all those who escaped the massacre, and
> took possession. (The number of dead was such) that they
> blocked all the streets and one could not make a way for
> himself without crossing over them. The number of
> prisoners was not less than 50,000 souls.
>   I wanted to enter the city and see it with my own eyes.
> I tried to find a street without having to walk over the
> corpses. But that was impossible.
>
> *Purported eye-witness account of the capture of*
> *Ani, quoted by Arab historian Sibt ibn al-Gawzi*[1]

Writing in 1971 with pride on the 900th anniversary of their
forebears' victory at Manzikert, some Turkish historians
declared that the Seljuk incursions into Byzantine territory in
the eleventh century were in furtherance of a systematic and
premeditated plan to topple the Eastern Roman Empire and
to seize Asia Minor, or a deliberate attempt to fulfil a per-
ceived national destiny to reach the Mediterranean.[2] The
Islamic historian Abbas Hamdani declares that the Turkomans
'were unmistakably in search for a permanent home and not
simply grazing grounds for their animals'. In addition, he
writes that the Abbasid caliph of the time urged Sultan
Tughril to make a reality out of his title, 'King of the East
and West', by conquering not only the Fatimids, which he was
already eager to do, but also Byzantine lands.[3]
Certain other modern Turkish scholars[4] deny any prior

intent by the Seljuks to occupy Asia Minor, as does, most insistently, Claude Cahen, among the most respected of modern European authorities on early Turkish history. His contention would seem to be validated by the nature of the Turks' operations against Byzantium both before Manzikert – exclusively raiding and no attempt at conquest beyond Armenia whose history, they felt, made it rightfully subject to their suzerainty – and after the battle, when the Seljuk sultans made no effort to occupy the Byzantine lands that lay helpless before them.[5] Although Turkoman bands moved at once to expoit a defenceless Asia Minor, they appear to have acted without official sanction or direct control of the Seljuk rulers, and even then their emirs did not come to the idea of carving out domains for themselves until a decade or so later. Until then, plundering sufficed them.

Cahen does not go so far as to say that the Seljuks took Armenia and then Anatolia in a fit of absent-mindedness, but he implies something of the sort: invasion seemed natural, indeed almost automatic, when the circumstances amounted to a virtual invitation and when little if anything stood in the way. Armenia and Anatolia beckoned with irresistible treasures: grazing land, booty, potential slaves and a near riskless opportunity to fulfil God's command to exterminate or convert a host of infidels. Although after Manzikert the Turks entered a military vacuum even as nature fills an atmospheric one, Professor Cahen insists that it never crossed the minds of Sultan Tughril and his successor, Alp Arslan, that 'Rum' (as the Turks referred to the Byzantines' 'Roman' Empire) was to be overthrown; indeed, by the reign of Malik-Shah, Alp Arslan's son, the operations of Seljuk commanders in setting up principalities for themselves in Anatolia and on the Aegean caused him serious problems. The Great Seljuk sultans thought of the Byzantine Empire as being as enduring, as eternal an institution, as Islam itself and, with it, one of the world's two permanent great powers.

Why, then, did Tughril, his half-brother Ibrahim Inal and his successor Alp Arslan themselves lead raids on Armenia? Most European scholars of Turkish history feel that they did not engage in those operations for conquest but for what they saw as their own defence imperatives.

E

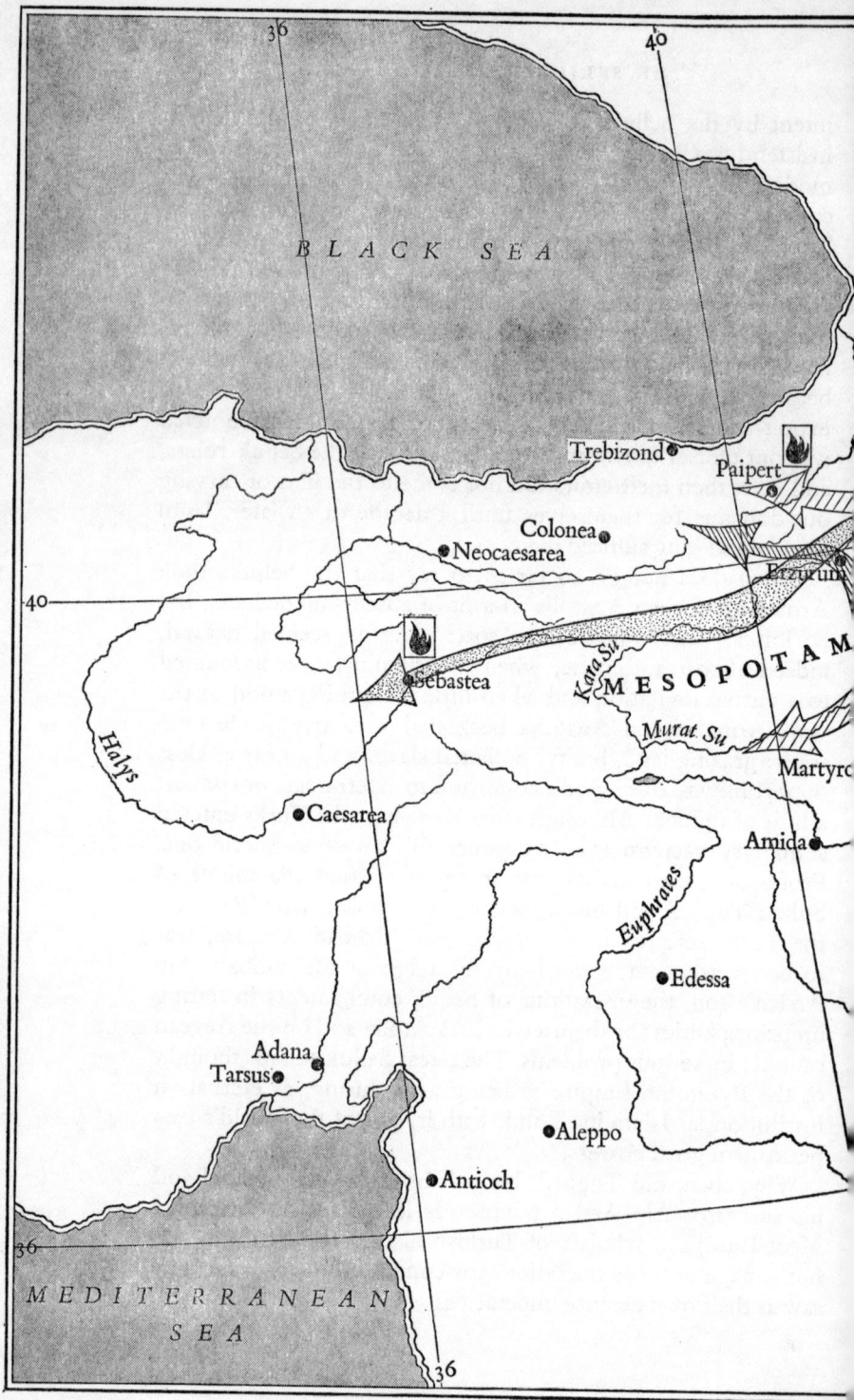

5 *Seljuk raids, 1048–64*

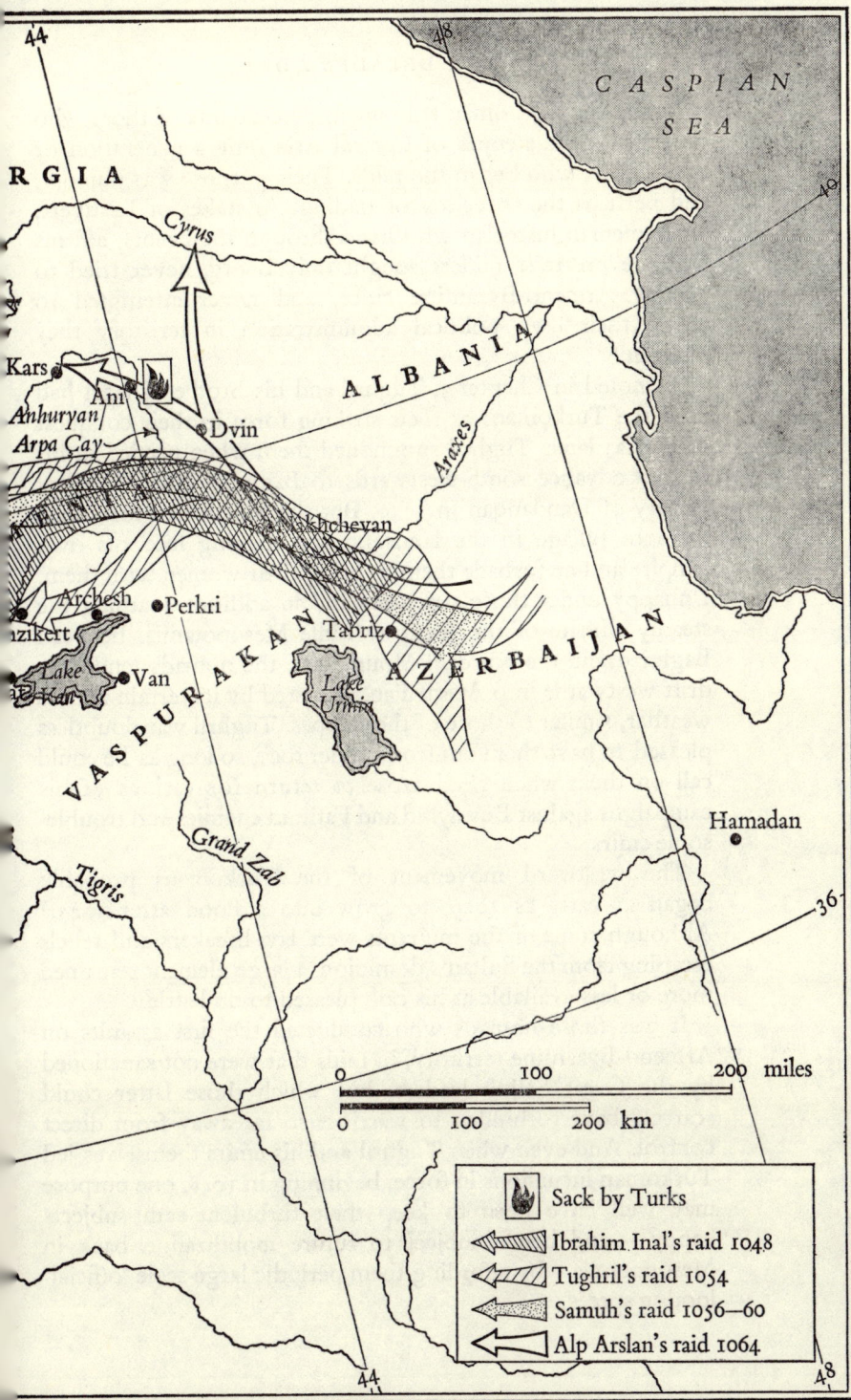

CASPIAN
SEA

RGIA

Cyrus

ALBANIA

Kars
Ani
Anhuryan/
Arpa Çay
Dvin

Araxes

ENIA
Nakhchevan

Archesh
Perkri
Tabriz
AZERBAIJAN

azikert
Lake
Van
Van
Lake
Urmia

VASPURAKAN

Hamadan

Grand Zab

Tigris

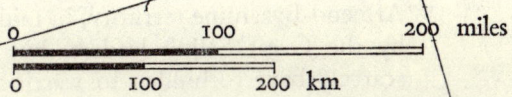

| 0 | | 100 | | 200 miles |
| 0 | 100 | | 200 km | |

🔥 Sack by Turks

Ibrahim Inal's raid 1048

Tughril's raid 1054

Samuh's raid 1056–60

Alp Arslan's raid 1064

It was the Turkoman tribesmen, descendants of those who came from the steppes of Central Asia only a generation or two before, who began the raids. Their purpose was plunder, and perhaps the sheer joy of raiding. Aristakes of Lastivert, an Armenian historian who lived through the events, affirms that the pre-1071 raiders sought only booty, never tried to occupy Armeno-Byzantine cities, and never attempted to create their own political administration in territory they overran.[6]

As noted in Chapter 3, Tughril and his brother Chagri had used the Turkomans as their striking force in their conquest of Persia; later, Tughril summoned them when needed in his further advance south-westwards to Baghdad after the great victory of Dandanqan in 1040. But the Sultan had forbidden them to pillage in the lands he was making into his own Empire and he forbade them to bring their women with them. Unhappy under those strictures and in addition loathing the steamy climate of the Jezire (Middle Mesopotamia, between Baghdad and the Kurdish Mountains), the nomads tended to drift westwards into Azerbaijan, attracted by its terrain and its weather, similar to those of the steppes. Tughril was doubtless pleased to have them out from under foot, so long as he could call on them when need arose to return for various of his campaigns against Buwayhid and Fatimid enemies and troublesome emirs.

The westward movement of the Turkomans probably began as early as 1029, to grow into a flood after 1043.[7] Although some of the migrants were law-breakers and rebels escaping from the Sultan's dominion, a large element remained more or less available at his call, pleased to do battle.

It was those nomads who conducted the first assaults on Armeno-Byzantine territory, in raids that were not sanctioned by the Great Seljuk leaders, but which those latter could scarcely have forbidden to warriors so far away from direct control. And even when Tughril and his emirs themselves led Turkoman incursions in force, beginning in 1048, one purpose may well have been to keep their turbulent semi-subjects happy – and hence subject to future mobilization back in Mesopotamia – by affording them periodic large-scale 'official' looting sprees.

But by that time, there was a new element in the picture: Byzantium had begun to appear to Seljuk eyes as an aggressor, beginning in mid-century to annex lands that had been under Moslem domination for centuries. Therefore, when the Great Seljuk rulers could spare the effort from other matters, and later when they had settled affairs to their satisfaction in Persia and Mesopotamia, they turned to what was for them close to a military necessity: the recovery of strong-points in Armenia and the upper Euphrates, and a response to what appeared to the sultan as a menacing prelude to further Byzantine attacks against Moslem emirates east and south of the Araxes, in Persarmenia and Azerbaijan.

That response was the application of the technique, so successful in Transoxania, Khurasan and Persia, of first capturing or destroying strong-points, then harassing the inhabitants and despoiling their lands until they would accept the dominion of the invaders as the lesser of two evils. The aim of the sultans, after those preliminaries were effectively performed, was what they saw as recovery of areas rightfully theirs rather than new conquests of traditional Byzantine lands.

The dates of the first raids into Vaspurakan and the identity of those who conducted them are in dispute, but those razzias in the first quarter of the century were not in the mainstream of the Seljuk attacks that ultimately overran Armenia. Those latter date from about 1045 or 1046, when a body of Turks from the region of Tabriz in Azerbaijan invaded and devastated Vaspurakan. Its Byzantine governor appealed for help from the governor of Ani; their combined forces ultimately defeated the intruders by a ruse: they fell upon the Turks who were sacking a Byzantine camp left undefended, as bait.*

In 1047 the general Leo Tornicius, of Armenian royal blood, revolted against Constantine IX in Macedonia and Thrace. Proclaimed emperor by his troops, he marched to the walls of Constantinople itself (see Chapter 5, p. 92). To oppose him, a panicked Constantine summoned his armies from the east, denuding it of imperial troops. Taking advantage of that situation, and perhaps urged to the effort by the Abbasid

---

*Alexius I Comnenus used the same trick against a pretender to the throne, Nicephorus Basilacius, thirty-nine years later.[8]

caliph,[9] in 1048 Ibrahim Inal, Tughril's half-brother, moved with a large force north from Azerbaijan and then west along the traditional invasion route to the Araxes valley to the region of Theodosiopolis/Erzurum, and overran Arzn or Ardzen, then a metropolis and trading centre guarding the entrance to Upper Mesopotamia, with routes from there as far north as Trebizond/Trabzon and as far south as the valley of the Murat Su, the southern branch of the Euphrates.*

Arzn, the first of a multitude of large cities to suffer the same fate in future years, was horribly sacked. Aristakes and Matthew of Edessa vied in describing the horror. According to the former:

Like famished dogs, bands of infidels hurled themselves on our city, surrounded it and pushed inside, massacring the men and mowing everything down like reapers in the fields, making the city a desert. Without mercy, they incinerated those who had hidden themselves in houses and churches. . . .

A pitiful and harrowing sight was to be seen. All the city, the market stalls, the lanes, the inns, all were filled with bodies But who could count the number of those who perished in the flames? For those who escaped the flashing swords and hid themselves in their houses found themselves in flames. They burned priests whom they seized in the churches and massacred those whom they found outside. They put great chunks of pork in the hands of the dead to insult us, and made them objects of mockery to all who saw them. . . .

Such was the unhappy history, oh happy and famous city, renowned throughout the world. Lift your eyes and your looks to your sons taken into slavery, your infants smashed without pity against the stones, your youths given to the flames, your venerable ancients thrown down in public places, your virgins, raised gently and in comfort, dishonoured and marched off on foot into slavery. . . .[10]

Matthew tells of 150,000 people massacred, of forty camels required to carry off Inal's booty and of some 5000 cattle taken. At that time, he continues,

there were in Ardzen 800 churches where the mass was celebrated. It was by this cruel disaster and after a frightful carnage, this

---

*After the sack the inhabitants fled to the nearby city of Theodosiopolis and began to call it by the name of their old home, Arzn ar-Rum (Arzn of the Romans), i.e. Erzurum. It became a key defence point and has so remained in modern Turkey.

beautiful and noble city fell. How to relate here, with a voice stifled by tears, the death of nobles and clergy whose bodies, left without graves, became the prey of carrion beasts, the exodus of women of high birth led with their children into Persian slavery and condemned to an eternal servitude! That was the beginning of the misfortunes of Armenia. So lend an ear to this melancholy recital. The extermination of the eastern nation progressed from year to year, and Ardzen was the first city that was captured and disappeared in that ruination.[11]

The Armenian chroniclers were not given to understatement, but even allowing for exaggeration, the carnage must have been ghastly.

Such local troops as there were in Iberia, Vaspurakan and Mesopotamia consolidated and were able to catch the raiders on their return, but the Turks forced a passage and escaped.

Just as the annexation of Greater Armenia lost for Byzantium a buffer state between it and the Seljuk Turks, so had Basil II's earlier annexation of Bulgaria removed a buffer between the Empire and the Turkic Patzinaks/Pechenegs. Now on Byzantium's northern borders, they attacked ceaselessly. They seemed to Constantine IX, not unreasonably, the more serious threat. But unlike his great Macedonian precursors, he was scarcely in a position to fight a defensive war on one front, let alone two. In 1050 troops were again brought out of the east to strengthen the Balkan theatre. But the Patzinaks attacked again and again and, as late as 1053, the emperor was obliged to deploy his eastern troops against them once more. Meantime, he had no option but to try to negotiate a peace on the other front with Tughril. The Sultan's envoy, coming to Constantinople, had the satisfaction of hearing his leader's name read in the *khutba*, the Friday prayer, in place of that of the Fatimid caliph, with whom Byzantium had had excellent relations ever since the time of Basil II.

The negotiations in no way prevented further raiding by the Turkomans; Tughril could always maintain, truthfully or otherwise, that the marauders were rebels, acting beyond his writ.

But, engaged in struggles closer to home, Tughril sanctioned no 'official' invasions until five or six years later. Then, in 1054, he himself led a large force into Armenia. The probable purpose was to consolidate his hold on his vassals in Azerbaijan and particularly on the important emir of Tovin/ Dvin in Persarmenia (Constantine IX had made him an ally in 1044 as part of his machinations to dispose of native princes still ruling in Armenia). And, as always, the sultan needed to keep the Turkoman bands, concentrated in the hill country between Hamadan and Tabriz, under his discipline, especially on the eve of projected, crucial politico-military operations in Irak, where he would need them.

Tughril's equipment suggested that he intended to make a lasting rectification of the Persarmenian frontier, thus taking pressure off the Emir of Tovin, but he seems to have abandoned the idea rather promptly. According to Aristakes,[12] he sent three groups to ravage the centre and north of Armenia, the plain of Erzurum, the valley of the Murat Su and the mountain areas behind Trebizond as far west as Paipert/ Bayburt, which was sacked. He himself took Perkri and Archesh/Ercis on the north shore of Lake Van and then moved some sixty miles to the west to attack Manzikert/Malazgirt.* The large and heavily walled city, a strong-point on a bend of the Murat Su, commanded one of the two traditional military and trade passages into Byzantine territory, that of the lower course of the river itself.

Except for passionate jeremiads and reports of wholesale terror such as those of Matthew and Aristakes, the historians who wrote of the events in the eleventh century rarely animated their accounts of a lugubrious succession of battles and sackings with human and tactical details. But Matthew and Aristakes give us something more in their descriptions of the month-long siege of Manzikert.

After his invariable preliminaries – Tughril with an army 'as numerous as the sands of the sea' launching his assault on the walls 'like a serpent consumed with malice' – Matthew turns to the city's ingeniuous defence under its valiant Byzantine commander, Vasil, half-Armenian, half-Georgian.

Manzikert is the usual English rendering today, but I have encountered no less than fifteen different versions of the name in nineteenth- and twentieth-century historical accounts and translations. *Malazgirt* is the modern Turkish designation.

Against the sultan's attempts to mine the walls, Vasil thrusts a counter-mine, capturing the enemy's sappers, among them one of Tughril's generals, his own father-in-law. Vasil thereupon takes the captives to the ramparts and massacres them in sight of the besiegers.

Deeply afflicted by the loss, the sultan sends to Balesh/ Bitlis to have fetched a huge catapult left there by Basil II thirty years or so before. Once installed, it terrifies the city and drives the sentinels from the ramparts. Whereupon a priest inside the town constructs a catapult of his own, its first shot smashing the fore-part of the enemy machine.* The defenders take fresh courage, but not for long; after a few days the Turks make repairs and protect their artillery piece with a revetment, rendering it invulnerable to further missiles from the city. Once again, deep despair in Manzikert.

Vasil asks for a volunteer who will set the enormous stone-thrower on fire. A 'Frank' (i.e. European mercenary) responds to the promise of rich rewards for himself or, as the case may be, his widow and orphans. He is fitted out with armour and sword, mounted on a fast horse, and rides out with a letter attached to the point of his spear. Hidden inside his shirt against his breast, however, are three pots, presumably clay or glass, filled with a petroleum incendiary.

As intended, the Turks take him for a messenger. His arrival is during the noonday heat, when most of the soldiers are asleep in their tents; those who see him approach the catapult think only that he is admiring it. Suddenly, swift as an eagle, he circles it thrice, hurling one of his incendiary pots each time and then making good a get-away back to the city walls. The dreadful machine is reduced to ashes.†

*Aristakes adds a staggering embellishment: the priest's machine actually hit Tughril's projectiles seven times in a row *in flight*, suggesting an accomplishment which seems not yet to have been achieved in the twentieth century by the USA and the USSR. More incredible even than Aristakes's account is the fact that Canard, his translator, seems to believe it.[13]

†Matthew's account leaves a question to which there is no easy answer: how were the grenades ignited?

Recent research and experimentation suggest that the famous 'Greek fire', saviour of Byzantium time and again, particularly against enemy navies, consisted of a form of petroleum of about the same viscosity and

Summoned to the court of [Constantine] Monomachus, he received honours from him. The sultan himself was not able to deny his admiration for the doer of such a deed and made known to Vasil his wish to see and reward him. But the Frank refused the invitation, to the great regret of Tughril.

Nevertheless, the sultan ordered resumption of the mining of the ramparts; but those besieged redoubled their efforts, facing all the machines he had at his disposal. They manufactured iron clamps with which they seized the miners, whom they massacred on the spot. Seeing himself so vigorously repelled, the mortified Tughril was forced to end the operation. To defy him, the inhabitants took a pig, placed it in a ballista [*sic*; it could only have been a catapult and one hopes it was that built by the priest-engineer], and hurled it at the enemy camp, shouting in one voice, 'Oh Sultan, take this pig for your wife and we will give you Manzikert as dowry.'

On hearing those words, the prince flew into a rage, cutting off the heads of those who brought him the pig and laying out their bodies in front of Manzikert. Then he returned to Persia, enraged by his failure. Thus by the mercy of God, that city was saved from the hands of the Turks.[15]

According to Aristakes, there was a traitor, or Armenian sympathizer in Tughril's camp who shot arrows into the city

---

about as flammable as paraffin (US: kerosene), collectable here and there in Byzantine territory in Asia from natural seepages, and that its 'secret' was less its composition than the sophisticated methods and machinery for its projection: a pre-heating in a closed chamber, then pumping under pressure through a swivelled nozzle. Even then, however, it had to be ignited at its point of ejection or by a flaming missile once it splashed against its target.[14] It is not to be believed that the Byzantines had developed any substance that ignited spontaneously on exposure to air. Incendiaries in the form of grenades, probably filled with somewhat the same kind of petroleum fluid, were also used by both Byzantines and Arabs, and thus known to the Turks too. But they must have been set alight, once the containers smashed against their objectives, either by a burning wick or wrapper (even as are today's petrol (US: gasoline) Molotov cocktails), or else they were ignited moments after they were hurled by fire-arrows shot from a distance.

Conceivably a flaming arrow or catapult bolt could have been shot from the walls by Manzikert's defenders after the daring horseman pitched his pots. Yet Matthew's account declares that the Seljuk's catapult had been protected against such missiles by a revetment. If, however, the Frank carried his pots corked or wrapped with an already smouldering material, he must have worn a remarkably protective undershirt.

carrying messages of the Turks' battle plans for the next day, telling where the attack would come and how and when, thus helping the city defend itself.*

Negotiations were resumed between Tughril and the Empress Theodora, who returned briefly to the throne on the death of Constantine IX in 1055. It is assumed, from terms demanded in later years, that the sultan called for the restitution of major cities formerly in Moslem hands, such as Manzikert, Antioch and Edessa, and the payment of tribute, to which last exaction Theodora apparently agreed.

Great events for both adversaries ensued in the next three or four years. In 1055 Tughril achieved his long-intended triumph, entry into Baghdad. The caliph conferred on him the title of 'King of the East and West', giving him the right and the mission to conquer all Moslem lands, and named him sultan. His entry was peaceful; the mere presence of Turkoman troops in the neighbourhood, summoned by Tughril to his forces, was a powerful persuader. Buwayhid forces fled, freeing the caliph from their long dominion over him. Although he now found himself equally under a military master, the new one was at least more orthodox in his Sunni persuasion and could maintain order in his lands.

Almost at once, however, Tughril was involved in a new series of battles, some of them desperate. The difficulties were revolts by his unruly half-brother, Ibrahim Inal, and the sons of the sultan's brother, Isra'il, disgruntled at their share of the spoils. The Buwayhids, backed by the Fatimid Caliphate, took advantage of the sultan's troubles to fight back and for a time they reclaimed Baghdad. With the help of more loyal

*Some insight into the martial attitudes of the times is provided by another story of an event during the siege of Manzikert told by Aristakes: A young Armenian nobleman captured in battle was taken before Tughril, who was grieving over the severe wounding of the son of one of his emirs. The sultan told the prisoner that he would be executed if the emir's son died; otherwise he would be spared. The Armenian warrior declared that if it had been his blow that struck down the wounded man, he would certainly die, but otherwise he could not be sure. After a few days, the wounded man died and the captive was accordingly executed. The sultan cut off his right arm and sent it to the bereaved emir, with the message: 'Your son was not killed by the arm of a weakling.'[16]

nephews, the three sons of Chagri Bey, Tughril succeeded finally in establishing unquestioned rule. But to maintain it, it became necessary to concentrate his strength and activity in Iran and on its Kurdish borders and to content himself with the vassalage, rather than direct rule, of the emirs in Mesopotamia. For the time being, he no longer ventured further afield towards Armenia.

But, after all, conquest in that direction was not his heart's dream. However greatly his Turkomans were incited by visions of sugar plums in Armenia and Anatolia, Tughril saw as his God-given duty the extinguishing of the Fatimid Caliphate. Just as the Byzantines tended to think of the Armenians as embracing a more villainous theological doctrine than the infidels, so the sultan and his Sunni peoples abhorred the Shi-ites more than the Christians.* There is no indication in any of his acts after entering Baghdad that he entertained any notion of a holy war against the Eastern Empire (even though he had fought to recover Byzantine cities once held by Moslems). Nor is there evidence of such a thought by his successors, Alp Arslan and Malik-Shah. The goal of all of them was to bring Egypt into their Empire and under the rule of the Abbasid Caliphate.

But the different aspirations of the Turkomans remained a problem, to be solved as before by sanctioning, or at least not preventing, even if that were possible, further forays into Byzantine lands.

The risk to the raiders was rendered minimal by the Byzantines themselves. After Theodora's death in 1056, the throne passed to her nominee – or rather that of the civil bureaucracy – the incompetent Michael VI the Aged. The Empire's military magnates, aghast at the succession of successful Turkish raids on the eastern frontier, joined Isaac Comnenus in the revolt which overthrew the emperor (see Chapter 5, p. 95). But, in an act that for the time being undermined the basic purpose

---

*The attitude persists. Half a millennium later, the vizier of Sulayman the Magnificent explained to Busbecq, the Holy Roman Empire's ambassador, 'I assure you that we abhor the Persians [by then Shi-ite] and regard them as more unholy than we regard you Christians.'[17] The deep antagonism, occasionally flaring into armed combat, continues today in both Turkey and Iran.

of the revolt, the rebellious general gathered the armies of the east and took them to Nicaea in the far west of the country for his decisive battle with Michael's forces. Armenia was thus again stripped of imperial soldiers. It was further weakened by its perpetual internal altercations and the rivalries of frontier chieftains. In the Empire itself there were outright civil wars among Greeks, Armenians and Syrians. Discipline was lost among the shabbily treated mercenaries; their leaders began acting as free agents, snapping their fingers at commands from the capital.

For the bellicose Turkomans the opportunities were irresistible. From about 1056 onwards it became normal for them to carry out razzias. Each foray served as reconnaissance for the next one, and each succeeding one had to penetrate deeper to reach areas not already pillaged. The only risk entailed was crossing the frontier, but even that was not great inasmuch as the defensive garrisons, although often large, were in widely spaced fortresses and of little use for intercepting light, hard-riding armed horsemen.

Thus the raids began as before but plunged deeper. In about 1056–7 a Turkish chief known as Samuh or Samoukht, in connivance with a turncoat Norman mercenary, Hervé Francopoulus (driven to desert to the Turks by the foolish refusal of Michael VI to give him a promotion), devastated the valleys of the upper Araxes and Murat Su. With nothing to prevent him, Samuh apparently stayed some years in Armenia with a force of possibly 3000 men, ravaging and pillaging. In 1059 or 1060 he took the age-old access route in the north to the headwaters of the Araxes and across to the upper Halys/Kızılırmak, and deep inside Anatolia, sacked Sebastea/Sivas horribly. At the outset of a particularly grievous lament, Matthew of Edessa explains that the attackers at first mistook the domes of the unwalled city's churches for tents of an opposing army but, seeing their mistake, entered, burnt it to a cinder, massacred one and all, and rested a week from their exertions before going home.[18]

Those attacks, it appears, were launched by chieftains acting more or less on their own initiative, perhaps with Tughril's assent but not under his orders or with his help. But by the early 1060s official sanction seems to have been vouchsafed.

Every year from 1065 on, Edessa and Antioch had to save themselves from Turkish sieges.[19] It was probably under a son of Chagri that devastation was carried on between the Tigris and Euphrates below Melitene – the captives being sold in the slave markets of Amida. And in 1064 the new sultan, Alp Arslan took the field himself for a renewed assault on Armenia.

Chagri Bey died in about 1058, leaving his portion of the Seljuk realm – Khurasan and Khwarizm – to one of his sons, Alp Arslan ('Heroic' or 'Valiant Lion') who for some years before had been the *de facto* ruler. When Sultan Tughril died in Rai/Tehran in 1063, rich in years (he was said to be seventy but apparently did not know his own age) and honours, Alp Arslan established himself as heritor of his title and of almost all the rest of his Empire. That achievement was not without difficulty: he had first to defeat rival claimants including his half-brother, Sulayman, his father's vizier, al-Kunduri, who had backed the wrong horse, an uncle and a cousin, Kutlumush.

Moslem historians have left us very little information about the person of the man who was to inflict on Byzantium its most decisive battlefield defeat ever, although they tell us a considerable amount about his exploits. He was about thirty-three when he succeeded to the sultanate and – such is the inevitable encrustation of legend – is represented by Moslem writers in the same terms as the great Arab traveller, al-Idrisi, used in characterizing the Turkish princes a century or so later: warlike, provident, firm, just and distinguished by excellent qualities (in a nation he considered cruel, wild, coarse and ignorant).[20] But his reputation in the Christian lands that felt his heavy hand was that of a brutal, cruel and merciless tyrant. Matthew called him 'a drinker of blood', and Aristakes saw him as one of the forces of the Antichrist. Michael the Syrian, however, termed him a just man.[21]

That he was less than observant of the Prophet's interdict against the drinking of wine is evidenced by an account of the Moslem historian, Ibn al-Adim.[22] At Aleppo in 1071, a few months before the Battle of Manzikert, the sultan, deep in wine, demanded the head of a local emir resisting pressure to convert from Fatimid to Abbasid loyalty. Alp Arslan's vizier, Nizam al-Mulk, attempted to reason with him but was rewarded for his pains by a blow on the head from his master's drinking-bowl. The sultan's wife persuaded him to sleep off his drunkenness; when he awoke next day he professed to have no memory of the events the night before and to abhor the proposed cruelty he was charged with. When, soon after, he spied his vizier with a massive bruise on his face and inquired of the cause, Nizam al-Mulk replied that he had been struck by a falling tent pole. All in attendance, says the historian, approved the answer, testimony to that great and remarkable man's unfailing diplomacy.

Nizam al-Mulk himself wrote of a happier side of his sultan's character in his book *Siyaset Nameh*. Asked why he did not appoint a *sahib-khabar* (spy or informer), normal practice for a court such as his, the sultan replied:

If I appoint a *sahib-khabar* those who are my sincere friends and enjoy my intimacy will not pay any attention to him nor bribe him, trusting in their fidelity, friendship and intimacy. On the other hand my adversaries and enemies will make friends with him and give him money: it is clear that the *sahib-khabar* will be constantly bringing me bad reports of my friends and good reports of my enemies. Good and evil words are like arrows, if several are shot, at least one hits the target; every day my sympathy with my friends will diminish and that to my enemies increase. Within a short time my enemies will be nearer to me than my friends, and will finally take their place. No one will be in a position to repair the harm which will result from this.[23]

The disquisition is unlikely to have passed the lips of an almost certainly illiterate man in such an elegant piece of rhetoric; one suspects literary aid from the vizier's pen. But the sound judgement, that of a man not contaminated by civilization, we may trust was the sultan's own.

Cruel or just, murderous or moral, what is beyond dispute is that he was a superb military commander. He led his father's forces to victories over their Ghazanavid neighbours in 1058 and his timely arrival at the side of his uncle soon after the latter was made sultan saved Tughril from a grave situation, deep in the hostile Jezire and beset by a revolt from less loyal relations, including Ibrahim Inal (ultimately captured and strangled).

Once firmly in the saddle, Alp Arslan moved against Armenia probably for the same reasons as had his uncle: to reinforce the frontier and strengthen his hold on the Turkomans and on the restless emirs in Azerbaijan and the area west of the Caspian. Runciman suggests also that he may have been nervous about a possible alliance between the Byzantines and his prime enemy, the Fatimid Caliphate.[24] Two armies were involved, one which he led himself and the other under the nominal command of his son, Malik-Shah, but under the tutelage of Nizam al-Mulk.

The forces set out from Rai in February 1064, proceeded to Azerbaijan and had boats for crossing the Araxes built at Nakhchevan.[25] The sultan's force then moved against Georgian mountain strongholds while his son's operated further south. After those campaigns the two groups reunited, together reduced other fortresses, and thereupon moved against Ani.

Isolated and amid ravaged territory, the city nevertheless put up a resistance of some twenty-five days. The great Armenian capital, the key to the defence of the nation, enjoyed a superb defensive position behind enormous triangular walls on the top of an escarpment protected on three sides by the formidable gorges of the Akhuryan/Arpa Çay and one of its tributaries. Arab historians, no less prone to exaggeration than the Armenian, claimed it encompassed 500 churches – some said 700* – and 700,000 inhabitants. The figures must be heavily discounted but even so there is no doubt that for its times it was indeed a very large city.

The (more or less) contemporary historians of the three peoples involved differ in their emphasis on the reasons for the city's fall. The Byzantine chroniclers, Attaleiates, Scylitzes-Cedrenus, contend that Pancratius (Armenian: Bagrat), the governor of Ani, an Armenian, provoked the sultan's attack when his troops fell upon the rearguard of the Turkish army which until then had given no injury to Pancratius's territories, thus inciting Alp Arslan to vengeance. They charge as well that Pancratius had received his position by promising the imperial administration in Constantinople that he could defend

*Matthew of Edessa said 1001.

Ani on the cheap, without need of any military reinforcements or additional supplies. Attaleiates adds an implication of a lack of unity or political difficulties between the governor and Byzantine officials and the people of the city.

Aristakes, writing of an event which occurred in his lifetime, strongly implies a lack of will among the inhabitants to resist, and fatal internal disorders. He suggests that the city's fall was divine punishment for the sins of the citizens (he offered the same reason for the sack of Arzn), the logical corollary of which would be a doctrine of non-resistance. Another Armenian historian of the twelfth century, Samuel of Ani, makes the same point.

The third Armenian, Matthew, writing some sixty or seventy years after the event, concedes that, although they fought bravely at first, the defendants lost heart. But, as would be expected of him, he declares that the real culprits were the 'infamous' Byzantine officers who had been installed by Constantinople, and who abandoned the defence to take refuge inside the citadel or fortress of the city, leaving the rest of it to be taken by the Turks. Thereupon it was *sauve qui peut*. The sultan at first refused to believe that the city was his, until the invaders entered and seized a child from its mother's arms to bring to him as evidence. Astonished, he declared that it was 'their God' who delivered the invulnerable city into his hands.*

The Arab historians who describe the fall of Ani stress the tremendous difficulty facing the sultan in trying to break a way into the city towering above them, and give the defenders some credit for an initially stout resistance. They erected road-blocks and other obstacles to prevent access but the besiegers, who also knew the use of incendiaries, were able to destroy them or to build ramps over them. As part of his siege technique, Alp Arslan built a wooden tower covered with vinegar-soaked padding – the standard defence against attempts to

---

*J. Laurent, writing early in the present century, defends the Byzantine administration to some degree against the complaints of the contemporary Greek and Armenian writers. Byzantium, he notes, was at that time pressed by Turkic tribes on the Balkan front and had no troops to spare; and the commanders of Ani, after all, were Armenian and Georgian, not Greek, even though given the posts by Byzantium.[26]

set such structures on fire – manned it with archers and a ballista or catapult, and moved it against a portion of the wall. Whereupon, by what some Arab chroniclers saw as an act of God, others as the effects of an earthquake and what was instead almost surely the result of mining operations under it, a tower or skirt of the wall collapsed.

It was presumably at this point that the Byzantine commanders took to their citadel, only to be burned out and massacred. According to one highly unlikely account, the desperate city sent out its loveliest girls and handsomest young men to the Sultan's camp in the notion that captives of that kind would prevent his troops from carrying on the fight; the sultan simply imprisoned them and went on as before, with the murderous consequences described in the epigraph to this chapter – and, of course, chronicled with infinitely more anguish by Matthew and Aristakes.

Alp Arslan put the city (which was to revive in times to come) under the governorship of an emir of the region and, to consolidate his hold over the entire area, took to wife the daughter of the King of Georgia. Other princes, hitherto under Byzantine sovereignty, ceded their lands to the sultan. In one way or another, the large city of Kars, some forty miles west of Ani, and several times previously attacked and pillaged, fell into Seljuk hands. Matthew of Edessa would have it that the lord of that city, another Gagik, summoned by the sultan to render homage, contrived a deft defence. He garbed himself in mourning robes to greet the arrival of Alp Arslan's envoys. Why, they asked, was a king so clothed. 'I went into mourning,' Gagik replied, 'when my friend Sultan Tughrıl, brother [sic] of Alp Arslan, died.' Delighted when he was told of the response, the sultan visited Kars at the head of the army for a round of rejoicing, bestowal of rich presents, pledges of eternal friendship and feasting. A more credible passage in the account declares that Gagik placed his troops at the sultan's disposal whenever he called for them. Later, after Alp Arslan had departed from the area, the wily Gagik fled to Byzantium and was there given new territories by the emperor.[27]

For his victories, the Abbasid caliph gave the young sultan the name Abu'l-Fath, 'Father of Conquest'.[28]

*

While Constantine X, succeeding to the throne after Isaac Comnenus, attempted again to negotiate with the sultan, and while the latter doubtless used the same excuses as his uncle about his inability to control rebel chieftains, the Turkoman attacks increased year after year. Also, probably with the sultan's official sanction, raids increased in fury and effectiveness under the direction of powerful Turk and Arab emirs in the area of Aleppo and Antioch. An army was sent against them but, as Attaleiates notes, 'again stinginess made it ineffectual and contemptible'.

For those in power did not want to pay the full salaries of the warriors who would have to endure the hardships of battle, and they tried to encourage them to risk their lives by giving them only the tiniest recompense. The result was that they missed everything. The money the soldiers received was not enough to get them to march against the enemy. . . . They raised some meaningless shouts and dispersed to their homes. Once more the barbarians raided the Roman country with impunity.

The government then assembled a band of young men at very little expense . . . but nothing really could be expected of them; they had no combat experience, their horses were in sorry shape, and they were practically without weapons. After suffering many hardships they returned ingloriously to their homes.[29]

The general commanding at Antioch, Nicephorus Botaniates, raised some local troops and for a time turned back the onslaughts largely through his own bravery and skill. But, on his resigning or being relieved of command, the assaults were renewed and, cutting off supplies, reduced the cities to miserable straits.

Significantly, however, the Turkish attacks tended to skirt rather than enter deeply into Byzantine territory, and kept to the east of the Euphrates. The sultan must have felt that he had done the necessary in rectifying his Persarmenian frontiers and had protected his north-western flank so that he could now turn to his all-important goal, the conquest of the Fatimid Caliphate. Byzantine lands west of Greater Armenia were there for his taking, but he did not try to take them, for all the tempting booty they offered. His holy war was against a different enemy in a different direction.

One incursion (1067–8) demonstrated just how incapable Byzantium was of defending itself against assaults deep into

Anatolia. The leader in this case was a bona fide renegade, a certain Afşin who killed his superior, one of the sultan's chamberlains. Fleeing Alp Arslan's wrath but making the best of it in the process, he sacked Caesarea/Kayseri, turned south into Cilicia and thence Syria, devastated the country around Antioch and, escaping Byzantine forces under the new emperor, Romanus, who was moving into Syria, dashed northwards across all of Asia Minor almost to the Black Sea to sack Neocaesarea/Niksar. Thereupon he moved west, beyond Cappadocia to Amorium (now abandoned), a hundred miles south-west of Ancyra/Ankara. Returning to the east after this incredibly deep foray into Anatolia, he received the sultan's pardon as his due for his exploits.

The state of the Byzantine armies had become chaotic. As at Melitene, 'these tattered remnants of the military forces simply retired to the safety of walls and refused to march out and oppose the Turks'.[30] Edessa survived capture from yearly raids, it can be assumed, only because of the deep and wide moat carved out of solid rock that protected its acropolis. From 1066 on, the Turks were in full control of Greater Armenia.

Except for the brief reign of Isaac Comnenus, Byzantine policy had been in the hands of the civil bureaucracy ever since the death of Basil II. By the record of those years, 1025 to 1068, that policy stands condemned.

9

The Feckless Response:
1068–70

Here one could see an appalling sight: the famous units of the Romans who had reduced both East and West to subjection, now consisting of a few men, and men, at that, bent over with poverty and ill-condition and deprived of their full armour. Instead of swords and other weapons of war they had – in the Biblical phrase – only pikes and scythes, and this not even in a period of peace; they were short of war horses and other equipment because no Emperor had campaigned in this area for a long time. And since they were considered useless, they were without their remittances for provisions and their former customary allowance for grain. For they were regarded as weak and cowardly and good for no important service. Their very standards gave a dull ring when struck, and looked filthy as if they had been blackened with smoke, and they had few men, and poor men, to care for their needs. All that caused great despondency in the hearts of those who saw them when they reflected on the state to which the Roman armies had come and from which they had fallen.

John Scylitzes[1]

The legacy of the civilian bureaucrats and of the emperors who were their nominees and puppets – profligate spenders on their own ostentations and miserly providers for their armies – was a defenceless Asia Minor. Turks raided at will, ever further to the west. Interior cities, without even the garrisons of the frontier forts, were helpless; local resistance forces had collapsed. Worse, Constantinople remained blind to the Empire's nakedness, the blindfold having been stripped from its eyes only once since the death of Basil Bulgaroctonus, and that but briefly, by Isaac Comnenus.[2]

Constantine X died in 1067 after presiding over the policy of disaster for seven and a half years and doing his best to perpetuate it even from the grave. On his death-bed he required his wife Eudocia – younger than he – to swear she would never re-marry, and made his relations and henchmen sign commitments that they would recognize no other emperor except his sons. One suspects strongly that those oaths were the doing of Psellus and John Ducas, the Caesar,* Constantine's brother. Now head of the family and like his late brother no friend of military life or of those who followed it, Ducas was instead a political intriguer and power-broker. Psellus, co-*éminence grise* with Ducas during Constantine's reign, was head of the civil party and the tutor of the heir-apparent, the future Michael VII, as much under Psellus's influence as his father had been. Together the two men could, and for a few months did, manage Eudocia and thus the course of state; even if Michael succeeded to the throne, they could be confident of maintaining their positions and authority. By the same token, they would lose all if someone not of the house of Ducas or of the civilian party became emperor. Psellus, in particular, had fallen from palace favour once before and loathed the monastic life to which he was temporarily relegated; he did not intend that any such fate should befall him a second time. There is a certain sour and inadvertent humour in his disclosure in the *Chronographia* of his efforts to hold on to the reins, a transparency scarcely to be expected of a man deemed the greatest writer and most gifted politician of his age.

In Psellus's chronicle of the year 1067, Eudocia first appears as the epitome of modesty, virtue, intelligence and diligence, having cherished 'an extraordinary respect for me'. But she began to lose 'some of her old precision' because 'her tower of wise counsels' was violently shaken by 'evil counsellors'.

---

*Nominally or ceremonially, the deputy-emperor, a post deriving from the tetrarchy of Diocletian. Scylitzes makes clear, however, that in John's case he was deputy in fact – if not more – to a ruler who knew nothing about running an empire.[3]

Rumours abounded that she planned to re-marry but – sin of sins – she did not so much as hint her plans to Psellus. When at last she told him, he was 'filled with instant consternation'. From that moment her husband-to-be was the object of his most venomous abuse.

Eudocia's 'evil counsellors' were, no doubt, those military figures who still had influence in the Empire and even members of the bureaucracy and senate who at last realized the danger of the barbarian hordes ravaging the whole of the east and the need of a forceful military professional to take the throne. The assaults in northern Syria that Botaniates had tried to repel and the horrible sacking of Caesarea by Afşin, deep inside Cappadocia, had finally raised the alarm. Death-bed oath or no, Eudocia determined, or was obliged, to re-marry.*

Apparently, the first choice as Eudocia's mate had been Botaniates, but for reasons not clear another man was chosen, Romanus Diogenes. We know more about him from contemporary Byzantine historians than we do about the sultan he was to face. Romanus IV was of a distinguished military family with large landholdings in Cappadocia. Psellus, who, as noted, loathed him, declares that his father had revolted against Romanus III and, on arrest, committed suicide. More

---

*Just how 'Byzantine' were the methods in Byzantium is illustrated by Eudocia's contrivance to be released from her promise of perpetual celibacy. Opposition was feared from the senate and from the Patriarch of Constantinople, the famous Xiphilinus, custodian of her signed pledge. It was arranged with one of the eunuchs of the palace women's quarters to bamboozle the Patriarch by proposing that the latter's brother, 'a lecherous fellow', should become her husband. Scylitzes's account of what happened reaches high comedy:

'When [the eunuch] had the Patriarch all his own, taking the bait and all but arranging the marriage, he advised him to inquire of the Senate about this matter. So the Patriarch summoned the Senators to himself one by one, set forth the necessity of his proposal, and denounced the [death-bed] document as unjust, unlawful, and framed to gratify the vanity of one man, with no view toward the common good. This common good can only be achieved, he said, if the Empress marries some noble and brave man. The affairs of the Romans will flourish again, which now are expected to wither and die.'

When the consent of all had been obtained, some by persuasion and flattery, others by money and gifts, the chosen husband, not the Patriarch's brother, was brought to the marriage altar. Xiphilinus, irremediably swindled, could not object.[4]

credible is the account of Attaleiates, who admired Romanus greatly from many years of campaigning with him. He asserts that when his hero was governor of Sardica/Sofia and won victories over Patzinak invaders, he conceived a plot against Constantine but was betrayed. Brought to Constantinople and tried, he received a death sentence, commuted however to exile. Much admired in influential circles, he was interceded for by friends and brought before the empress. She appears to have been taken by the youngish officer: 'As he stood before the imperial throne, unrestrained mercy took hold on the Augusta, and streams of tears fell from her eyes.' Little wonder, if Attaleiates is to be believed:

The man not only surpassed others in his good qualities but he was also pleasant to look at in all respects. His broad chest and back gave him a fine appearance, and his very breath seemed noble, if not actually divine. He seemed more handsome than others, and this was enhanced by his bright eyes. His complexion was not exactly white nor very dark, but as though mixed by artifice with nature and somewhat ruddy. In all these his gentleness could be observed, and he gave evidence, as the Comedian [Aristophanes] says, of a form worthy of worship.[5]

Freed and his dignities restored, he set out to return to his Cappadocian lands, but was recalled, to take wife and throne on 1 January 1068.* 'An error in judgement,' Psellus snorted, 'she ought to have put him to death.' A more fatal error in judgement was that of the new emperor: he should have put John Ducas to death, an idea that occurred to him more than once.

Romanus fell to work diligently trying to restore Byzantine affairs to some sort of order, but struggled against formidable difficulties, not the least of which were 'the very large number of relatives about him who sat in counsel' – or, according to

---

*Evidence about Eudocia's motives is conflicting. Matthew of Edessa, happy to believe the worst about any 'Roman', but having the least reliable information about Byzantine affairs, claims Romanus was the empress's lover. Attaleiates implies, to the contrary, that it was a wrench for her to take a husband because of her aversion to sexual intercourse. The probable explanation is that given above: realization of the need for a general on the throne.

Attaleiates, 'it would be more accurate to say they lay in ambush' – principally, his new stepsons (children of Constantine X) and the Caesar John Ducas.[6] Equally malevolent was the disloyalty of large sections of the army, the mercenaries in general and the Varangian Guard in particular, deeply resentful at Romanus's favouritism toward native troops of the Empire. This animosity was to manifest itself with disastrous results again and again and doubtless accounts for the otherwise inexplicable lack of co-ordinated military action over the next three years.

By early spring 1068 Romanus made ready to march against the Turks in the east, with 'an army not such as became a Roman Emperor', but a mixed bag of Macedonians, Bulgarians and Cappadocians, plus Patzinak and Frank mercenaries and the Varangian Guard. Its sorry state was as Scylitzes describes it in the epigraph to this chapter. Without adequate provisions and obliged to live off the land it traversed, the army could be taken for a band of beggars out to search for bread rather than soldiers marching against the enemy; it was fortunate only in the fact that the Turks were ignorant of its wretched condition.[7]

The chronicle of events of the next two years by Attaleiates who accompanied the emperor as a member of the military tribunal, is a prolonged cry of anguish, relieved only by the image of a heroic leader. For the rest it is a story of missed opportunities, chaos and cowardice. On occasion, it is an account of the mercenary Franks fighting bravely while the native troops of the Empire stood idly by; on occasion it is exactly the reverse. Only rarely, it appears, did the forces act in valiant co-ordination; more often, one group, sent to fulfil a given task, scuttled back in terror, or an entire regiment sought to hide while another unit was being demolished. Above all else, the history is of Turkish bands here, there and everywhere, least of all where they were expected, either taking the initiative to press attacks or escaping Byzantine pursuers when not actually routing them.

The emperor first led his army – Bar Hebraeus put the number at 200,000, which must be a great exaggeration – into Cappadocia, intending to push towards Armenia to undo Alp Arslan's and his emir's conquests there. But, hearing of the

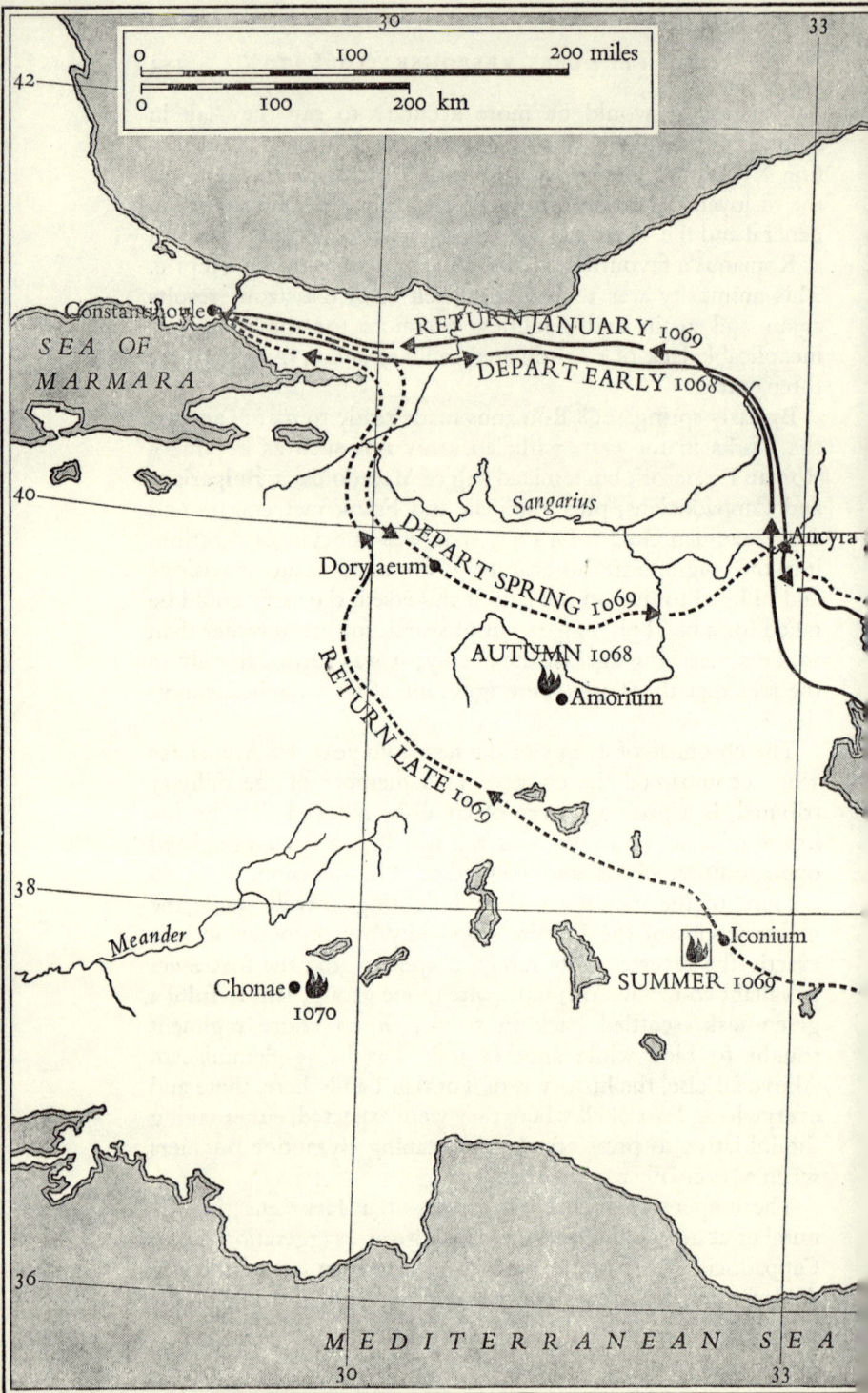

30

33

42

0   100   200 miles

0   100   200 km

Constantinople

SEA OF MARMARA

RETURN JANUARY 1069

DEPART EARLY 1068

Ancyra

40

Sangarius

Dorylaeum

DEPART SPRING 1069

AUTUMN 1068

Amorium

RETURN LATE 1069

38

Meander

Iconium

Chonae 1070

SUMMER 1069

36

M E D I T E R R A N E A N   S E A

30

33

6   *Campaigns, 1067–69*

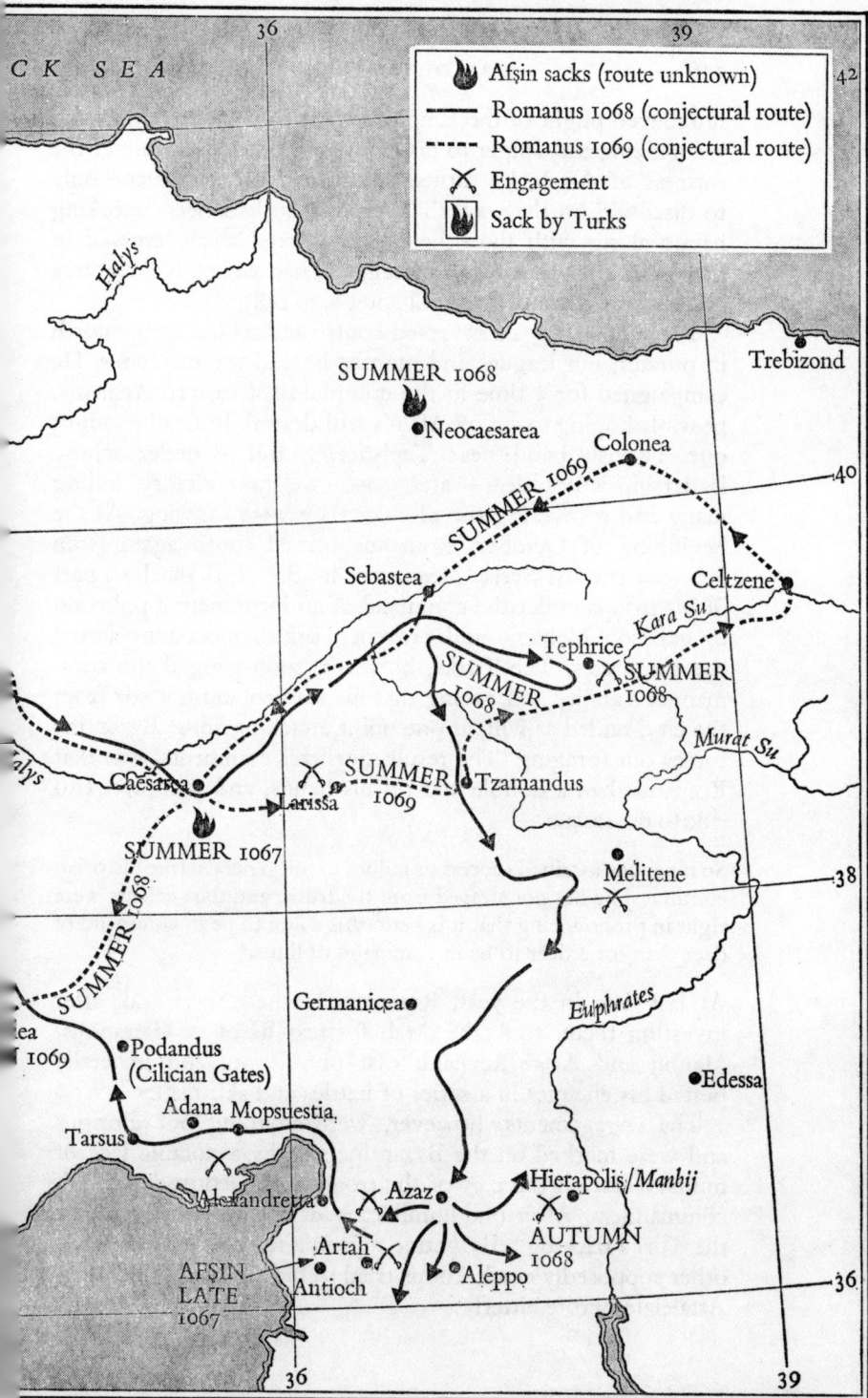

Legend:
- 🔥 Afşin sacks (route unknown)
- ——— Romanus 1068 (conjectural route)
- - - - Romanus 1069 (conjectural route)
- ✗ Engagement
- 🔥 Sack by Turks

BLACK SEA

Halys

Trebizond

SUMMER 1068
Neocaesarea

Colonea

SUMMER 1069

Sebastea

Celtzene

Kara Su

Tephrice   SUMMER 1068

SUMMER 1068

Murat Su

Caesarea

Larissa   SUMMER 1069   Tzamandus

SUMMER 1067

Melitene

Germanicea

Euphrates

Edessa

Podandus (Cilician Gates)

SUMMER 1069

Adana Mopsuestia

Tarsus

Hierapolis/Manbij

Azaz   AUTUMN 1068

Alexandretta

Artah   Aleppo

AFŞIN LATE 1067   Antioch

unrelieved plight of the Empire's cities in northern Syria, and recognizing the danger to his frontiers from the capture of the fortress of Artah, he turned south-east to their rescue only to discover, on the way, that Afşin, who had been wreaking havoc along with the others, had ducked away, crossed in front of Romanus's line of march, and had sacked Neocaesarea Niksar far to the north (see Chapter 8, p. 148).

The emperor again reversed course and set out to the north in pursuit, but leagues and months behind the marauder. He campaigned for a time in the mountains of eastern Armenia, possibly hoping to cut off Afşin's withdrawal. In fact he caught one Turkish band near Tephrice/Divriği – under whose leadership is not clear – and won a welcome victory, killing many and recovering the plunder they were carrying. At the beginning of October, Romanus turned south again from Sebastea toward Syria. Meantime, he detached the best part of his troops under the command of an incompetent poltroon to garrison Melitene and prevent Turkish incursions across the Euphrates. The Turks, however, soon gauged the commander's ability and, seeing that his soldiers did not stir from the city, raided at will, at one point attacking some Byzantine forces out foraging. The result, Scylitzes comments, was that Romanus had a double war on his hands, and was forced to ride to the rescue.

So if anyone ascribed success or failure to the generals, [the historian continues] he has not strayed from the truth; and the ancients were right in pronouncing that it is better for a lion to be in command of deer than for a deer to be in command of lions.[8]

At last, late in the year, Romanus reached Syria and, after investing them, took the Arab fortress bases of Hierapolis/Manbij and Artah/Reyhanlı east of Aleppo, and generally bested his enemies in a series of battles and skirmishes.

The engagements, however, were anything but glorious and were marked on the Byzantine side by a notable lack of military zeal on the part of the troops and ineptitude by unit commanders. After one humiliating defeat brought about by the Turks tricking a Byzantine unit in a feigned retreat, while other supposedly crack troops tried to hide instead of helping, Attaleiates wrote bitterly:

It was then that I despaired not so much of my own safety as I came to despise the cowardice, ineptitude or wretchedness of the Romans. Although the Romans had suffered an overwhelming defeat before the encampment, none of the remaining companies or commanders was stimulated to action. Instead, they all sat around inside, all attending to their own business as though they were camping in a friendly country, and no emotion or anguish could stir them at all.[9]

Romanus soon reversed the defeat and sent the enemy fleeing back to Aleppo, but his own troops failed to pursue them and missed a chance to vanquish the enemy in his own nest. The best Romanus could do was to fortify Hierapolis and Artah and leave garrisons there before turning back, via Alexandretta/Iskenderun and the Cilician gates, at the end of the year. His march to Constantinople was in no way cheered by news on the way that the commander at Melitene had again let the Turks through – presumably Afşin's group – and that they had reached and sacked Amorium (see Chapter 8, p. 148). Romanus and Afşin, it becomes clear, were in separate compartments of a revolving door, Afşin regularly exiting for devastating forays half a turn ahead of his pursuer. When the raider was despoiling Neocaesarea, the emperor was setting out for Syria; when he sacked Amorium, Romanus was at Hierapolis.

Romanus's operations in Syria were not, however, entirely in vain. His capture and garrisoning of strong-points there, Cahen concludes, covered Antioch and secured its line of communications with Edessa, and threatened Aleppo. That was sufficient pretext to warrant a triumphant entrance for the emperor into the capital late in January 1069. As could be expected, Psellus noted the event, and the year's campaign, with a paragraph of sneers.[10]

Remaining in the capital only a few weeks, Romanus set out again in the early spring of 1069 on a campaign that yielded even fewer results than that of the year before. His first task, however, was not to fight against the Turks but to quell a mutiny in Armenia by a Frankish mercenary, Robert Crispin. A *condottiere* who had fought well for Byzantium against the Normans in Italy, he returned to Constantinople at the head of a considerable military force. Already feeling insufficiently rewarded for his services, Crispin was sent to Armenia to cover the frontier during the winter, only to be denied pay and provisions. Forced to live off the land, he began pillaging the official tax-collectors and others with wealth to be taken. The emperor twice sent troops against him, under subordinate commanders, who were twice trounced. Crispin spared his captives and, still quasi-loyal to his pledges, fell upon a large band of Turks and cut them to pieces. Crispin ultimately sent envoys to Romanus, then camped at Dorylaeum/Eskişehir, who argued the case for their leader and won him pardon. Jealous members of the emperor's entourage, however, set about poisoning Romanus's mind against him, with the result that Crispin was dismissed from his command and exiled. Attaleiates, failing to distinguish mote from beam, excused the emperor's decision on grounds that 'by nature the Frankish race is faithless'.[11] Justified or not, the decision was a grave mistake: the emperor not only lost a gifted and valiant commander but also Crispin's forces. Enraged by their leader's dismissal, they revolted and fell to ravaging Byzantine Mesopotamia on their own.

Romanus marched on to the east through Caesarea and Larissa forty miles further to the east, and won something of a victory there over a band of Turkish raiders which he caught unawares. Except for executing his prisoners to the last man, he failed to follow it up, giving those of the group who had escaped a chance to fall back across the Euphrates, looting as they went.

On the march once again, Romanus headed towards the Armenian mountains, intending a descent on the Seljuk fortress of Khilat/Ahlat on the north shore of Lake Van. First, however, he divided his army, entrusting the larger part to an Armenian-born general, Philaretus, to prevent Turkish forays from crossing the Euphrates and moving west. As it turned out, the Byzantine forces did nothing to prevent them. At the first sight of Turkish groups approaching, they deserted and scurried back in terror to the emperor, by then near Celtzine/Erzincan, leaving their equipment behind them to fall into the enemy's hands.

Bitterly discouraged, Romanus gathered in the fugitives and set out again, marching through Colonea as far as Sebastea.

There, once again, his plans were aborted: news came that the Turks whom Philaretus should have stopped at the Euphrates above Melitene were pressing into Cappodocia, with Iconium/ Konya as their goal. Abandoning his programme for pushing further into Armenia, the emperor turned back towards Cappadocia in pursuit of the intruders. He marched south-west as far as Heraclea/Ereğli only to learn that he was too late: Iconium had been sacked and the plunder-laden Turks were making good an escape through the mountains of Cilicia towards the Mediterranean coast.

Romanus had had enough foresight to order the Byzantine commander at Antioch to move with his forces to Mopsuestia/ Misis, a river city east of Adana, to cut off an expected Turkish retreat in that area; the emperor also dispatched some of his own troops to join the Antiochenes. As so often before, the plan failed: although the retreating Turks had been badly mauled in the Cilician defiles by the migrant Armenians there and had lost their booty, the troops at Mopsuestia dawdled, letting the Turks cross the mountains by night. They reached Syria with no further trouble.

Learning of their escape and with no further purpose to serve where he was, Romanus led his ineffective army back to Constantinople in the autumn. Once again he had been evilly served by his subordinates, while he himself had been in the wrong section of the revolving door.

Psellus's sneering, now mixed with gloating, took on renewed impetus:

This second war of his was no more successful than the first. It was, in fact, altogether indecisive and the enemy held their own every-where. If our men fell in their tens of thousands, while a mere handful of our adversaries were taken prisoner, at least we were not beaten – and we succeeded in making a lot of noise at the barbarians! The result of all this was that Romanus became more proud and more insolent than ever, because, forsooth, he had twice commanded an army.[12]

Evil counsellors had helped lead him astray, the out-of-power philosopher concluded. Romanus, he decided, instead of admiring Psellus, had been so arrogant as to try to surpass him in military expertness and, in envy, had not listened to his advice, although 'I was throughly conversant with the science of military tactics, [and] had made a complete study of everything pertaining to military formations, the building of war-machines, the capture of cities and all the other things that a general has to consider',[13] including, as he was later to demonstrate, treachery.

The political circumstances in the capital in 1070 were apparently such that Romanus would not risk leaving it on another expedition. As Scylitzes makes clear, Psellus, John Ducas and others were plotting against him and 'if it lay within their power, they would have chosen that he not even live, for he was an annoyance to them and they hated him as a noble and brave man'.[14] Nevertheless, the emperor was obliged to send a force against a Turkish band raiding in Anatolia as far west as the upper reaches of the Halys. The Turks' leader was a certain Erisgen (Chrysosculos to the Byzantines), uncle or brother-in-law of the sultan,[15] but in rebellion against him and thus operating as a free-booter.

Manuel Comnenus, grandson of the Emperor Isaac, was put in charge of the eastern armies by Romanus and was sent against the rampaging Turks. He had some initial success against raiding bands he encountered and won a considerable acclaim which, Attaleiates and Scylitzes hint, may have provoked the emperor's envy. Whether out of spite or of necessity Romanus ordered part of Manuel's forces to be detached and sent to Syria to relieve Hierapolis, then under siege.

Some time before that advance in the later summer of 1070, however, it appears that a truce of sorts had been concluded between the Empire and the sultan, either as a consequence of the stalemate of the campaign the year before or because of the minor successes Manuel had scored more recently.* Whether or not he had negotiated the truce in good faith, and unaware that Erisgen was actually in revolt against Alp Arslan, the emperor had every reason to conclude that the

---

*The evidence is meagre but uncontestable. There is no record of it by Byzantine historians, possibly because they considered the armistice merely a dodge engineered by Romanus to gain time for his campaign of the next year. But it is recorded by Bar Hebraeus and Sibt Ibn al-Jawzi, most reliable of all Arabic sources on this period. The matter is summarized by Cahen.[16]

emir's raids, which were vicious, rendered the agreement invalid; hence his dispatch of Manuel to the east to confront him.

Manuel Comnenus, weakened by the departure of a major section of his army to Syria, marched from Caesarea to Sebastea and there encountered the rebel emir. It is conceivable that Erisgen actually tried to tell the Byzantine general that he was approaching him as a friend, indeed, as someone wishing to make common cause with him against the sultan. But in view of the Seljuk warrior's depredations, Manuel could be excused for doubting his protestations of amity. In any event, the two forces clashed in fierce battle. The Turks pretended to retreat and Manuel, like Byzantine commanders before and since, fell into the time-worn trap. Capturing some, including Manuel himself, and massacring others, Erisgen descended on the Byzantine camp, destroyed and pillaged it, while remnants of the Byzantine army fled for safety behind Sebastea's walls.

As Erisgen's prisoner, Manuel proved a better diplomat – or intriguer – than general. He and the rebel agreed to join forces to overthrow Alp Arslan and to return together to Constantinople to make arrangements to that end. Thus, to the capital's enormous surprise and relief, the loser came back with the winner in tow. Erisgen's followers, however, would have no part of such a deal and went on their way, despoiling.

The sultan, meanwhile, had sent the redoubtable Afşin in pursuit of his disloyal relative. He entered Byzantine territory with his forces, whom he had restrained from pillaging. When he discovered Erisgen's plot with Manuel, Afşin demanded that the emperor deliver the traitor to him and threatened that if he did not obtain satisfaction, he would consider the recent Seljuk–Byzantine treaty invalid and with a joyous heart would fall to plundering. Romanus refused to render up Erisgen on grounds that it was contrary to his honour to surrender someone who had come to Byzantium for asylum.

As might have been expected, Afşin was as good as his word. He moved west from Sebastea, devastating everything in his path, until he reached Chonae (now abandoned), a city on the upper Meander less than a hundred miles from the Aegean, famed for its trophies and miracles attributed to the

F

Archangel Michael. Its sacking was rendered particularly horrible because, fortuitously, its underground waterworks flooded at the same time, drowning the population that took refuge in them.

On his withdrawal, Afşin was held up by winter in the Taurus but made it back to Seljuk lands in the spring of 1071. The legend arose, which Bar Hebraeus reported as fact, that he had actually reached the walls of Constantinople itself.[17] Again, according to Bar Hebraeus, Afşin told Alp Arslan that there was no force capable of withstanding him in Byzantium; Asia Minor was his for the taking.

The sultan, however, had a different goal in mind and was not to be deterred; the conquest of Asia Minor was simply of no interest to him. Instead, and thinking his north-eastern frontiers no longer menaced thanks to his truce agreement with Romanus, he had finally found the moment opportune to return to the dream cherished by his uncle Tughrıl ever since that sultan had entered Baghdad in 1055: the destruction of the Fatimid Caliphate. His motives, no doubt, were a mixture of religious zeal, the sheer pleasure of territorial conquest and enlarged power, and considerations of defence, for he knew that the Fatimids remained determined to conquer the Abbasid Caliphate in Baghdad.

Seizing the excuse of an invitation from a Fatimid rebel, the sultan commenced preparations in 1070 for an invasion of Egypt. Whether as a response to news that the truce with Byzantium was no longer operative, or to the rebuff that his emir Afşin suffered, or simply as a sensible military precaution to guard his rear against attack, Alp Arslan began operations by setting out from Khurasan (either late in 1070 or early in 1071) and capturing the Armenian strong-points of Manzikert and Archesh. Thence he marched southwards along the routes of the upper Tigris and Euphrates that had been explored and opened up by his emirs' raids in the years immediately preceding. Taking other lesser Byzantine cities on his way, he moved on to Amida, in Moslem hands, settled some problems there and by March of 1071 brought his armies to the formidable walls of Edessa.

He was soon to discover that he had moved in the wrong direction.

10

Twilight at Manzikert

No matter how few we may be, and no matter how great in numbers the Byzantines may be, I shall fling myself upon the enemy at this hour when the Moslems are praying for us. . . . Either I shall be victorious and fulfill my goal or I shall be a martyr and enter Paradise. Those who desire to follow me, come with me; those who wish to go back may do so freely. There is here no Sultan commanding and no soldier being commanded. For I am today only one of you. . . . When some of you who follow me and dedicate their lives to the most high God die, they will enter Paradise, and those who stay alive will acquire great riches. Eternal fire and infamy await those who desert us.

Alp Arslan's speech on the eve of the
battle of Manzikert[1]*

Romanus's priority was as firmly fixed in his mind as Alp Arslan's but, unlike the sultan's goal of conquest, it was of necessity focused solely on national defence: the recovery of the Armenian strong-points and the restoration of the barrier to invasion across the eastern frontiers. It was indispensable for the protection of Anatolia.†

*No surviving Moslem account of the battle was written until the twelfth century, and the most reliable ones date from at least a century after the event. The words above may be seen in the same light, therefore, as those attributed to Pericles by Thucydides.

†Hamdani speculates that the Fatimid Caliphate had a hand in the matter, sending a secret mission to Constantinople urging Romanus to

Early in 1071 he began planning for a huge military force, larger than he had ever taken into the field before, of between 60,000 and 100,000 men.* Its equipment, hauled in an enormous baggage train, appears to have been lavish: included were such numbers of siege machines as to have required almost one thousand carts to transport them.† Otherwise, however, the army was probably as low in morale and lacking in training as those of the three preceding years. In principle, its organization may have differed little from patterns laid out centuries before in the manuals of Maurice and Leo, but, in Fuller's words, in fact it was 'the shell of a blown egg'.[5] And, also as before, the levies were disparate and non-co-operative: Frankish, (i.e. European) mercenaries, Armenians, Bulgars, Patzinaks and other non-Seljuk Turks, called by the Byzantines *Uzes* or *Ghuzz*, from the northern frontiers of the Empire.[6]

As throughout man's history, auguries, omens and prophecies are remembered only when they are fulfilled, and conveniently forgotten when they are not. It may be doubted that the portents seen early in the emperor's fatal campaign were more numerous and ominous than had marked a hundred other Roman campaigns in the past, but on this occasion they were validated by the events and hence remembered and recorded by chroniclers of that intensely superstitious age.

When Romanus left the capital and crossed the Bosphorus in the second week of March 1071 (about the time that Alp

---

attack Alp Arslan in Armenia, thus diverting the threatened invasion of Egypt. The thesis is plausible: the Seljuks were the common enemy of both the Byzantines and the Fatimids, who had had comfortable relations with each other since the time of Basil II. But it is hard to believe that Romanus launched his campaign of 1071 principally because of instigation from Cairo; he had reason enough, solely for purposes of defending his Empire, to march towards Armenia.[2]

*So estimated by, among others, Gibbon, Laurent, Lebeau, and Runciman. Lot and Delbrück consider the figures much too high, but offer no estimates of their own. Moslem historians, writing from legend and oral tradition, give wildly exaggerated estimates ranging from 200,000 to an impossible 600,000 while Matthew of Edessa proclaims a total of one million.[3]

†Moslem historians of the time, and not a few modern Turkish ones, persist in declaring that one catapult alone needed a thousand men to drag it; they apparently took their information directly or otherwise from Attaleiates's contemporaneous account, but misread it.[4]

Arslan was besieging Edessa), a dove alighted on his vessel and came to rest on his right hand; it must have portended something, not necessarily good.

The emperor moved his headquarters to the naval base of Helenopolis, a name pronounced by the locals 'Eleeinopolis': thus not the city of Helen but, in the Greek play on words, a pitiable or miserable city.

There, the centre pole of the imperial tent suddenly broke and fell. There could be no doubt in the soldiers' minds of the meaning of such a portent.

Leading his troops eastwards, on one occasion the emperor set up his quarters at some distance from the main encampment, whereupon the most symbolic event of all took place: a fire broke out in the imperial quarters, consuming his rich equipage – armour, chariots, saddles and bridles – and making living torches of his fine horses and draught animals.

Once across the Sangarius/Sakarya River, Romanus rounded up such fighting men as he could from the area, scattered in hiding places as a result of earlier Seljuk raids. Some he kept, but in a reorganization of his forces he dismissed a good number of men and officers, including Nicephorus Botaniates (who might have been useful, or might not – Romanus had been chosen in preference to him for the throne) and those whom he thought to be battle-weary or, in fact, plotters and potential traitors. But, perhaps because Romanus thought it would be safer to have him in the field under military command and, so to speak, a hostage for his family, rather than leave him in Constantinople to foment rebellion, he kept Andronicus Ducas, eldest son of the Caesar, John Ducas, as one of his principal commanders. The decision was, literally, fatal. Before leaving the capital, Romanus had bound the Caesar and his sons to him by oaths of loyalty (but nevertheless exiled the elder Ducas across the Bosphorus[7]) although he could not have expected much from those pledges: in the Byzantium of that day oaths of that kind carried about the same likelihood of fulfilment as the assurances of an itinerant horse-trader.

Attaleiates, the only chronicler who was an eye-witness to the events and who remains by far the most reliable source, was, as noted earlier, a keen admirer of his leader. But, along

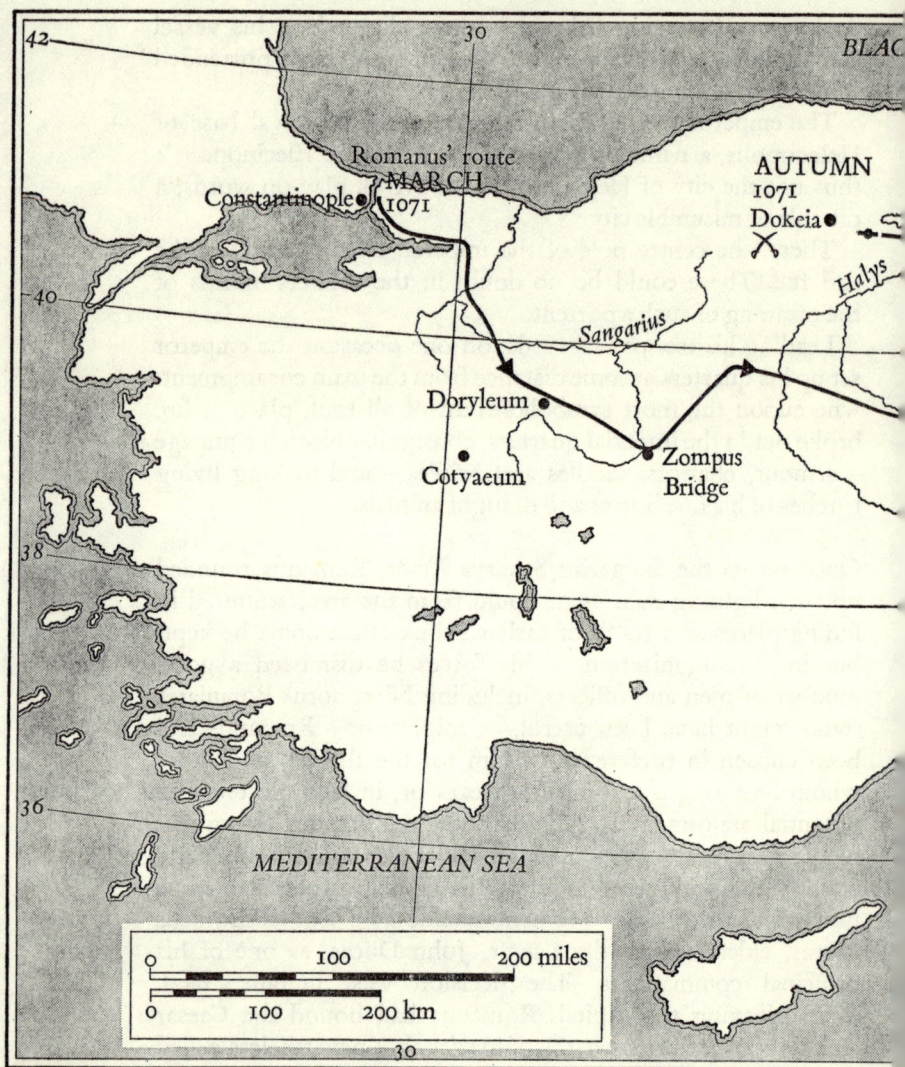

7 *Campaign routes, 1071*

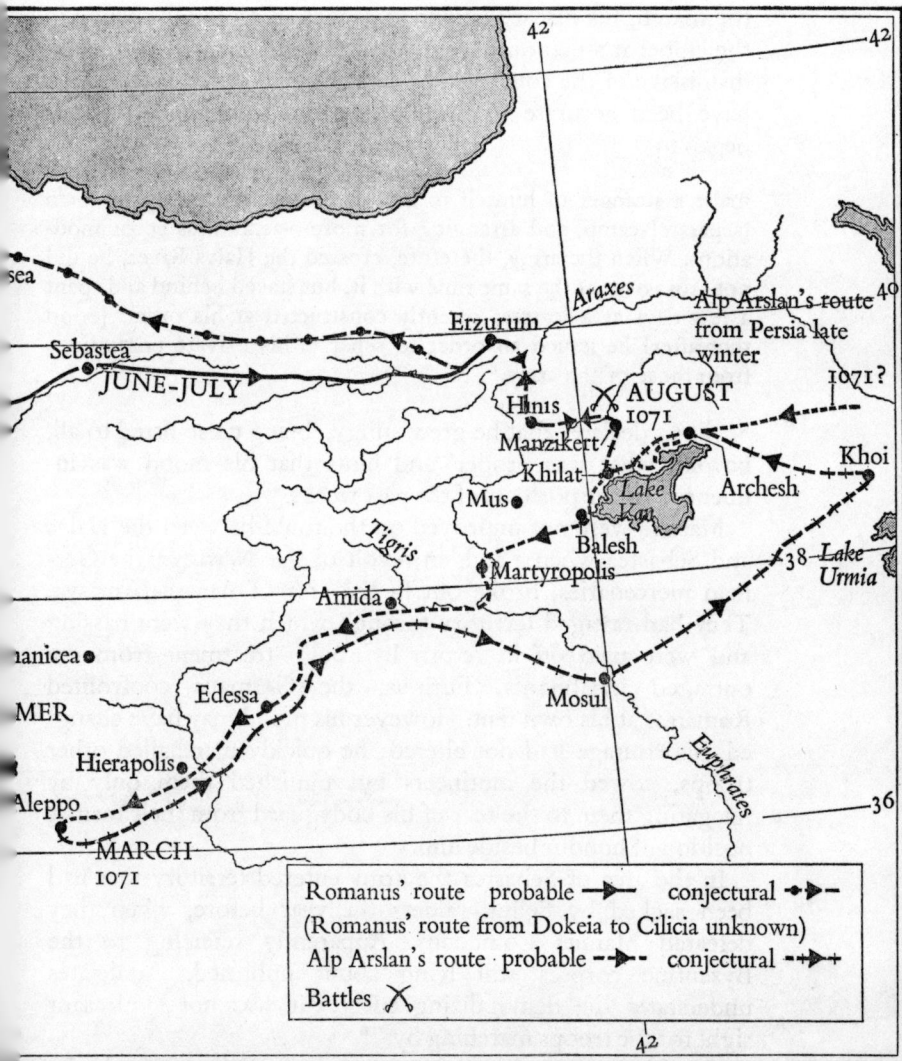

sea

Sebastea

JUNE-JULY

Erzurum

Araxes

Alp Arslan's route
from Persia late
winter

1071?

Hınıs

Manzikert

AUGUST
1071

40

Khilat

Mus

Balesh

Lake
Kan

Archesh

Khoi

Tigris

Martyropolis

Lake
Urmia

38

Amida

manicea

MER

Edessa

Mosul

Euphrates

Hierapolis

36

Aleppo

MARCH
1071

42

Romanus' route   probable ⟶   conjectural ⟶
(Romanus' route from Dokeia to Cilicia unknown)
Alp Arslan's route · probable ⟶   conjectural ⟶
Battles ✗

42

the march, his history begins to report an ominous change in the emperor's demeanour. Always rash, overly self-confident, dismissive of the counsels of prudence and – here Psellus may have been accurate – vainglorious and arrogant, Romanus began to

make a stranger of himself to his own army, setting up his own [separate] camp, and arranging for more ostentatious accommodations. When the army, therefore, crossed the Halys River, he did not cross over at the same time with it, but stayed behind and spent a few days at a fortress recently constructed at his order. [Soon thereafter] he issued an order to separate his private possessions from those of the army.[8]

Scylitzes declares that he grew stingy, 'being close-fisted to all, beyond what was proper' and hints that his mood was influenced by the portents of the past weeks.[9]

Matters were not improved on the route between the Halys and Sebastea when a sudden revolt of the *Nemitzoi*, the German mercenaries, broke out in the area of Amasea/Amasya. They had ravaged territory through which they were passing and were paid off in return by rough treatment from the outraged inhabitants. Furious, the Germans confronted Romanus at his own tent. However his mood may have changed, his courage had not altered; he quickly marshalled other troops, cowed the mutineers but punished them only by relegating them to the rear of his bodyguard from their former position of honour beside him.

In the area of Sebastea the army entered territory that had been sacked by Seljuk raiders the year before, when they defeated Manuel Comnenus. Apparently referring to the Byzantine corpses still lying about unburied, Attaleiates understates the demoralizing effect: 'It was not a pleasant sight for the troops marching by.'[10]

Trouble was a constant companion. In Sebastea itself the Greek inhabitants complained bitterly that at the time of Afşin's raid the year before the Armenians in effect made common cause with the enemy and 'set upon us furiously, more merciless than the Turks themselves'. According to Matthew of Edessa, the only source on this matter, Romanus ordered his troops to sack the city and swore to take furious vengeance on it on his return from that year's campaign. Meantime the priests uttered terrible maledictions upon him. The details are cloudy but an episode of considerable turbulence is probable. Romanus's rage is said to have been abated when the practical fact was pointed out to him that a large contingent of the troops he depended on were Armenians.[11]

Either at Sebastea or, when the army moved forward into Armenia, at Erzurum, the last large Byzantine bastion facing Seljuk-dominated land to the east, there was a council of war. The debate is not mentioned by Attaleiates but is reported by Nichephorus Bryennius,[12] grandson[13] and namesake of one of Romanus's principal commanders and head of the Army of the West, who may have had a family account of his ancestor's deeds.

He declares that the question was whether the emperor and army should wait in Byzantine territory or move forward into 'Persia', i.e., into enemy lands. To understand the considerations that underlay the question we must return to the history of Alp Arslan's action in the spring of 1071.

As noted in the last chapter, the Seljuk leader had moved south-west from his conquests in Armenia across the Tigris and laid siege to Edessa in March. Whether he actually intended to capture the city or merely to besiege it in order to be bought off is not clear. At the end of a month he withdrew on the promise of the city to pay a large tribute provided he would burn his siege machinery. He did so, whereupon the city welshed on its side of the bargain and Alp Arslan, enraged, moved on.*

But while he was encamped before Edessa he received an emissary from Romanus, proposing a truce, or the restoration of the truce of the previous year. The terms are not known but they may well have been those that Romanus was to propose a few weeks later: the restoration of Manzikert and Archesh to Byzantium in return for the relinquishment of Hierapolis/Manbij, taken by Romanus in 1068, to the sultan. Alp Arslan's anger at the trickery of the Edessans was cooled by his vizier, Nizam al-Mulk, and he seems to have given a

---

*The account is that of Matthew, who may have been boasting about what he saw as a praiseworthy bit of one-upmanship by his home town.[14]

favourable reply. He thereupon marched on across the Euphrates to Aleppo in continuation of his planned campaign against Egypt.[15] That he was confident that he had an agreement with Romanus is suggested by the facts that *en route* to Aleppo he took no hostile action against Hierapolis and that he was taken completely by surprise when he heard the news, two months later, that Romanus had launched a campaign into Armenia.

Early in May, when the sultan was before Aleppo attempting to bring its Fatimid ruler to heel, a second Byzantine envoy, Leo Diabatenus, reached him, proposing the exchange of the cities already mentioned and, of course, a pledge from the sultan to prohibit all further incursions into Byzantine territory – a pledge he could not have enforced, given the incorrigible habits of his Turkomans. But this time the proposal was made almost as an ultimatum, to be brought about by force of arms if not by agreement. For, by then, Romanus was well on the road to Armenia.

If in fact Alp Arslan had agreed with Byzantine's offer of a truce in March, by May he would have seen in Romanus's campaign a double-cross. In his eyes it was an attempted invasion of his land. He recognized at once the critical danger the emperor's sally into Armenia posed to the safety of his realm and immediately abandoned his projected operation against the Fatimids and faced about for the speediest possible return. He seems, indeed, to have panicked for the moment, dismissing his local levies and re-crossing the Euphrates so precipitously with his personal guard of only 4000 men that most of his horses and pack-animals were drowned in the process.

In June or July Romanus received word at Erzurum from his envoy to Aleppo that Alp Arslan had turned back to the east in what seemed to be a rout. That news may well have been a major factor in leading the emperor to the decision he reached.[16]

'Flatterers', according to the younger Bryennius, urged the emperor to move forward, get behind the sultan and give battle, whereas the historian's ancestor and another leading general, Joseph Tarchaniotes, 'found that advice very dangerous, and implored him to wait'. He should fortify the cities and lay waste to the surrounding countryside so that the enemy could find no means to live off it. In any event, they argued, he should fortify Erzurum with an entrenchment and delay in order to force the sultan, his troops without sustenance, to attempt an engagement in circumstances more advantageous to Byzantines.[17]

The historian may have been trying to exculpate his grandfather from responsibility for the disaster that followed (or the general may have let his wish be mother to his memory for the same purpose in relating the events in later years), for the recommendation would not have struck Romanus as making good sense at the time. A ruler does not make a desert of country he is intent on reclaiming as his own unless he is expecting an assault from a manifestly superior enemy and has no other recourse, just as a farmer does not burn a swath in his own fields unless that is the only way to block a fire advancing on him downwind. Romanus had no reason to believe that Alp Arslan could muster an army more powerful than his. He also knew that the Turks always did their utmost to avoid a pitched battle with a Byzantine army, as they were always bested in such engagements; indeed, the mere news that an organized Byzantine force was in the neighbourhood had always made Seljuk raiders take to their heels. With the faulty intelligence he received about Alp Arslan's plans – he supposed that with only a small force in hand, the sultan would have to return to Persia for reinforcements – the emperor could reckon on capturing and fortifying strong-points further east in Armenia and garrisoning them before the enemy could reach them.

Moreover, he had not assembled a huge army and taken it to the east merely to hold what he already had of western Armenia or to repeat the relatively indecisive toing and froing of the three previous years. (He could not have been oblivious either of the political consequences in plot-ridden Constantinople if he returned after having marched his army up a hill only to march it down again.) The overriding necessity was to protect the Empire from any more of the raids that had been playing havoc with the cities of the interior. What was needed was to re-fortify points that could block the approach routes of the raiders, both in the upper Araxes and in Vaspurakan. If that would bring about a direct engagement with the Seljuk army, so be it.

The prudence urged by the generals Bryennius and Tarchaniotes was, to be sure, the 'safe' posture, but to what purpose? It would not have prevented the Seljuk emirs and the Turkomans from mounting new raids, if not that year, then the next or the next after that. Once they were over the frontiers, there were no defences in the interior of the Empire to stop them.

Romanus chose to advance. He instructed his troops to collect provisions for two months to sustain them in the semi-desert country through which they would pass. He then separated a portion of his force, mostly Frankish mercenaries, and ordered it off ahead of him to forage in or pillage the area of Khilat/Ahlat on the north shore of Lake Van, commanding access to the pass above Balesh/Bitlis and the routes from there over relatively easy country to Syria or Anatolia. They were under the command of the renowned Roussel of Bailleul, who was endowed with all the attributes appropriate to a mercenary captain, including the tendency to desert his paymaster when he saw fit and to hire out to another.

Romanus probably marched some miles to the east of Erzurum and then turned south along a southern branch of the Araxes through present-day Hınıs (Xenophon's route in reverse) and, just north of Muş, turned eastwards to Manzikert, the prize he had marked for himself. Either on arrival there or somewhere *en route* to it, he decided that Manzikert, weakly garrisoned, would be easy to capture but that Khilat might be a harder nut to crack. Accordingly, he dispatched Tarchaniotes, with the army's best troops and almost all of his infantry, to cover Roussel and capture Khilat.* The emperor was thus left with what seems to have been less than half of his forces, and of inferior quality.

Tarchaniotes had vigorously opposed the emperor's deci-

*The absence of details, especially of dates, in the accounts of the Greek historians bedevils attempts to reconstruct the sequence of events of Romanus's army between Sebastea and Manzikert. The inconsistencies of Moslem historians who wrote about Alp Arslan's movements perform the same disservice to precision for the Seljuk side, as will be seen.

sion to split the army, but lost out to Romanus's 'obstinacy' and departed reluctantly.[18] Latter-day historians, with the advantage of hindsight, join in condemning the division.[19] Reflecting on the situation at the time, however, Attaleiates defends the decision as 'not unreasonable nor inconsistent with the notions of strategy'.[20] The great mistake was a faulty assumption reached in the absence of intelligence about the enemy's whereabouts. Romanus could conclude that if either he or Tarchaniotes ran into trouble they would be a bare thirty miles apart, able to call on one another for help. That the sultan would have reached the scene before then with a formidable army was not foreseen.

What is clear about Romanus's strategy is his intent to capture, garrison and fortify Manzikert and Khilat. What his next moves would have been can only be assumed: the logical step would have been to march about sixty miles to the east along Lake Van and recover Archesh, taken by the sultan only months before. Then he could either have called it a day and, leaving garrisons behind, return to Constantinople, or thereupon move south to Vaspurakan to strengthen defences there against the perennial Turkoman raids.

Romanus was right at least about his contempt for the Seljuk strength in the fort of Manzikert. It was weakly garrisoned and surrendered without a fight. The inhabitants asked for mercy and the permission to evacuate the city with their personal possessions. The emperor agreed and occupied the fort.

His mood, however, was savage. A Byzantine soldier was brought before him in chains, accused of stealing a donkey from one of the Turkish inhabitants. Instead of assessing a fine or inflicting some other condign punishment, Romanus ordered the culprit's nose to be severed. The luckless man invoked the intercession of the Sovereign Mother of Blachernae, holiest of the icons carried by the emperor, but to no avail; Romanus let his sentence stand 'without respect for the inviolability of the divine image'.[21] The onlookers were horrified and Attaleiates declares that he then truly had a presentiment that some awful divine vengeance would follow.

Swelled with pride by his easy conquest, the emperor garrisoned the fortress and returned to his camp outside the city to the accompaniment of paeans, acclamations and songs

of triumph. Manzikert was indeed a key strong-point to have
and to hold, sited on a sharp bend of the Murat Su and commanding entrance to its plain to the west, the easy route for
both trade from the Caspian or, as the Seljuks had shown, for
armed incursion into the heart of the Empire. What Romanus
did not know at this moment of triumph was how badly
matters had gone thirty miles to the south at Khilat, how strong
his adversary was and, most important, how close at hand.

If Alp Arslan were to give battle – by no means a certainty –
he would have to muster an army, and would therefore return
to Persia to do it and would sally forth only after that. Or so
Romanus calculated.

Alp Arslan did *not* return to Persia but, at most, only to the
border of Persarmenia, not more than a hundred and twenty
miles east of Lake Van.* Instead, he sent that energetic and
able man, the vizier Nizam al-Mulk, back to Azerbaijan to
recruit a force for him.

Moslem sources vary widely in defining Alp Arslan's return
route from Aleppo, some contending that he speeded by the
most direct route – Edessa, Amida, Martyropolis, Balesh to
Khilat – which would not explain how or where he obtained
reinforcements in the number he possessed when he got there
or why that relatively direct passage would have taken more
than two months to traverse. More credible are accounts
declaring that from Amida he followed the Tigris to Mosul
and thence to Khoi/Khvoy, then as now a node of east-west
and north-south routes, slightly north of Lake Urmia, and
that it was from there that he sent his vizier (and his wife)
back to Tabriz or Hamadan. *En route* he had picked up some
10,000 Kurdish cavalry; later, presumably, further reinforcements hurried to him from Persia. The agreement is general –
and the figure may be accepted as credible – that he assembled
a total force of about 40,000, mostly cavalry, each trooper with
an extra horse.

*Writing a century or more later, Moslem historians explained the
decision on grounds that the sultan thought such a deep withdrawal
would be cowardly or appear as a retreat.[22] It is hard to believe that those
reflections would ever have crossed the mind of as pragmatic and hard-
headed a commander as Alp Arslan.

From Khoi he would have returned to the west along the north or, more probably, the south shore of Lake Van. An advance detachment of 10,000 men under one of his commanders, Sundak, who had previously shown his mettle fighting in Syria and Asia Minor, seems to have arrived in Khilat only hours ahead of the sultan, almost exactly when Roussel and Tarchaniotes approached it. That, in turn, would have been about the same time that Romanus fell upon Manzikert or, at most, a few days before, in mid-August 1071.

Of all of the gaps in our knowledge of details of the Manzikert campaign, what next ensued is the widest; of all the elements difficult to explain, it is the most enigmatic. Only two things are certain: first, the Byzantine troops turned tail and pelted full speed back to Melitene on the Euphrates; second, no word of their rout reached the emperor.

To the question 'why?' for each of those facts, one can only respond with a variety of speculations – none of them satisfactory.

But still another question must be asked first: was there even a battle at Khilat? The Moslem writers of the twelfth century, one taking his material from another, even as Scylitzes and Cedrenus did from Attaleiates, would have it that Alp Arslan's advance force valiantly defeated its enemy, captured and sent back in triumph the great cross carried by the Byzantines into battle, and sliced off the nose of the commander, 'a Russian' (perhaps taking the name Roussel to mean 'Russe').[23] There is no reference to any such engagement by the Byzantine historians; Attaleiates says that Tarchaniotes fled the scene on the mere word that the sultan was in the field preparing for an attack on Romanus; there is also no indication in the history of Roussel's future swashbuckling that he did so with his face bereft of its Norman-Scottish nose.[24]*

Battle or merely threat of battle, why did the Byzantines flee? Cowardice? Yet Roussel and Tarchaniotes, with perhaps

*The imprecision of the Moslem accounts, however, makes it possible that the capture of the cross and the Byzantine officer and the severing of his nose may have occurred a few days later, during the immediate preliminaries to the main battle itself.

half of the emperor's army and the best troops at that, should have been at least as numerous as Alp Arslan's whole army, and were certainly numerically stronger than the advance guard. After the flight, Attaleiates called Tarchaniotes a scoundrel[25] but Bryennius described him as 'an excellent man for advice and military stratagems'.[26] He may, however, have been so embittered at having his counsel twice rejected – first on proceeding into Armenia itself and second on the division of the army – that he had no desire to save the emperor from a potential catastrophe of his own making. As for Roussel, we can assume he had no stomach for a chancy fight: he could save his skin and that of his mercenaries and find future work from other employers – as indeed he did in later years, both from Romanus's successor and then from the Turks.

Or was the flight dictated by good military reasons, despite the superiority of the Byzantines postulated above? There is some indication that the forces of Roussel and Tarchaniotes were scattered when word came of an impending Turkish attack; it may have become a matter of *sauve qui peut*. But why, then, the precipitous flight to the west rather than a retreat to the north to rejoin Romanus and his main force?

Or, finally, was it outright treason? The answer can be considered along with the question of why no word about the flight was sent back to Romanus.

If, on hearing of the sultan's approach at or near Khilat, the commanders did not know their leader's exact whereabouts, they certainly knew his route and knew he was to the north of them. It would have been a simple matter to dispatch a courier, or several, to make a good day's ride to Manzikert to bring the bad news. Or, if Roussel and Tarchaniotes were not aware of that city's fall, and thought it still in Turkish hands, their couriers could easily be instructed how to skirt the city on the way further north to meet the emperor. Tarchaniotes and Roussel were neither simpletons nor tyros in war; they knew the need for communications – a desperate need as matters then stood – and how to conduct them.

If, as may well have been the case, Turkish forces had blocked the road north from Khilat to Manzikert before Tarchaniotes and Roussel had organized their dispersed forces, those commanders had the duty either to harry the enemy's rear or else seek to reunite their troops with Romanus's by a northwards march via routes further to the west. The roads would have been more roundabout and hence longer, but the terrain would have been entirely passable by foot and horse.

Roussel, as indicated above, may simply not have cared what happened to Romanus. But what about Tarchaniotes? Bitter he may have been, but surely not so bitter as to let Romanus proceed without any warning of impending danger. Was he, then, one of the Ducas party, hoping and plotting for Romanus's downfall, and thus happy to desert if his desertion might accomplish the cabal's objective? There is no indication that he was Romanus's political enemy, but there is no indication that he was not. If he was hostile, however, was he so indifferent to the possible fate of a Byzantine army that he would have been content to have it destroyed? After all, Andronicus Ducas and doubtless others in the opposition party within the emperor's army might go to their deaths through lack of warning, along with the principal target of their plot.

These questions remain unanswerable.

Even though the events of the next few days near Manzikert are more fully reported by the Greek and Moslem chroniclers than the affair at Khilat, many aspects remain puzzling and the area in which only speculation is possible is too wide to allow a tidy and precise account. The production of official reports, regimental histories and memoirs of generals was not the practice of the age. The account given by Attaleiates, as an eye-witness, must be taken as the most reliable (Scylitzes's history seems to have been lifted from Attaleiates almost entirely), but in many points it is inconsistent with that of Bryennius who, one is entitled to suppose, had a vivid enough recapitulation, directly or indirectly, from an ancestor who was in the thick of things. And their accounts, in turn, often run on different tracks from those of the Arabic and Persian writers. Those latter wrote a generation or two – or three – after the event, by which time oral tradition and legend had left an embroidery on the facts which, though rich, is not particularly persuasive (the most trustworthy of them seem to have worked from documents, now lost, by writers almost as contemporaneous and as close to the affair as Attaleiates).[27] One is left to cut the best path one can through a thicket of uncertainty.

Besides the fact of Romanus's catastrophic defeat itself, almost the only other item that is beyond question is that the battle fell on a Friday, but whether it was Friday, 5, 19 or 26 August remains in dispute.*

Another uncertainty is how many days were taken up by the preliminaries to the battle: Cahen produces a chronology indicating that three days passed between Romanus's capture of Manzikert and the final engagement, but it can also be argued that the latter followed more closely on the heels of the former. A far more important unanswered question is the number of troops on each side: wildly divergent statements by the Moslem writers and complete silence on the point by the Greeks have not prevented modern historians from making guesses of anything from 40,000 to 100,000 on each side – but they are no more than guesses.

The battlefield itself remains unidentified but lack of that information does not seriously cloud an understanding of what took place: most or all of the battle was fought on the steppe; level or slightly rolling country, remarkably uniform for several miles south and south-east of Manzikert.

The scene was the high plateau of Armenia, 5000 feet or more above sea level. The fortress of Manzikert stands on a slight rise about two and a half miles to the east of the broad,

---

*Almost all latter-day European historians accept 19 August as the date; almost as unanimously, modern Turkish scholars conclude it was the 26th. In their favour is a point made by Attaleiates (p. 156): shortly – one or two days – before the battle, the night was 'moonless' (*aselenos*). Conceivably, he could have meant merely that the sky was overcast, a condition possible but unlikely at that place in that season. If we take him literally, however, he meant that the time was in the dark of the moon. In August 1071 the full moon was on the 13th (Julian – old-style – calendar, as used by the historians throughout) and thus would have been bright during most of the nights of the 17th or 18th, but would have been visible only just before dawn, and then only as a small crescent, on the nights of the 24th and 25th. One Arab historian, Ibn al-Adim, who is credited by Ramazan Şeşen[28] as being the most trustworthy, puts the date on 5 August, but the moon would then have been almost half full.

(I am indebted to the Nautical Almanac Office of the Royal Greenwich Observatory for this nine-hundred-year retrospective ephemeris.)

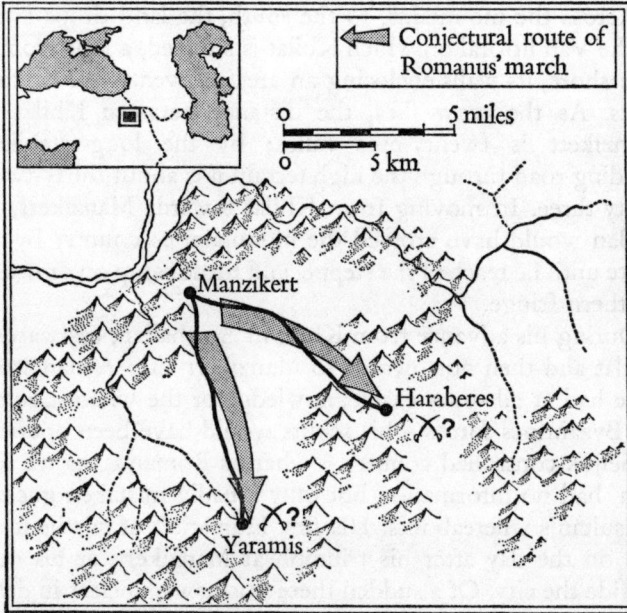

8 *The Battle of Manzikert, August 1071*

south-flowing Murat Su which at that point makes an almost ninety-degree turn to the west about at the juncture of two tributaries, one coming in from the south, the other from the north-east. The rocky plain extends for about eight miles in the south-east quadrant until it gives way to rising terrain that culminates in weather-worn mountains climbing to more than 7000 feet. The mountains are barren except for bits of arable land in the bottoms of seasonal streams that cut the area into a tangle of ravines and small canyons. The plain is ideal cavalry country, the uplands ideal for ambushes. That the battle moved from those plains towards the high country is strongly suggested by Bryennius, who speaks positively about the Byzantine forces running into ambushes.[29] Almost the only places where ambushes could be laid within half a day's ride of Manzikert are the foothills of those mountains.

Across the mountains, to the south, the land drops swiftly to the Van littoral on which Khilat is situated, a mile from the lake shore, its walls enclosing an area of twenty-five or thirty acres. As the crow flies, the distance between Khilat and Manzikert is twenty-nine miles; by the long-established winding road through the high terrain it is about thirty-two or thirty-three. In moving from Khilat towards Manzikert, Alp Arslan would have crossed the mountainous country by that route until he reached the steppe, and made camp on or near its southern fringe.

During his advance from Khoi, in Azerbaijan, eastwards to Khilat and then northwards to Manzikert, Alp Arslan would have had at all times exact knowledge of the whereabouts of the Byzantines forces – his scouts would have been operating in Seljuk-controlled country – whereas Romanus, as we have seen, had no information but only a badly mistaken guess of the sultan's whereabouts. His first intimation of hostile forces was on the day after his triumph at Manzikert, at his camp outside the city. Of a sudden there was news, unclear in detail, that some of his foragers were being beset by Turks, coming from no one knew where. They were in fact the forward elements of the sultan's army which only a day or two before – or even the same day – had sent Tarchaniotes fleeing.

Romanus assumed, however, that the harassers were merely a small Turkish detachment. To drive them off, he sent out Bryennius with what was considered an adequate force. With infantry and horsemen, the general attacked in small units. Confused by encountering rather more of the enemy than they had expected, they soon found themselves in difficulties. With their usual tactics, the Turkish archers were shooting from a distance, killing some of Bryennius's men and wounding more. The Turks engaged in the affair, Attaleiates notes, were far more vigorous and determined than those met in the past and stood up to their opponents in hand-to-hand combat. Becoming aware of what he was facing, Bryennius sent back for reinforcements.

The emperor's sour frame of mind – one senses again the change in his temperament from earlier years – seems by now to have degenerated into petulance and anger. To those around him he accused Bryennius of cowardice and refused to send him help. Instead he assembled his army – a curious act at that moment but perhaps he saw morale crumbling under his eyes – and addressed them on the conduct of the war, 'using words of extraordinary violence'.[30] At this point the chaplain of the army saw fit to deliver a sermon; those hearing it thought its text alluded to the emperor's behaviour on the outcome of his current undertaking. It was from John 15: 20-1 and 16:2: 'If they persecuted me, they will persecute you . . . the hour is coming when whoever kills you will think he is offering his service to God.'

The fighting grew heavier and at last the emperor sent out a reconnaissance in force under the command of an Armenian officer, Basilacius. He was a hot-headed, impulsive commander, according to Bryennius,[31] and as his behaviour proved, a reckless fool; he had assured Romanus of what he wanted to hear, namely that the attackers were only a detachment of the Khilat garrison. With a body of horsemen as eager as himself for action, Basilacius began a pursuit of the Turks, breaching a fundamental Byzantine doctrine forbidding a commander to advance ahead of the body of his troops. They lost communication with Bryennius behind them. Now, instead of standing firm as before, the Turks fled, giving the appearance of undisciplined fugitives. But, unlike Basilacius, they were following *their* tactical precepts to the letter, feigning retreat and drawing their pursuers on. When the Byzantines had charged far enough forward to be beyond immediate rescue, the Seljuks turned and snapped the trap shut. The madcap officer's horse was killed and he was quickly surrounded. Encumbered by his armour, he was easily captured. Almost none of his troops escaped with their lives.

When word of the disastrous sortie was brought back, along with litters bearing wounded, Romanus ordered Bryennius to advance in full force with the entire left wing of the army to attempt a rescue. The general moved forward, but for a time saw neither friend nor foe. Eventually, however, he came on the bodies of Basilacius's men and learned from one wounded survivor, breathing his last, what had happened. Suddenly, once again, the Turks appeared as if out of nowhere

– Bryennius must have ridden to a point where the steppe gives way to broken country and where an ambush could have been laid – and went on the offensive. They were a substantial segment of Alp Arslan's main force.*

Retiring in good order until he neared the Byzantine camp, Bryennius then commanded a portion of his troops to gallop to safety and, to cover their escape, he himself and a few other soldiers turned about and again went on the attack, actually forcing the Turks to flee. But they, in turn, soon received reinforcements, regrouped and formed a new attack. In the see-saw engagement, Bryennius suffered three wounds – a lance blow in the chest and two arrows in the back – but none so serious as to keep him from the field a day or two later.

When he and his valiant rearguard finally made it to their camp he reported what had happened to the emperor, who must by then have seen that he had been served by a warrior and not a coward. He ordered his general to his tent to have his wounds treated and, realizing at last that he was face to face with Alp Arslan's entire army, marshalled his own and prepared to fight.

But 'the Turks are wicked by nature, and masters of deceit', Attaleiates fumed.[32] They had quickly withdrawn and although the Byzantines remained posted in observation points until the evening, they could see no sign of the enemy.

Romanus returned to camp, obliged to consider his next steps. But the night was not one for quiet contemplation. As quickly as they had disappeared, the Turks returned when darkness fell and charged on some Uz mercenaries (Turkic, presumably non-Moslem Patzinaks and other Oghuz from the area of the Danube and north of the Black Sea) who were dealing with local traders outside the camp. Attaleiates's account resembles the scenario of a western film:

With irrational howling and shooting of arrows [the Turks] rode around greatly endangering [the mercenaries] and killing some. The victims of the attack were forced to run inside the fortified camp.

---

*Bryennius the Younger gives a somewhat different account, reporting that it was Basilacius who first rode out against the Turks, was defeated and that only then was the general Bryennius dispatched to discover what had occurred.

All jammed together one after another; they were chased into the entrance way, which caused tremendous confusion among the troops within. They thought it was a full scale attack by the enemy and that the whole camp and all their belongings would be captured. For there was no moon that night, and you could not tell who was being chased and who was doing the chasing, or who was on the other side. The Scythian [i.e. Uz] mercenaries, moreover, looked exactly like the Turks, which made the situation that night all the more confusing.*

It was then that a tremendous fear took over; there was talk of disaster, there were incoherent cries, meaningless shouting; it was a scene of utter confusion and impending doom. Death would be, so everyone felt, preferable to what we then witnessed; being absent was regarded as a stroke of luck, and happy were they who did not have to look on such a sight.[33]

For those inside there was no sleep that night, but at least the Turks failed to break through the defences.

As would have been necessary, Romanus had pitched his camp beside a river, probably the Murat Su or one of the large watercourses flowing into it near Manzikert. The following day the Turks attempted to gain control of its banks but were driven off by such infantry as the emperor had retained in his army. At about the same time, however, a portion of his Uz contingent deserted to the Seljuks: blood – or fear of defeat – was thicker than whatever other ties existed. It is not clear how many defected – Aristakes says an 'important' detachment, but no Moslem historian mentions the event. Attaleiates declares that the desertions caused grave concern, instilling fear that other Turkic contingents in the Byzantine forces were on the verge of doing the same. With the emperor's blessing, Attaleiates took it on himself to harangue them and obtain renewed pledges of loyalty. In the event, they remained faithful.[34]†

*The Seljuks and their distant cousins, separated for centuries since their various migrations from Central Asia, appear to have retained their common garb of old, their language and racial appearance.

†A curious account of an event not easily explicable and not reported by any other source, but which may have a bearing on this episode, is that of an Italian or Norman poet writing around the turn of the eleventh century. He is William of Apulia, author of the *Gesta Roberti Wiscardi*, the *Deeds of Robert Guiscard*, implacable enemy of Alexius I (see Chapter 12).

Romanus was tempted to give battle at once but held off, awaiting the return of the troops from Khilat to whom he had sent messengers urgently ordering them back. The commands were, of course, too late, but the emperor did not know it.

At the same time, either one or two days before the final battle there arrived at the emperor's camp a totally unexpected delegation from the Caliph of Baghdad, led by one of his principal dignitaries, al-Muhalban, seeking a parley. The mission was doubtless instigated by Alp Arslan in the belief that it would be better received if it appeared to come from a personage whom Romanus was known to consider as a friend and with whom he had previously negotiated. But the delegation was coldly welcomed and its members forced to make the *proskynesis*, a bow to the earth, demanded by Roman emperors since Constantine's times and before.

Allowed to approach the emperor for conversation, the embassy proposed a truce. Romanus expressed himself as pleasantly surprised by the suggestion but added magisterially that the Seljuk army should first withdraw from its nearby camp to a location further off; he would then occupy the position that the Turks abandoned and fortify it with a palisade. Thereupon, the two sides could meet to begin discussions.

*

Realizing the relevance of Byzantine affairs to those of Robert 'The Weasel', the poet begins his account with verses describing the rise and fall of Romanus IV. He does not seem to have seen Attaleiates's history, but appears to have been informed by those who had. Though his recitation is full of errors and meagre in detail, he follows Attaleiates's story with some fidelity, and from the same point of view, i.e. as a partisan of the emperor.

Uniquely, he reports that at one point, presumably a day or two before the final battle, Romanus distributed all of his wealth and treasures to his troops, in the hope that should his camp be taken, the Turks, seeing the riches to be grasped, would not harm the Byzantines themselves. But, the poet continues, 'The silver was gathered in by the mercenaries, who fled. The Greeks were obliged to spend the night without sleep.' The 'mercenaries' referred to may have been the turncoat Uzes. The alleged distribution of all the emperor's wealth could be simply an exaggeration of a bribe or bonus Romanus may have offered to men he felt were wavering.[35]

The question is why he gave a reponse guaranteed to precipitate a full-scale engagement.*

With no word of the whereabouts of Tarchaniotes's forces, including his best troops and most of his infantry, after the mauling that Basilacius and Bryennius had undergone, after the terrible night around the camp, and after the desertion of some of his Turkic mercenaries and the distinct prospect of others following suit – why, after all that, was Romanus so intent on precipitating what he knew would be the decisive engagement with the sultan's main army?

Attaleiates offers the explanation that even before the discussions with the caliph's delegation were finished, those 'close to the emperor' persuaded him that the offer was a deception, a trick rather than a constructive proposal, made by the sultan because he feared a fight and was only intent on gaining time to assemble a larger force.[37] Bryennius identifies those advisers as the usual 'flatterers' and declares that the more judicious members of a council that Romanus hastily convened advised him to wait the return of the troops he had sent to Khilat.[38]

Romanus may indeed have been subject to flattery but there were surely weightier considerations that led to his decision:

If Byzantium were ever to be freed from the devastating Turkish invasions, the core of Seljuk power, the nourishing source of its emirs and Turkomans, which is to say the sultan and his main armed force, would have to be destroyed. Hitherto, that had been impossible because, among other reasons, the Turkish army had never been willing to stand and fight in hand-to-hand battle. Here, at last, was the chance.

Romanus's expenses in assembling his army had been enormous; he would not be able to muster another of that strength in the foreseeable future.

Yet, strong as that army might be, it was doubtful if it would retain what strength it had for much longer. Morale,

*Writing a century after the event, Bar Hebraeus no doubt invented the words he put into Romanus's mouth in his reply to the caliph's envoy: 'Now that I have brought out my treasures, and collected all these troops, and the victory was mine, shall I go back? For you there is nothing but the sword.' But he was certainly not far off the mark in reflecting Romanus's attitude.[36]

bad to begin with, would degenerate further under the daily harassment in prospect. Restrained from effective reply, the army's spirit would plummet even further, and desertions would become more probable.

Leo Diabatenus, Romanus's envoy at Aleppo some months before, had reported Alp Arslan's army as being weak and frightened. Thus, the truce offer might indeed be a trick to avoid battle until reinforcements were gathered. Alp Arslan was in a position to bring them over short distances from Persia; Romanus was far from Constantinople and in any event could not call for more levies to be brought up.

As mentioned earlier, to return to Constantinople with nothing to show for the huge expeditionary effort but a truce – necessarily shaky, given the nature of Turkish promises and the sultan's only half-obedient Turkomans – would have meant political suicide for Romanus, or something worse and more painful.

Finally, caution was alien to Romanus's nature.

But we must ask, equally, what were the sultan's motives in proposing a truce. Two possible answers suggest themselves:

The first is that he himself was much in doubt about winning a pitched battle with the Byzantines. The Greek army still enjoyed a formidable reputation despite all the deflationary evidence; in past hand-to-hand combat, it had always bested the 'barbarian' tribesmen. Moreover, even after dividing his forces for the foray on Khilat, Romanus may have had a larger number of troops to put in the field than Alp Arslan.*

*Such is the consensus of all near-contemporary Moslem historians and most of the later European ones except for Oman, who puts the sultan's forces at 100,000 and the emperor's at 40,000, exactly reversing the usual estimate.[39] His judgement, however, may have been the closest to the truth with respect to the emperor's strength, if not the sultan's. The Islamic sources' tally of Byzantine numbers may be discounted, for they obviously would have been inclined to make the sultan's victory appear as glorious as possible, a victory over great numerical odds. If Romanus had taken some 100,000 men into the field initially, but had dispatched what Bryennius said was 'a part' and Attaleiates says was 'a very large unit' of his army to Khilat; if he had scattered his forces at the time of the battle, as Psellus alleges, so he had less than half his effectives about him; and if, as some sources indicate, he had previously detached a unit of 10,000 to forage for supplies in Iberia, then Alp Arslan could indeed have deployed a stronger force at the battle itself.

Certainly the sultan's preliminaries on the day of the battle do not suggest that he was over-confident. He spoke of finding martyrdom in the field; he dressed in white so that his garb might serve as his shroud; he made his entourage swear to recognize his son, Malik-Shah, as his heir should he die in battle; his prayer, cited as the epigraph to this chapter, was not that of a man revelling in the contemplation of a sure victory. He may well have been stalling for time or hoping for a way out.

Alternatively, he may have sincerely hoped for peace with Byzantium and have thought that it was obtainable. His only quarrel with Byzantium was its renewed effort to retake more of Armenia than he felt it was entitled to, including territory that endangered his rear and his western flanks. He might have hoped that he could persuade Romanus that he had no aggressive designs on Anatolia and, that being the case, that he could reach an acceptable settlement on a division of Armenia. That obtained, he could turn back to his main objective – the business of conquering Fatimid Syria and Egypt.

The rebuff of his truce proposal, however, left Alp Arslan no option. It served simply to inflame Seljuk ardour.

Assuming for some weeks that a battle to the death was likely, the Abbasid caliph had circulated a prayer for victory to be offered every Friday in all the mosques of his domain. Departing from that fact into projections about the sultan's piety, the early Moslem chroniclers declared that Alp Arslan deliberately launched his major assault on that holy day of the Islamic week at the moment when prayers from the Faithful for his triumph were wafting heavenwards. The assertion is doubtful; more probably the engagement came when Romanus chose to take his army out of its encampment, form them in line of battle and advance on the enemy. That moment was, Attaleiates indicates, immediately after the truce delegation's departure; Cahen believes it was a day or two thereafter. Whichever, the fateful day was Friday.

The morning was given over in both camps to preparations, military and religious. Mass was celebrated in the rich tent of the emperor, prayers were said by the troops and the cross was paraded through the camp, all being normal preliminaries when the Byzantines made ready for battle. The ceremonies in the Moslem camp were analogous. As the troops passed in review they were fired by the declaration that the insolence of the Greeks was no longer to be tolerated and that the forth-coming conflict was to be fought not merely for the sultan but for the sake of all Islam. Alp Arslan made his do-or-die adjuration, tied up the tail of his horse (a symbolic and perhaps practical act before the battle), ostentatiously threw his bow and quiver aside and seized his sword and mace.*

No one has located with certainty the place where the two forces faced each other shortly after noon and, in the absence of detailed topographical indications or the finding of relics no one is likely to.

The engagement took the form of a running fight, with the Byzantine army moving forward the entire afternoon, ad-vancing for what must have been several miles from its starting point at Romanus's camp. The terrain and what general descriptions there are in the works of Greek and Moslem writers suggest that the emperor led his forces across the steppe country to, or partly into, the steeply rising and rugged hills on the borders of the plain to the south or south-east. The direction would have been determined by the Seljuks, withdrawing towards the quarter where they had laid ambushes and posted their reserves.

The modern Turkish writer Feridun Dirimtekin provides a map showing the scene of the climactic engagement about eight miles south-east of Manzikert where the plain rises gradually to about 200 yards above the level of the city at the foot of a loftier spur of hills. Above is a site from which Alp Arslan could have commanded the battle and behind and below which, within canyons and gullies, he could have concealed his assault troops. An equally possible location could have been about the same distance almost due south, where the terrain is of similar configuration. Most authorities place the end of the battle there rather than east of Manzikert.[40]

---

*His choice of weapons seems to have been a symbolic guarantee of his intent to remain on the battlefield to the end; the Seljuks fought and won the battle with mounted archers, until the last stages when they closed in to surround and slaughter the vanquished.

Sword and mace in his hand notwithstanding, Alp Arslan, as a good commander would, took no part in the fighting itself but directed it from a vantage point on a summit from which he could observe the entire scene. Command in the field, according to Bryennius, the only source for this information,[41] was given over to a eunuch named Tarang. He deployed his army in a wide crescent which permitted, in the usual Turkish fashion, an orderly withdrawal of the centre while the horsemen in the wings harassed the Byzantine flanks with a steady rain of arrows. Bryennius adds that Tarang also set up ambushes, a tactic as time-honoured among the Seljuks as it was intelligent.

Romanus's formation and tactics were just as traditional in Byzantine practice and, at the beginning, just as intelligent as the Turks'. The army formed in a straight and wide front, doubtless several ranks deep. The emperor commanded the centre, with the army corps of the guards regiments and possibly the native troops whom he favoured more than the mercenaries. A Cappadocian general, Alyattes, led the right wing, presumably with levies from Anatolia. Bryennius headed the left wing, and, as commander of the Army of the West, would have had troops from Byzantium's European territories. Andronicus Ducas had a strong rearguard under his charge, comprised of the levies of 'allies and the nobility', and thus must have included what were by that time the almost private or personal soldiery of the aristocrats' great estates. According to the younger Bryennius, Andronicus 'exceeded those of his age in wisdom and was surpassed by no one in courage. He was marvellously trained in ruses and stratagems . . .' (as he was soon to demonstrate in the most malign fashion). But, the historian continues in a staggering bit of understatement, 'he was not very favourably disposed towards the emperor'.[42]

In the *Tactica* of Leo the Wise, observed in principle by all Byzantine commanders since his time but often forgotten in execution, precepts were laid down for fighting the 'Turks' (a term that in Leo's day referred to the Patzinaks, Magyars and other tribes north of the Black Sea): engage the enemy at close quarters as soon as possible to take advantage of the Byzantines' superior weight and skill in hand-to-hand fighting; protect the army from enemy archery by using the infantry with its heavier and longer-ranging bows; beware of heedless pursuit and of falling into ambushes; keep the forces in close juxtaposition and communication lest detached units be subject to separate attacks and encirclement by superior forces; keep the flanks protected and guard the rear, if possible by natural defences such as a marsh, river or defile.

But by Romanus's time Byzantine skill in archery had greatly degenerated and in any case most of his infantry with their distance-keeping bows had gone off to Khilat. His rear was covered by nothing so useful as a river, marsh or defile, but by a traitor awaiting his chance.

Romanus commenced the hostilities by trying to observe the *Tactica*'s command to engage the enemy frontally as soon as possible. But the Seljuks, probably better mounted and certainly better commanded than their Turkic cousins of other times on the northern frontier, steadily withdrew, in good order, in the centre. Romanus found the enemy melting away before him and he advanced over what had been Alp Arslan's camp, abandoned and emptied of all contents, doing little harm to opponents constantly keeping out of range and avoiding contact.

It was a different matter, however, on the flanks. There the Turkish horsemen made minor sallies from time to time but occupied themselves principally with showering the Byzantine cavalry with a rain of infuriating arrows. Bryennius tells of the consequences: the soldiers, he writes, 'having been harassed by the Turks, were obliged to pursue [the enemy archers] because otherwise they would shoot from afar and kill their horses. But in pursuing them thoughtlessly, they fell into an ambush.'[43]

While the Turks abided by their rules, the Byzantine flanks forgot theirs – and so did their leader.

Romanus rode on, never finding an organized opposition to hit at. It is understandable – although it was catastrophic – that in his frustration he took no note of the time until 'the twilight took him by surprise'.[44]

Having taken every fighting man of his army into the field, he realized that his camp was undefended and vulnerable to attack, pillage and even capture by Turkish horsemen riding around and behind him. His troops were exhausted and without provisions. Further pursuit into the darkness would be futile as well as dangerous. He gave the order to turn back, employing the usual signal of reversing the imperial standards.

But the wings had somehow become detached and some units at a distance interpreted the reversed standards to mean that the emperor had been defeated. With confusion prevailing among the Byzantines, the Seljuks, stationed on the heights, sprang their trap. Withdrawing no longer, they turned, attacked, broke the Greek right wing and cut between it and the rearguard, which was already in retreat instead of doing what a rearguard is supposed to do: move forward, engage the enemy that had ridden behind the army's front lines, and squeeze him in a vice.

Andronicus, so 'marvellously trained . . . in stratagems', seized the moment. To fulfil 'the plot he had already hatched for the emperor's destruction, he personally spread the word' to his troops that Romanus had been defeated.[45] They fled back to camp. The units near them saw their flight and followed their example; still others, one after another, caught the same infection. The left wing, attempting a rescue of the emperor in the centre, found itself charged from behind; it too, was forced to flee.

Seeing what was happening and that the reversal of his banner had precipitated a panic, Romanus turned about again and attempted a last stand with his personal guard. His rallying call to other troops fell on deaf ears.

Attaleiates continues the story:

Outside the camp everyone else was in flight; all were shouting incoherently and riding about in disorder; nobody could say what was going on. Some claimed the emperor was firmly resisting with what was left of his army and that the barbarians were running away. Others said that he had been killed or captured. Everyone had something different to report, claiming victory for each side and then denying it. . . .

It was like an earthquake with howling, sweat, a swift rush of fear, clouds of dust, and not least hordes of Turks riding all around us. Depending on his speed, resolution and strength, each man sought safety in flight. The enemy chased them, killing some, capturing some and trampling others under the horses' hooves. It was a terribly sad sight, beyond any lamenting or mourning. What could be more pitiable than seeing the entire imperial army in flight, defeated and chased by inhuman and cruel barbarians, the emperor defenceless and surrounded by armed barbarians, the imperial tents, symbols of military might and sovereignty, taken over by men of that stripe, the whole Roman state overturned and knowing that the Empire itself was on the verge of collapse?[46]

The internal divisions in the army, manifested from the moment Romanus had taken the throne and demonstrated throughout the long march from Constantinople, reached their fatal climax. The mercenaries, jealous of the emperor's favouritism to his native troops, did not ride to the rescue. The Armenians, seething with hatred for the heretic Byzantines who had persecuted them for their resistance to Orthodoxy, were among the first to take flight, and Andronicus's nobles, also at odds with the emperor, simply abandoned the battle.[47]

By all accounts, even including that of Psellus,[48] Romanus fought like a lion until, with a wound in his hand and his horse brought down, he could defend himself no longer and was made captive. Andronicus, his noble entourage and his troops escaped, as did some other officers and men. Psellus declares that those who escaped were but a tiny fraction of the whole,[49] and Bryennius states that 'the great part of the soldiers were put to the sword; some others escaped'.[50]

Romanus was left to lie among the wounded throughout the night. He would have been more fortunate had he shared the fate of most of his men.

11

'All They that take the Sword . . .'

> 'Yes,' the Sultan cried, 'the Romans are atheists; from today on, the peace with them is broken and the oath which linked them with the Persians no longer exists. From now on, the worshippers of the Cross will be immolated by the sword and all Christian countries will be delivered into slavery.'
>
> *Matthew of Edessa*[1]

The Moslem historians of the Seljuk period, for whom the victory at Manzikert was the most glorious episode they would ever relate, enjoyed telling the story of a slave so miserable that when a Turkish chieftain tried to force him on Nizam al-Mulk as a gift the vizier refused to accept him.

'What good would this mamluk do?' the great man scoffed. 'Would he bring us the Byzantine emperor as prisoner?'

Yet, as has happened before with words spoken in scorn, 'the Almighty God decided that this should be so'.[2] The wretched *gulam* was Romanus's captor.

Told of the emperor's capture, an event unprecedented in a thousand years of Roman–Byzantine history, the sultan would not credit it until the prisoner was brought into his presence, garbed as a common soldier, and in chains. He was identified by envoys who had seen him in the imperial court and by Basilacius, the hot-headed general captured earlier, who threw himself at his former leader's feet in miserable lamentation. 'Like a madman', Scylitzes reports, Alp Arslan leapt suddenly from his throne, commanded Romanus to

G

kiss the earth, and placed his foot on the prisoner's neck.[3]

Gibbon doubts that the sultan committed such an indignity upon his vanquished adversary – although it was no more than what a Byzantine emperor would have done if the roles had been reversed. Indeed, Romanus had required the *proskynesis* of the caliph's envoys only a day or two before. But, Gibbon continues, even if the sultan did in fact act as Scylitzes related, it was only 'in a moment of insolence' and in conformity with national custom.[4]

What then took place has been described, with kaleidoscopic variations of detail but with extraordinary unanimity in the essentials, by all the Greek and Islamic historians who wrote on the subject; there can be no doubt about the basic facts. Gibbon's account reminds one of the 'new journalism' of the late twentieth century, with seemingly clairvoyant insight into minds and manners of men at a scene he did not witness, and he embroiders no little on the information provided by the works he read – especially with respect to the sultan's stately *politesse*. Nevertheless, Gibbon's version is as close to the fundamental truth as any other. And, as would be expected, it is the best-written:

. . . the rest of [the sultan's] conduct has extorted the praise of his bigotted foes, and may afford a lesson to the most civilized ages. He instantly raised the royal captive from the ground; and thrice clasping his hand with tender sympathy, assured him that his life and dignity should be inviolate in the hands of a prince who had learned to respect the majesty of his equals and the vicissitudes of fortune.

From the divan Romanus was conducted to an adjacent tent, where he was served with pomp and reverence by the officers of the sultan, who, twice each day, seated him in the place of honour at his own table. In a free and familiar conversation of eight days, not a word, not a look, of insult escaped from the conqueror; but he severely censured the unworthy subjects who had deserted their valiant prince in the hour of danger, and gently admonished his antagonist of some errors which he had committed in the management of the war.

In the preliminaries of negotiation Alp Arslan asked him what treatment he expected to receive, and the calm indifference of the emperor displays the freedom of his mind.

'If you are cruel,' said he, 'you will take my life; if you listen to pride, you will drag me at your chariot wheels; if you consult your interest, you will accept a ransom and restore me to my country.'

'And what,' continued the sultan, 'would have been your own behaviour had fortune smiled on your arms?'

The reply of the Greek betrays a sentiment which prudence, and even gratitude, should have taught him to suppress.

'Had I vanquished,' he fiercely said, 'I would have inflicted on thy body many a stripe.'

The Turkish conqueror smiled at the insolence of his captive; observed that the christian law inculcated the love of enemies and the forgiveness of injuries; and nobly declared that he would not imitate an example which he condemned.[5]

But Gibbon missed the point – or rather two points: the emperor's and the sultan's.

Wounded, humiliated as no Roman emperor before him, his army destroyed and his power demolished, Romanus nevertheless kept his wits about him. A canting reply to Alp Arslan's hypothetical question, oozing professions of intended mercy and generosity, would have been not only a transparent lie but also a demonstration that the emperor considered the sultan a fool. It would have provoked the contempt it deserved – and worse.

At the same time, Alp Arslan's renunciation of vengeance was not brought about by some unsuspected conversion to the precepts of the Beatitudes but because it was – as Romanus correctly pointed out – greatly in his interest. The Byzantine devil whom he knew stood before him harmless. An unknown devil coming to the throne in Constantinople, not having been taught the lesson just administered to Romanus, could be a nuisance or even a menace to the Seljuk–Byzantine accord that the sultan needed for his future plans. His purposes, as he saw them at the time, required stability and a humbled loser at the head of the Byzantine state, prepared to accept a peace treaty dictated to him.

The booty in the Byzantine camp that fell into the hands of the victorious Turks was beyond counting – even, in fact, beyond the army's ability to haul away. The supply was so huge that prices dropped to ridiculous levels: a helmet sold for half a dinar, three cuirasses for one dinar. Jewels were peddled for a pittance. Inhabitants of nearby towns such as Manzikert and Khilat busied themselves for days carting off what the army could not carry; the treasures they amassed were still to be seen among them a century later.[6]

The peace treaty imposed by the sultan was an intelligent one, in that it left Romanus some remnants of dignity. It included a mutual non-aggression agreement, the return to Turkish hands of such cities in Byzantine possession as Manzikert, Antioch, Edessa and Hierapolis, the return of all Moslem prisoners of war in Byzantine hands, the freeing of certain of Romanus's officers captured in the battle, and an arrangement for the future marriage of a daughter of Romanus to the oldest son of Alp Arslan. The emperor also promised to supply troops to the sultan on demand.

These terms, principally taken from the history of Sibt Ibn al-Jawzi, most trustworthy of the Moslem chroniclers (his account reproduced a work, now lost, of his grandfather who, in turn, almost certainly had at hand the sultan's contemporaneous dispatches to the caliph's court[7]), also prescribed the payment of ransom for the emperor and tribute. According to Sibt, Alp Arslan originally demanded ten million gold pieces, a sum Romanus pointed out was impossible to produce since he had spent the major part of Byzantium's treasure in raising his army. The amount finally agreed on was one and a half million plus 360,000 in annual tribute – the equivalent of which in today's terms cannot even be estimated.

Romanus insisted that he could not put the treaty into effect merely by sending word ahead to Constantinople to carry out his orders, and proposed instead that he be released and allowed to return as soon as possible himself. Otherwise – such was the clear implication – he would be deposed and succeeded by a ruler unwilling to acknowledge the pact.

Alp Arslan saw the logic of his argument and held him for only eight days, setting him out on his return journey with pomp and ceremony. The sultan himself and his entourage rode with him for a short distance, refused to let him humble himself by dismounting to make his farewells, and sent him on his weary return with an escort of honour: two emirs and a band of a hundred Mamluks.

Not the least remarkable aspect of the week-long encounter between victor and vanquished was, as Cahen observes, that despite a total victory and the absence of further resistance, the sultan demanded no important conquest. He remained faithful to the concept of two empires, of different religions, neither encroaching on the other, but joined in an alliance.[8]

The scene in Constantinople was one of utmost confusion. Fugitives from the battle arrived one after another, all reporting the dreadful defeat but with conflicting stories on whether Romanus IV Diogenes was dead or a prisoner in the enemy camp. A conference of court officials was summoned and a decision was reached that whatever had become of the emperor, his fate and his person were to be ignored and that Eudocia and her sons should be vested with full imperial powers. Argument broke out at once, however, over whether the empress should rule alone or whether Michael and his younger brother should govern without her. Psellus claims credit for a compromise in favour of joint rule.

His solution did not last. 'The main cause of a multitude of [ensuing] disasters', he confesses innocently, 'was the sultan's magnanimous and dignified treatment of the vanquished emperor, releasing him and sending him back with an impressive guard of honour. No one had anticipated such a sequel; that the emperor was alive and fully intending to resume the throne – news brought by a letter to the empress in his own hand written on the return journey – was the last thing the power-hungry anti-Romanus faction wanted. Alp Arslan might have had the decency to have rid them of the fellow. Self-satisfied and self-important, as always, Psellus continues the account:

Immediately there was wild confusion in the palace, with comings and goings everywhere. Some professed astonishment at the news, others would not believe it. Eudocia found herself in an embarrassing position. She was unable to decide what to do next. When I myself arrived in the midst of the turmoil, there was a general demand that I should advise on the best policy. My beloved emperor [Michael] was particularly insistent and joined the others in urging me to speak. I declared, therefore, that it was no longer necessary to receive Romanus in the Empire: he should be outlawed, and instructions should be forwarded to every place in the Roman dominions that his reign was over. The moderate element was convinced that this policy was in our best interests, but the opposition favoured a different plan.[9]

Psellus does not disclose in so many words what or who the opposition were, but it may be inferred that the Caesar, John Ducas, hurrying back from his exile across the Bosphorus, wanted no continuation of an arrangement in which Eudocia had any part. His aim, of course, was total power for himself, easily exercised through the weak and malleable Michael, but subject to complications if the empress sought to exercise the authority she had become accustomed to as the wife of two emperors and when, for a short period, she ruled alone. Even though Romanus had been reduced to the status of a non-person, she might actually want him back.

Fearing for himself, his sons and his nephews if Romanus regained the throne, the Caesar secured the loyalty to him of the Varangian Guard. He placed one group under his command, another under that of his sons. The first, shouting war cries and pounding on their shields, marched on the apartments of the empress; the second, rushing into the palace, proclaimed Michael emperor. The date was 24 October 1071.[10]

Eudocia was terrified and so was Psellus, who initially had played his cards too much in her interest. They retreated to a cavern or crypt under the palace 'and she would have perished of fright had not the Caesar reassured her'. His reassurances, it soon appeared, were those of a prison warden.

Psellus himself was rescued by his 'beloved emperor'. In one sentence admitting that he cowered, frightened and unable to make a decision at the entrance of Eudocia's hideaway, in the next he relates that he was the first person Michael remembered and that the new ruler sent messengers to all parts of the palace to find him.

Having discovered me, they lifted me up in their arms and carried me in cheerful triumph to their sovereign, as if I was some lucky find, or some precious gift. And he, as soon as he set eyes on me, was like a man who heaves a sigh of relief when a storm has passed. At once he handed over to me the responsibility of taking all decisions that might be necessary.[11]

His claim to have exercised plenipotentiary powers was considerably less than the truth: it was John Ducas who ruled. Psellus merely made another of his lightning switches to join the winner.

One of Caesar's first acts was to order Eudocia's exile to a church she had built at the entrance to the Dardanelles. Scylitzes declares that the matter was principally engineered by Psellus and he 'glories in his deed in one of his books'.[12] A second order of the Caesar soon followed: Eudocia was tonsured and forced to become a nun, against her will. The Ducas clan was taking no chances with her.

Nor – to get ahead of the story by a few weeks or months – was Ducas taking any risks with the Comneni. A family that was endowed with more than usual courage and perception would be, *ipso facto*, dangerous to Michael and his puppet-master. Had not Manuel, the eldest, died in the service of Romanus? His brothers were too young to be slandered convincingly so the attack was made on their mother, the redoubtable Anna Dalassena. According to Bryennius, alone of contemporary historians to report the matter, a wretched intriguer was found to spread gossip against her, implying seditious tendencies; he then concocted forged letters from her to Romanus. These were brought to Michael who, acting solely on this *ex parte* evidence, ordered her to be brought to trial – but was too ashamed to attend it himself. Ushered into the presence of the court, Anna drew an image of Christ from inside her gown. 'Behold the Judge,' she said, 'who will today decide between you and me. Observe Him well when you utter your sentence and try to ensure that it is not unworthy of the Judge who knows the secrets of the heart.' The dignified statement did her no good: the craven judges, 'like the Sanhedrin of Caïphas', exiled her and her sons to one of the Princes Islands, in the Sea of Marmara.[13]

On the return march to Constantinople, Romanus soon heard what he may have failed to anticipate: not only would he not be received with open arms but he would have to fight to regain the throne. He somehow succeeded in reassembling a considerable military force out of fugitives from Manzikert and other troops in Anatolia by the time he reached Dokeia/

Tokat, about forty-five miles south-east of Amasea/Amasya, on the northern road to the capital. An equivalently formidable force was sent out by the Caesar to engage him, with his youngest son, Constantine Ducas, in command.

Accounts from contemporary sources of the events during this period vary considerably and tend to be internally inconsistent. According to the Arab historian Sibt, who may have drawn at second hand from communications between Romanus and his new ally, Alp Arslan, Romanus renounced all claims to the throne, clothed himself as a monk, and appealed to Michael to carry out the terms of the treaty with the sultan, beginning by paying the agreed ransom and tribute. Michael concurred but declared that the war had emptied the treasury so that immediate payment was impossible, but that he would pay up later, when he had the means to do so. Alp Arslan, Sibt continues, accepted the delay.[14]

At the same time, however, as all sources make clear, Romanus refused Michael's demand that he give up the fortress of Dokeia, hand it over to Constantine and retire to a monastery to make a reality of the monastic life he supposedly was adopting.

Bar Hebraeus, relying also on Moslem sources, gives something of the same story, reporting Michael's agreement to Romanus's proposals, but that 'after some days certain men worked on him' to demand that Romanus relinquish Dokeia and enter a monastery. Furious, Romanus refused, declaiming, 'Is there not one fortress which he would leave me?'[15] It can only be concluded that Romanus's professed intention of becoming a monk was a sham, and that he still aimed at recovering the Crown.

Whatever the preliminaries may have been, the outcome was a fierce battle with heavy casualties on both sides, ending in a victory for Constantine. Romanus's troops were commanded by Alyattes, the general who led the right wing at Manzikert; he was captured and, according to Scylitzes, his eyes were gouged out by iron tent-stakes.[16]

Either then or earlier, Romanus decamped and made his way to Cicilia, where he was succoured by the Armenian governor of Antioch, Katchadour. Borrowing money from local merchants to recruit other soldiers, Romanus once again assembled a sizeable force, basing himself in Adana. A new army from Constantinople was sent out against him under the command of Andronicus Ducas, the traitor of Manzikert. A battle ensued in which Katchadour was defeated; the dispirited garrison at Adana forced Romanus to surrender.

A treaty was agreed upon calling for Romanus to give up all further pretensions and to retire to a monastery as a monk. A letter from Michael, in effect guaranteed by the archbishops of Chalcedon, Heraclea and Colonea, promised that no injury would befall him. In monkish garb, he gave himself up to Andronicus. The magnanimous victor, Psellus, assures us, 'instead of receiving him in a high-handed, arrogant fashion . . . really sympathized with the prisoner. He shook hands and invited him to his tent. Finally, he asked him to be a guest at his own table, where a magnificent banquet was prepared.'[17]

The captor's civility scarcely survived the last bite of the feast. Andronicus mounted his black-garbed prisoner on a mule and led him, in degradation, 'through those villages and places in which he had formerly been recognized as god-like' as far as Cotyaeum/Kütahya, to await word on what should be done with him.[18] One can picture Psellus's crocodile tears as he penned the sequel:

To pass on to what happened thereafter is a most disagreeable task. I am reluctant to describe a deed that should never have taken place; and yet, if I may alter my words slightly, it was a deed that should have taken place by all means. On the one hand, the scruples of religion, as well as a natural unwillingness to inflict pain, would forbid such a deed: on the contrary side, the state of affairs at the time, and the sudden changes of fortune of both parties, proclaimed that it *must* be done.

The thing came about as follows. The more enthusiastic [!] element in the emperor's council were afraid that [Romanus] Diogenes might succeed in his plots and once more embarrass the emperor. So, concealing their intentions from Michael, they wrote a letter to a certain person who was conveniently able to carry them out, with orders to blind him.[19]

The 'more enthusiastic element' was Caesar John Ducas. Whether he acted with or, as Psellus insists, without Michael's consent, was immaterial; his was the power. As for the archbishops' guarantees, Scylitzes explains:

. . . although they wished to help [Romanus], they were weak and powerless when cruel and harsh men had taken him up and gouged out his eyes pitilessly and inhumanely.

Carried forth on a cheap beast of burden like a decaying corpse, his eyes gouged out and his face and head swollen and full of worms and stench, he lived on a few days in pain and smelling foully before his death, and finally died, settling his ashes in the island of Prote, [one of the Princes Islands, in the Sea of Marmara], where he had built a new monastery.

He was richly buried by his wife, the queen Eudocia, leaving behind himself the memory of trials and misfortunes which surpass hearing. But in such great misfortunes he uttered no blasphemy or curse but continued to give thanks to God, bearing cheerfully what befell him.[20]

He must have been comforted, just before his death, by a letter to him from Psellus, who on this occasion surpassed himself. The dethroned emperor was, Psellus assured him, a fortunate martyr whom God had deprived of his eyes because he had found him worthier of a higher light.[21]

Death came in the summer of 1072.

Alp Arslan was enraged at the treatment meted out to Romanus not only because it voided a treaty he believed would produce the stability and peace he wanted with Byzantium, but also surely because a man whom he trusted and had come to admire and cherish had been murdered. Hence his declamation reproduced at the head of this chapter. He gave his subordinates free rein to do their worst thenceforth in Anatolia but he himself did not attack a land to be conquered almost without effort. Presumably, he still held to his intention of overthrowing the Fatimid Caliphate and of carrying out the mission given to his uncle before him to unify all Moslem lands under the Sunni banner.

But again he was thwarted. After his victory at Manzikert, the sultan was obliged to turn back to the east, apparently to quell a rebellion of a vassal in Transoxania, birthplace of Seljuk power. After crossing the Oxus, he met resistance from a certain Yusuf al-Harani, commander of a fortress. Alp Arslan laid siege to it but it was stubbornly defended. He gained its submission only by deceit, promising Yusuf safety and the retention of his holdings. Yusuf submitted but, as becomes evident, without expectation that the pledge would be honoured. He was led into the presence of the sultan who at once commanded that he be tied hands and feet to four stakes, to be executed by a firing squad of archers.[22]

Yusuf had nothing to lose, but only vengeance to be gained, for he had secreted a dagger in his clothes, a remarkable achievement in itself, given the usual security precautions when an enemy was brought into the presence of a sultan. Bar Hebraeus continues the story:

The prisoner, in his rage, reviled the Sultan and said, 'O thou poltroon, is it in this way that thou killest those who are like myself?' Then the Sultan, with his blood boiling, said, 'Let him go free, so that I may shoot him when he is unfettered, and I will kill him.'[23]

Whereupon Alp Arslan (according to Gibbon, drawing on sources, if any, known only to himself), 'the most skilful archer of the age'[24] drew his bow, shot at point-blank range but lost his footing and missed.

Yusuf fell upon him with his dagger and before he was himself torn to pieces by the sultan's guard, inflicted mortal wounds.* The sultan lingered for four days and died on 24 November 1072 at the age of forty-one or forty-two. His vizier, Nizam al-Mulk, and his son, Malik-Shah, who inherited the realm, bore the body to Merv, and buried it with his ancestors.

Little more than a year after the battle that determined a Turkish future for Asia Minor and doomed the Byzantine Empire, both the victorious and the vanquished captains, violent men, met violent deaths. A tale, as has been observed, for the moralist.

---

*Matthew of Edessa provides an even more gruesome account, declaring that the night before his surrender Yusuf feasted with his wife at a banquet enlivened by song and entertainment. Later that night he strangled his wife and three sons, lest they be enslaved, and in the morning set out on his own journey to death.[25]

12

'...and yet I am mine own Executioner'

> The sheihk Salah al-Din one day hired some Turkish workmen to build the walls of his garden. 'Effendi Salah al-Din,' said the Master [Jalal al-Din Rumi], 'you must hire Greek workmen for this construction. It is for the work of demolition that Turkish workmen must be hired. For the construction of the world is special to the Greeks, and the demolition of this same world is reserved to the Turks. . . . God created the people of the Turks in order to demolish, without respect or pity, all the constructions which they see.'
>
> *Eflaki*[1]

A defeat bringing to a nation the gravest peril in its history should, one would think, have galvanized its leaders into mounting a single-minded programme of defence. Manzikert had no such effect. It only ushered in ten more years of civil war. The obsession to seize the throne was incurable. The response of power-mad partisans was business as usual, and for fifty years that business had been fighting each other for the Crown, a Crown rendered by that very process progressively less worth having.

After Manzikert, the tiger was not merely at the gates but inside them, prowling and devouring as he chose. No one pretended otherwise, no one claimed to be ignorant of his ravages. What strikes us today as horrifying – what may epitomize as nothing else could the degradation of Byzantine spirit and values – is that the palace, the nobles and the generals failed to unite to oppose the Turkomans' slaughter and ruination of the peoples of Anatolia; they focused instead on methods to enlist the invading barbarian bands in their own forces, where they would slaughter even more Byzantines in rival forces. If the Turkomans' swords were to be bought by Byzantine gold, if their appetites were to be sated by the blood of Anatolian peasants, that was unfortunate, but what really mattered was to acquire those swords in one's own interest.

'In recruiting their army from the Turks, the Byzantine leaders quite simply accomplished the loss of Asia Minor,' wrote Laurent.[2] The verdict stands unchallenged.

It was not Alp Arslan who consolidated his victory by taking over Asia Minor when Michael gave him every excuse by repudiating the peace treaty with Romanus. As we have seen, the sultan turned back eastwards, and had he lived, it can be assumed that he would have renewed his campaign toward the Levant and Egypt. Nor is there any evidence that his successor, Malik-Shah, still guided by his father's vizier, Nizam al-Mulk, inaugurated a changed policy. It was the Turkomans, not the Great Seljuks, who exploited the defeat at Manzikert.[3]

The crucial battle instituted a crucial change. Almost ever since its founding, Byzantium had been periodically subject to destructive raids from Arabs and then from Turks. But, having done their worst, the Moslems retired, leaving Asia Minor bleeding but for the most part intact, subject as before to the emperor's writ. But now, for the first time, the invaders no longer needed to return to their homelands after their forays; no opposing force was left to drive them back. Now the land was theirs, not merely to plunder of its portable treasures but to sustain them and their flocks. As they had done in Transoxania, Khurasan and Azerbaijan – all within the last two to three generations – they brought in their herds and their families. Anatolia was nomad heaven – or could easily be made to be so by ridding it of cultivated fields and the peasants who lived on them.

Only the walled cities remained unpenetrated because, unlike the Persian-tutored armies of the Great Seljuks, the nomad bands had no siege machinery. Thus, the large majority of the urban centres held out for longer or shorter periods, isolated Christian storm-cellars in the midst of the Moslem tempests, increasingly cut off from Constantinople and from each other until, with a few exceptions such as Trebizond, they were starved out. The last of them, however, did not fall for many years.

One thing the Turkoman bands did *not* do in the beginning and of their own accord was to set up an organized state under a government exercising territorial rule. Given the nomads' habits and way of living, that is not surprising. What need for a state when a tribe or band could wander unopposed, with flocks and families, wherever it chose? For that matter, what need for cities when defensive walls were irrelevant and when, after all, the proper way to live was in tents, to be struck overnight as the seasons changed and when better grazing grounds were discerned elsewhere? For practical purposes they were independent of Sultan Malik-Shah's government and had no need of an institution of countervailing power to maintain that happy state of affairs. Their position was convenient, if somewhat ambiguous; close to autonomous in fact without being rebels in name. To be sure, the sultan wanted a degree of control to the extent possible over the bands he set loose to ravage Asia Minor, and he encouraged the formation of frontier satrapies ruled by his relatives. Some years later, as it happened, he was forced into political and military action against adventuring Turkish emirs who set out to build Anatolian regimes for themselves and who hence emerged as potential rivals or threats to his authority. Initially, however, most of the Turkomans roved wild and free.

Within two years after Manzikert they penetrated the entire defenceless peninsula, grazing here, raiding there, from the environs of Trebizond on the Black Sea in the north-east to Miletus in the west on the Aegean, from Antioch in the far south-east to Chrysopolis/Usküdar (Scutari) – which became a veritable Turkoman lair – a mile across the Bosphorus from the emperor's palace. They held the roads and passes, coursed the country and extorted tribute from the travellers, the notables and the cities.[4]

All this is not to say, however, that the whole of Asian Byzantium was lifted from Constantinople's grasp in a trice. Although, as Cahen points out,[5] it is impossible to reconstruct the situation in Asia Minor immediately following Manzikert,

it is clear that in the first decade the Turks had not made a
'conquest' of the country in the classic sense of permanent
occupation and rule. Despite massacres, considerable depopu-
lation, extensive flight of the Greek population to cities and
coastal areas, steady destruction of farms and their conversion
to grazing ranges, and disruption of communications, there
were sizable segments of Anatolia, including most cities,
which remained nominally under imperial control and, when
the nomad bands were not in the neighbourhood, actually so.
Precision on which cities and which areas remained integral
parts of Byzantium, and during what periods, is not to be had,
but it is known that at different places and at different times
communications were possible; there was probably even some
trade with Constantinople and tax-gathering by its agents.
Army units, still nominally troops of the Empire, existed as
far east as Armenia although they, like the still unconquered
cities, doubtless acted for the most part independently of
central governance.

Military operations on the scale and to the extent mounted
by Byzantium over the preceding centuries were, however, a
thing of the past. Romanus's march with a considerable force
from Armenia westwards into Paphlagonia and then south
over the Taurus passes to Cilicia, and similar counter-marches
by the troops Michael sent against him over the same territory,
were the last movements of Byzantine armies ever made across
Asia Minor free from the threat of Turkish attack. After 1072
no such untrammelled expeditions were possible.

Although the Turkomans themselves had no interest in filling
the political vacuum that their havoc had created, other power
seekers were quick to exploit the opportunities. Those setting
out to carve up Anatolia into personal domains were Frankish
mercenaries, Armenians and adventuring Seljuk emirs and
princelings. The details of their attempts provide an abundant
history but for our purposes only a summary is needed.[6]

Roussel of Bailleul – he who was nowhere to be seen when
needed at Khilat – had visions of making a new Normandy
for himself in north-central Asia Minor, where he had estates.
With 400 Franks in his following he began by besieging cities
and exacting tribute from them and became such a menace that

Constantinople felt obliged to send an army against him, commanded by the veteran general Botaniates and the Caesar. Roussel whipped it soundly and, as other Normans flocked to his banner to the number of almost 3000, reached his high-water mark by marching across Bithynia to the Bosphorus and burning Chrysopolis.

The Emperor Michael's response established a precedent: he turned to the Turks for aid.

He hired as a mercenary force a large contingent operating in Bithynia under the command of a Seljuk emir, Artuk. His army succeeded in defeating and capturing Roussel but, on being ransomed by his wife, the Norman returned to his base in the Armeniakon theme and resumed his depredations and extortions. It was not until 1074 that the young Alexius Comnenus, by now one of Michael's generals, brought Roussel down – and he too used Turks as his instrument. Without money or soldiers, but in a foretaste of the 'Byzantine' manoeuvrings for which he became renowned, Alexius used guile and cunning to persuade another Turkish emir to betray Roussel into his hands.*

Alexius was able to restore some degree of imperial authority to the cities in northern Anatolia, but Turkish bands controlled the roads in the area so effectively that in returning with his prisoner, Alexius barely escaped capture himself and made the final stage of his homeward journey, from Heracleia to Constantinople, by sea.

Meantime, at the other corner of the Empire, it was the Armenians, rejoicing in freedom from the hated Byzantine yoke, who set about making domains of their own. In Cilicia, to which Armenians had flocked or were pushed in increasing numbers for at least two centuries, chieftains and princelings among them began to claim independent rule over various pieces of territory in the Taurus Mountains and in the southern plain below them.†

---

*Roussel's revolt, Runciman points out, 'left its mark on the Byzantines. It taught them that the Normans were not to be trusted, that their ambition was not bounded by the shores of southern Italy but they wished to found principalities in the East. It goes far to explain Byzantine policy fo hostility to the Norman leaders of the Crusades twenty years later.'⁷

†It was almost certainly at this time that Gagik, the de-throned King of

The most skilful player in this game, and the man who succeeded in agglomerating the embryo Armenian fiefdoms into a single grand duchy of his own, was Romanus's inept defender of Melitene, the Armenian general Philaretus. It is noteworthy that he too used Turkish troops against recalcitrant Armenian princes in the process of consolidating his domain, and ultimately even apostasized to Islam. He effectively ended Byzantine sovereignty over a large area of south-eastern Asia Minor, from as far north as Melitene on the upper Euphrates to Antioch, and maintained his rule there for many years.

Elsewhere, several Seljuk emirs established themselves as masters of various cities and territories. The most notable were four sons of Kutlumush, rebel cousin of Alp Arslan, ancestors of what was to become the Seljuk dynasty of Rum, ruling most of Anatolia for two centuries and setting an indelible Seljuk stamp on it. The longest surviving of the brothers was Sulayman, who was later to establish his capital at Nicaea, less than eighty miles by road from Constantinople. Whether he was delegated by Malik-Shah to exercise viceregal authority over Turkoman bands in western Asia Minor or whether, alternately, he was a fugitive from the sultan is a matter of dispute. Whichever was the case, he came to be regarded as the chief of several Turkoman tribes in western Asia Minor, received the unofficial title of 'Sultan' from them, and built up a formidable military force and an extensive territorial domain. Though in the main he was the most dangerous enemy to Byzantium in Asia Minor, even Alexius, on becoming emperor, had to turn to him for help.

Michael VII, 'Psellus's pitiful puppet', sat on the throne for not quite seven years, 'surrounded by court intriguers and long-winded pedants', presiding over a regime that 'had neither the strength nor the will to resist' the Seljuk advance.[8] It was during these years that he earned his unlovely sobriquet, Parapinaces, 'the Peck-Filcher': prices had risen to the point

---

Armenia, declared open warfare in Cappadocia, horribly murdering the Metropolitan of Caesarea and setting his soldiers to raping the women of the Greek aristocracy. (See Chapter 6, p. 113–14.)

that a *nomisma* would no longer buy a full bushel of wheat but only three-quarters of one.

At last there was a Byzantine military reaction. Revolt broke out in the east, led by the veteran general Botaniates, commander of the Armeniakon theme. The degree to which Byzantine military power in Asia Minor had been reduced is evidenced by the fact that the rebel could bring only 300 troops to Cotyaeum/Kütahya and, moving by night and not on the regular road in a further march toward the Aegean, was nevertheless caught by Sulayman's and his brother Mansur's forces, hired by Michael to oppose him. There ensued what by then was becoming commonplace: a bidding match for the services of the Seljuk troops. Botaniates switched the Seljuks' allegiance by paying them a higher price than Michael VII, and so conquered, aided by a revolt in Constantinople against the feeble emperor.

Botaniates entered the capital to be crowned in March 1078. Michael, broken and forced to abdicate, went into a monastery, there to find such comfort as he could with the iambic verses he wrote when he should have been ruling his country. The notorious and domineering eunuch, Nicephoritzes, who had thrust aside Psellus and the Caesar John Ducas to become Michael's new puppet-master, paid for having forced up the price of bread by being tortured to death by the mob just before the emperor's fall.

Almost simultaneously with Botaniates's revolt, the principal military figure in Byzantium's European territories also set out to become emperor. He was Nicephorus Bryennius, Romanus's general at Manzikert and by now installed as governor of Dyrrachium/Durres (Durazzo) but listed by Nicephoritzes for assassination. Bryennius entered his native city of Adrianople/Edirne in November 1077 with his troops, proclaimed himself emperor and marched on Constantinople. Alexius Comnenus, now serving Botaniates, marched to oppose him and won a victory only because he too had Turkish help: 2000 troops supplied by Sulayman and Mansur. Bryennius was captured and blinded. Alexius's next task, successfully completed, was to suppress still another rebellion by another old hand at Manzikert, Basilacius, who had succeeded Bryennius as governor of Dyrrachium and had backed his effort to seize the throne.

The new but aged emperor could not reverse the process of disintegration. If anything he aggravated it by consolidating Sulayman's hold in Nicaea and opening up city after city on the Aegean to him by having them garrisoned by Turkish troops. Vryonis concludes:

The rule of Nicephorus Botaniates spelled the end of Byzantine Asia Minor as the future recruiting ground for the armies and as the principal source of tax revenues; in fact, by the end of his reign Asia Minor was with few exceptions in foreign hands.[9]

Two years after Botaniates won the throne, still another military revolt broke out in Anatolia, led by Nicephorus Melissenus. He too made alliances with the rampant Turkish bands and opened up still further cities and towns to them in western Asia Minor. On coming to power himself the next year, Alexius, who was Melissenus's brother-in-law, came to terms with him.

By employing as mercenaries in their armies the Turkomans and the Seljuk emirs who so recently vanquished them at Manzikert, the Byzantines – both those on the throne and those seeking it – virtually invited the Turks to take over their Asian domain. Cities were opened to them that they could not have taken themselves; they were bidden further westwards than they had gone of their own accord; the mercenaries were not expelled when their employment was ended, but stayed where they were. Masters of Asia Minor by 1081, they became so in good part because the Byzantines had served it up to them on a silver platter.

One wonders, momentarily, why the Byzantines themselves so dreadfully engineered the loss of their richest province. But the answer quickly proclaims itself: greed for political power overwhelmed all other considerations and blinded the contestants to the consequences. To gain their selfish ends they supped with the Devil, neglecting even the precaution of a long spoon. Cahen suggests, in further explanation, that the Byzantines failed to acknowledge just how menacing that Devil was:

It does not appear that the Byzantines regarded the Turks as enemies in the full sense, as they did the Arabs. They had known them for a long time and used them in their army, and had assimilated them into their population. Those in Asia Minor were Muslims, but their Islam might still seem as something new and primitive, without mosques, scholars or the Arabic language. In time they would be absorbed, in the way that Byzantium had absorbed many peoples. And the temporary loss of central Asia Minor, costly as it was, mattered little so long as the ports which were a source of profit held out.[10]

Among all those in the military aristocracy coveting the throne, Alexius Comnenus was the ablest and the shrewdest manoeuvrer. Despite the long-standing Comneni feud with the Ducas family, he effected an alliance, marrying Irene, grand-daughter of Caesar John and daughter of Andronicus, Romanus's betrayer and conquerer. When he determined that the time was right to strike for the throne and set about assembling a military force to do it, he convened what amounted to a Comneni and Ducas family conference to prepare the plans.

Old, worn down and a failure, besieged behind his walls and betrayed by the German mercenaries in the Varangian Guard – Alexius had cunningly won them over – Botaniates was persuaded to abdicate. Alexius was crowned on Easter Day 1081.

He took power at a moment when Turks wandered throughout all Anatolia unopposed, from Cilicia to the Dardanelles. Of the situation a few years later, his daughter Anna wrote, 'The boundary of Roman power on the east was our neighbour the Bosphorus, and on the west the city of Adrianople.'[11]

That was to overstate the matter, but not greatly. Some parts of the coast and the plateau were still under Byzantine control, enough at least to tempt Melissenus: in seeking a deal with Alexius, he proposed a division of Byzantium in which he would be Emperor of the East and Alexius Emperor of the West (Alexius would have none of such a division; he succeeded in settling with Melissenus by giving him the position of Caesar). Even so, what Alexius possessed when he reached the throne was more of a memory of an empire than a reality.

The extent to which he restored what there was from the wreckage and recovered a good bit more, fighting not merely Seljuks but also Normans, Patzinaks and Crusaders, marks him as the greatest statesman of the age, and the greatest emperor since Basil II.

Some Byzantine scholars have suggested that Alexius might have been able to regain all that was lost at Manzikert and in the following decade had he not been assailed by the Normans in Italy immediately on taking the throne. He had, it is true, all the courage, skill and, particularly, the energy that could be demanded of the greatest ruler. Yet, as the argument to the contrary holds, the disintegration of Byzantium had reached such a point that with by far the strongest and most productive half lost to Turkish occupation the remainder had neither the muscle nor the will to drive the invaders out. Indeed, even when the Crusaders recovered for the Empire – thanks to Alexius's superb diplomacy – one-third of Asia Minor, the centre would not hold: when the Crusaders departed more than a century later it was the Turks who recovered their losses, not the Byzantines.

Speculation about what Alexius might have done had he not been attacked from the West is intriguing but idle. The reality was that only after fourteen years of almost uninterrupted warfare against Normans, rapacious Seljuk emirs and revitalized barbarian raiders in the Balkans could the emperor even dream of clearing Anatolia of its alien occupiers.

On coming to power he engaged in a limited war with the nearest enemy, Sulayman and his infant sultanate of Rum. But almost at once, the major threat arose in the West. The hugely successful Norman adventurer, Robert 'the Weasel' Guiscard, Duke of Apulia, set out on a campaign to make himself Emperor of Byzantium. After propagandizing in Italy for support in a fight against the Byzantine 'schismatics' (he had previously liquidated their territorial holdings there, including their main strong-point Bari), he launched a massive invasion across the Adriatic.

Alexius fought for four years to fend him off. He lost more pitched battles than he won and was saved at one critical point only by the Venetian navy, whose services he acquired at the price of rendering to the Doges trade and customs privileges that put them in a position far superior to Byzantine traders and merchants themselves. The concessions were greatly to weaken Byzantine commercial strength in the years to come; Alexius has been charged by latter-day historians with dreadful folly in granting them. Yet when the house is burning, one does not haggle with the fire department over its extortionate demands.

In battling against Robert Guiscard, the emperor was obliged to withdraw such Byzantine military forces as were still left in Anatolia's northern tier – thus allowing even further advances of Turkish occupation in that area.

It was only because of Guiscard's death in 1085 that the threat and the warfare in Thrace and Illyria were ended. Alexius had a second stroke of luck in the same year, when Sulayman was killed in a campaign to add Cilicia, Syria, Antioch and Aleppo to his dominions.

Earlier, Alexius had tried to drive Sulayman from the neighbourhood of Nicomedia/Izmit, but was forced to make a treaty with him when the Normans invaded. He was in no position to enforce its terms; the Turks pressed all the way to the Bosphorus. But following Sulayman's death and much to Alexius's advantage, independent Turkish emirs proliferated along the Aegean coast and elsewhere in Anatolia. Their rivalries and internal dissensions created exactly the sort of game at which Alexius could play as a grand master: he set one group off against the other and began to make some headway in regaining coastal areas.

He had barely flexed his muscles in that endeavour, however, when the Patzinaks, habitual raiders and invaders in Danubian and Balkan lands for centuries and increasingly menacing in recent decades, launched a tremendous attack that brought them to the very walls of Constantinople. To double the danger, a powerful Byzantine enemy, Tzachas, emir of Smyrna/Izmir and the first Turk to undertake maritime warfare, built a formidable navy, allied himself with the Patzinaks, and besieged Constantinople.

Attacked by land and sea, Constantinople was in terror and distress throughout the winter of 1090–1. Alexius's recourse was to fall back on the traditional if dangerous Byzantine technique for dealing with barbarians by employing one group of them to fight another. He engaged the Cumans, a Turkish-speaking people who had come into the steppes of southern Russia after the Uzes and Patzinaks. In a ferocious battle in April 1091 they effectively decided the fate of the Empire, annihilating the Patzinaks so completely that they thereupon disappeared from history.

As might be expected, the Cumans soon abandoned their alliance with Byzantium and set out to conquer it for themselves. They advanced as far as Adrianople, plundering as they went, until Alexius devised a ruse to do away with the man they proposed to set on the throne, someone purporting to be the son of the Emperor Romanus IV Diogenes. Rendered leaderless, the Cuman invaders were dispersed by Alexius's troops.

Once again employing the 'Byzantine' diplomatic methods at which he was so skilled, Alexius then disposed of Tzachas: he incited the emir's son-in-law, Abul-Qasim, by now Sulayman's successor at Nicaea, to turn against his father-in-law and put an end to the latter's plans.

Needless to say, Abul-Qasim, too, made the same attempt on Constantinople, but was defeated. He reconciled himself with Byzantium by a treaty that promised to bring about the withdrawal of all Turks from western and maritime Asia Minor.

Far to the east, however, Malik-Shah had recognized Abul-Qasim as a rebel, in opposition to the sultan's determination to impose his own control over all Turkish bands in Asia Minor. To that end he proposed an alliance with Alexius and at the same time sent out a force to put down Abul-Qasim.

Out of this welter of warfare, diplomacy and intrigue came further benefits to the emperor: Malik-Shah's general defeated the troublesome emir and, receiving the loser ostensibly to discuss terms of submission, had him strangled. A son of Sulayman, Kılıj Arslan, succeeded to power in Nicaea and was promptly called upon by Tzachas, seeking an alliance. The new Sultan of Rum chose to solve matters simply and had him strangled at a banquet.

Malik-Shah's proposal for an alliance with Alexius offered the restoration to Byzantium of all of Sulayman's former territory, from Nicaea to Antioch – a singularly generous grant, testifying once again to the lack of interest of the Great Seljuks in the imperial conquest of Anatolia. Although one of the conditions was the marriage of a daughter of the emperor to a son of the sultan – which, as a Christian, Alexius could hardly have accepted – the emperor nevertheless sent off a favourable response. But on the way to the sultan's court, Alexius's envoy was met with the news of Malik-Shah's death; the proposed alliance, which might have had enormous consequence for the future of Byzantium, died before it was born.

Malik-Shah's death was followed almost immediately by a disintegration of the Great Seljuk Empire, the consequence of which was to leave the Turkish emirs a completely free hand for independent action in Asia Minor. Kılıj Arslan kept possession of a great swath of coastal territory from the Dardanelles to Syria as well as much land behind the Taurus; a new dynasty, that of the Danishmends, amassed such an extensive area in north-western Anatolia, holding Ancyra, Caesarea, Sebastea and neighbouring lands, as to threaten to eclipse the power of the sultanate of Rum.

Despite those young quasi-nations, and despite continual harassment of Byzantine possessions near Constantinople, Alexius was able to hold his own – or better. The mutual hostility and suspicions among rival major and minor emirs were tailor-made for his particular skills. By 1095 he had removed the military danger to Constantinople and consolidated his position on the throne – in good part by the lavish distribution of gifts and the bestowal of staggering numbers of new titles of his invention to personages whose support he sought. In addition, and also by intelligent diplomacy, he had bettered his personal relations with the papacy, soured by the still abiding ecclesiastical conflict of almost three-quarters of a century before.

He was now in a position to consider military action to drive the Turks out of Asia Minor. He turned to western Christendom for help. It was granted, but in such an unwanted form and excessive volume as to have nearly overwhelmed him. The 'helpers' soon conceived the idea of helping themselves – to what was Byzantium's.

13

Contra Paganos

An embassy of the Emperor of Constantinople came to the synod and implored his lordship the pope, and all the faithful of Christ, to bring assistance against the heathen for the defense of the holy church, which had now been nearly annihilated in that region by the infidels, who had conquered her as far as the walls of Constantinople.

Bernold of St Blase on the Council of Piacenza, 1095[1]

Spiritual, political and social changes in late medieval Europe exploded into the Crusades. Religious feelings, profound but volatile, needed only a spark to touch them off and a directing call to channel them into a mission to free the Holy Sepulchre and the city of Jerusalem from the grasp of the heathen. That spark and that direction came from Pope Urban II at Clermont, in 1095, but what were the considerations that made him strike it and to focus its impact as he did?

Historians give varying emphasis to the factors involved. Some stress the political ambition of the papacy, grasping at a newly presented opportunity, to restore Rome's former dominant position over the Eastern Church. Others see the workings of what might be called a passionate compassion to free the Christian churches of the East from the hands of the Seljuks and to rescue the fellow-Christians whom they were oppressing. Still others hold that the principal motivation was to renew the possibility of pilgrimages to the shrines of the Holy Land, a traffic that had been large and deeply significant for many centuries but which was now gravely impeded if not virtually blocked.

What is impressive here is that whatever the forces were that brought about the birth of the Crusades and whatever the relative importance one chooses to ascribe to them, all owed their origin to the fact that the Byzantine defeat at Manzikert and its sequels of the following two decades resulted in the loss of Asia Minor to Christian rule. It was that fact as well, and not spontaneous combustion, that put fire to the underlying yearning to recover Jerusalem. That hope had simmered for a long time, perhaps ever since Jerusalem was captured by Caliph Omar in 638; only some concrete development at the end of the eleventh century could have converted the dream into an organized programme for its realization.

The thesis of these final pages is that whichever of these proposed explanations played the major role or whichever is more important to understanding the inception of that greatest of all medieval adventures, all derive from a single cataclysmic development: the degeneration of the Byzantine Empire, culminating in and epitomized by the Battle of Manzikert, was as surely responsible for the Crusades as the importation of slaves over the middle passage was responsible for the American Civil War.

Jenkins states the matter flatly:

A fact of prime importance, a fact without which no western Crusade would have been possible at all, was that in the middle years of the eleventh century had occurred a complete and final breakdown of the balance of power in the Near East. . . . The collapse of the Middle-Byzantine empire, consequent on the loss of Anatolia to Seljuk Turks and Turcomans (1071–1075), immediately opened the path of the first Crusaders (1095). . . . But, a bare seventy years before this date, such an enterprise would have been regarded, both in the west and in the east, not merely as impracticable but as altogether chimerical.[2]

Church blessings bestowed on Christians warring against heathens ever since the days of Charlemagne can be seen as a kind of pre-history of the idea of crusade. But the concept as we have come to think of it – a holy war urged by the papacy and to be fought for the triumph of Christendom *in partibus infidelium* – did not take recognizable form until about 1010, when the mad Fatimid Caliph Hakim destroyed the Church of the Holy Sepulchre as part of his terrible persecutions. Pope Sergius IV reacted by issuing an encyclical, the ideological burden of which came close to the papal appeals in the last part of the century. His proposal, for winning back Jerusalem by a great sea-borne invasion, was ill-conceived and impractical; it died aborning.

It is, however, Hildebrand, Saint and Pope Gregory VII, who must be credited with first proposing massive military assistance to Byzantium for the holy cause of aiding oppressed Christians in the East. It was that conception that was at the root of the vastly more exalted and inclusive vision which, twenty years later under Urban II, resulted in the Crusades. But it is probable – and one of history's small surprises – that the relatively modest initial notion, destined to explode into such transcendental proportions, was put into Gregory's mind by a relatively prosaic request, devoid of inspirational overtones, by, of all people, the bumbling Emperor of Byzantium, Michael VII.[3]

There is no evidence that the suffering Christians in Asia Minor themselves ever hoped for or sought a great rescue mission from the West, and Michael had no such idea when he wrote Gregory in 1073 for help. The profound antagonism of more than half a century between pope and patriarch ruled out any dream of an outpouring of brotherly Christian love in the shape of a mighty succouring military force from Europe at that time. Michael could have asked only for the help of some mercenary soldiers.

Gregory, however, was impressed by the appeal and sent envoys to Constantinople for discussions. In the event, nothing so concrete and useful as a contingent of troops came from the talks, but the request for aid to Byzantium must nevertheless have left a strong imprint on the Pope's thinking.

For by March 1074 Gregory was pressing 'all those who wish to protect the Christian faith' with the argument that the heathens were advancing with violence against the 'Christian empire' of Byzantium and that the Christian faithful in Europe must give their lives to liberate their brothers in Christ. He himself, Gregory said, would lead in person a campaign to help the Easterners and urged all others to do the same under the banner of St Peter.

Gregory agitated vigorously for the idea throughout the year, proposing fantastic plans in which he would serve as spiritual and military leader of a vast expedition in which clerics, kings and their followers would join him in rescuing the Christians being slaughtered in Asia Minor.

Although the notion of marching all the way to Jerusalem makes its appearance in Gregory's correspondence, that was clearly not a major element in his aspiratons. His immediate and principal aim was to aid in the recovery of Byzantine lands overrun by the Turks and the freeing of the Eastern churches; those goals were to be achieved by furnishing auxiliary troops to the Byzantine army.

Behind that objective, it appears, was Gregory's ardent determination to bring about a reconciliation between the Greek Orthodox and the Roman Churches, with an acceptance of the latter's primacy. Antagonisms, political and ecclesiastical, festering for half a century, had solidified into the famous schism of 1054. Now, Gregory could calculate, the dire straits in which Byzantium found itself and its desperate need to be extricated from them might bring the throne and the patriarchate to accept Roman supremacy.[4]

A combination of political and military conflicts in Europe thwarted Gregory's plans. His attempted revival of the project in 1080–1 also ended in failure. It was not until two decades after Gregory first preached the idea of holy war against the Turkish heathens that it came to fruition under another pope as dynamic as himself.

Again, the beginnings may well have been in Constantinople: Alexius stood in need of military aid and, like Michael, appealed to the Pope for it.

'There is, indeed, good reason to think that [the Crusaders'] enterprise took shape in the mind, not of Pope Urban, but of the Byzantine Emperor Alexius I,' Jenkins has written.[5] The proposition is stated much too broadly. One thing Alexius certainly did *not* want was to be host to tens of thousands drunk with religious exaltation for a holy war and the recovery of Jerusalem. Driving out the Turks was to him a political objective, not a holy war, even though he may have embellished his supplications for papal help with pious murmurings. Furthermore, his interest in Jerusalem seems to have been no more than tepid. Yet, paradoxically, he would not have been pleased at the prospect of Latins intruding into what had traditionally been a Byzantine bailiwick: Jerusalem and its Christian affairs had always been the responsibility of Byzantium and of none other. Finally, and doubtless most important, Alexius would have had a lively anticipation of the events that in fact later took place, those arising from the Crusaders' quickly-conceived lust for the golden treasures of what was still the richest city in the world.

What Alexius *did* request of Urban was no more grandiose than what Michael asked of Gregory: he wanted mercenaries, and had pleaded for them from the West before. In 1089 or 1090, for example, he won a promise, subsequently fulfilled, for the services of 500 Flemish knights sent to him by Count Robert of Flanders.

Alexius was, however, in a better position than Michael to apply for papal support. As early as 1089 he had responded with intelligent compromises to an initiative by Urban to heal the breach with the patriarchate, again, of course, on the condition of Roman supremacy; negotiations had made some progress. It was probably during this period while Alexius was steadily improving his personal relations with Urban that he began appealing for military assistance. Anna Comnena mentions in passing that in 1091 'mercenaries [were] expected to arrive from Rome'.[6] It is generally assumed that they could only have been troops mustered by the Pope, although it is possible that the reference was to the band of knights promised by Robert of Flanders.[7]

Modest though the emperor's entreaties were to the Pope, we may nevertheless ask – recasting Jenkins's statement into a less sweeping form – whether they were in fact the operative factor that put the infinitely larger conception of crusade into Urban's mind.

Unfortunately, there is no documentation that discloses the inception of Urban's transcendent resolve before he first preached an early form of the idea at the Council of Piacenza. He was, of course, an avowed disciple of Gregory – *pedisequus*, to use his own word – and may have cherished his precursor's dream without broaching it until he felt the time was ripe. Or the trigger could have been stories of hardship and persecution brought back by pilgrims who still, twenty-five years after the Turkish occupation, tried to push their way across Asia Minor to Jerusalem. Those journeys to the Holy Land, important in Urban's thinking, had been of great significance in medieval life in Europe; they were central to the psychology of the Crusades. Many historians, Runciman perhaps the principal among them, suggest that the barriers raised to pilgrim traffic and the worsening of the pilgrims' treatment in the Holy Land after 1071 was one of the most profoundly influential causes of the First Crusade.[8]

Pilgrimages to Palestine's holy shrines were made to gain sanctity, to worship and, with luck, perhaps to collect a relic or two to be brought back home in awe and glory, and most particularly to obtain remission of penance ordered for one's sins, and they had been undertaken almost ever since there was an Eastern Roman Empire. The volume of traffic varied during the succeeding centuries according to the changes in the reception accorded the voyagers and, more importantly, the hazards of the journey. Passage by sea was possible at times when the Saracens did not control the Eastern Mediterranean but travel by land, being cheaper, was more popular. By the fourth quarter of the tenth century, with the conversion of the Hungarians to Christianity, a pilgrim from Britain, France, Germany, Italy and even Scandinavia could count on simple and inexpensive land passage throughout Christian countries as far as Constantinople, wearisome but without much greater discomfort or danger than was normal in his daily life at home. Once at the Bosphorus, he moved by relatively good roads to his first meeting with the heathen at the Syrian border. From there on he might experience some harassment and extortion but for the most part the Arab emirs knew a good commercial opportunity when it was on their doorstep and permitted further passage.

Except for occasional periods such as when the mad Fatimid Caliph Hakim launched his horrible persecutions early in the eleventh century, the pilgrim was decently received in the Holy Land and permitted to visit the sacred shrines and to worship in the many Christian churches functioning there under Moslem tolerance.

By the middle of the eleventh century the pilgrimages had grown to enormous volume, generally in big groups. The largest ever made was the Great German Pilgrimage, led by an archbishop, three bishops and a solemn mass of lesser clerics, with a following of somewhere between 7000 and 12,000 penitents. Only about 2000 survived the ordeal, but they appear to have suffered from extremes of persecution.[9]

Surprisingly, no great additional obstacles to the journeys emerged in the years immediately following Manzikert nor was there any marked change in the treatment accorded visitors in Palestine when Seljuk emirs displaced Fatimid governors in Jerusalem in the same year. But when the Great Seljuk Empire began its swift deterioration on Malik-Shah's death in 1092, firm, unified rule gave way to that of petty emirs on the roads north of Jerusalem, harassment increased in the city itself and passage over Asia Minor, where Turkomans held the roads, may have become more painful and difficult. Evidence on the state of affairs is scanty, but it is known that Peter the Hermit, that most effective inflamer of popular ardour for the First Crusade, had been mistreated by the Turks on a pilgrimage some years before and doubtless spread accounts of his miseries far and wide.

As Runciman points out, successful pilgrimages were dependent on two factors: an orderly life in Palestine where the travellers could move and worship in safety, and an open and inexpensive passage to the Holy Land.[10] By the last decade of the eleventh century neither of those conditions remained.

The reports of the difficulties must have had a trenchant impact on Urban's thinking, schooled as he was in the Cluniac Order, the most ardent promoter and protector of the pilgrimages for more than a century.

Delving for the seed, or several seeds, that germinated in Urban's mind into the call for Crusade makes interesting historical detective work. But no specific resolution of the problem is needed to support the thesis of this chapter. Whatever the fuse that touched off his explosive adjuration for a holy war – whether Alexius's appeals, devout reaction to news of Christian suffering in Asia Minor, deep grief at persecution of pilgrims or cold political seizure of a chance to restore Roman primacy over a unified Church – each and all derived from the fact that a defeated Byzantium could no longer defend Christendom in the East. Perhaps the only exception, and certainly of secondary importance, was the chance to stop incessant warring by French nobles with each other by sending them out of the country to fight another enemy.

It could be argued that one of the central purposes of the Crusades, the lifting of Jerusalem from heathen hands – a dominant consideration in Urban's mind and in his appeals* – was not a product of Byzantium's disaster. Yet, as noted above, the project did not arise simply as the anonymous author of the *Gesta Francorum*, one of the major contemporary chronicles of the Crusades, would have it, because 'the time was at hand'. The ardour for freeing the city was, to be sure, growing strongly in the years before the Crusades, but it was only a part of the general picture, and one not at the burning point in earlier years. As Runciman points out:

In the middle of the eleventh century the lot of the Christians in Palestine had seldom been so pleasant. The Moslem authorities were lenient; the Emperor was watchful of their interests. Trade was prospering and increasing with the Christian countries overseas. And never before had Jerusalem enjoyed so plentifully the sympathy and the wealth that were brought to it by pilgrims from the West.[11]

The liberation of Jerusalem and the Holy Sepulchre was then not in the air. It was the drastic change in conditions in the East that set the idea aflame.

The Council of Piacenza in early March 1095, the first great synod summoned by Urban, was principally concerned with ecclesiastical affairs and church reforms. Some 200 bishops,

---

*Erdmann vehemently denied that it was and devoted his major work to arguing his point, holding that the *Kampf-* or *Kriegsziel* – the fundamental aim of the Crusades' instigators – was freeing the Christian churches of the East in general, and that the *Marschziel* – the campaign goal – came later, almost as a propaganda cry to inspire a body of warriors not overly sympathetic to the 'schismatic' Byzantines. Most later historians find his distinction too subtle and his emphasis on it excessive.

4000 other clerics and 30,000 of the laity – Gibbon's figures[12] – far too many for the largest of cathedrals to accommodate, assembled in the open plain. There they heard – if human voice could carry to such a throng – the appeal of Alexius's envoys quoted in the epigraph to this chapter. Urban supported the request but made no attempt to broaden it.

It was not until November of that year, at the second great council of his pontificate, at Clermont in his native France, that he broached his immense conception in its fullness. Fulcher of Chartres, the only one of the contemporary chroniclers believed to have actually been present, declares that the Pope asked the valorous in his audience to go to the aid of Christians in the Byzantine Empire because the Turks had 'advanced as far into Roman territory' as the Mediterranean and were killing the Christian population. Standing alone, such an altruistic argument for action was unlikely to stir the sentiments of the Western knights, whose preferred way of life was robbery of their neighbours and slaughter of their rivals. More persuasive, therefore, was the remainder of Urban's address, a story of the desecration of churches and holy places, related perhaps, as Duncalf comments, because he knew that 'injuries to sacred places and things seemed greater atrocities to his contemporaries than the suffering of human beings'.[13] He then turned to what was to be his most effective inspirational theme: the Crusaders would be a new brand of fighting pilgrims on the greatest conceivable pilgrimage, that to open the road to Jerusalem and reclaim if for Christ. *Deus le volt, Deus le volt,* was the famous response.

Too many scores or hundreds of volumes on the Crusades have been written to require repetition of the history here. It is enough to recall in a few words the consequences of the Crusades on Asia Minor and the battle for its control.

Alexius's awesome statesmanship, unfailing in judgement, brilliant in execution, largely succeeded in turning the Crusaders' power to his own purposes. The greatest stroke of his genius, accomplished as the situation demanded by lavish gifts, promises, subtle manoeuvrings, threats and even armed combat, was to extract pledges from the Western leaders to restore to Byzantium those Anatolian lands they conquered that had formerly been in the Empire's possession; he left the Crusaders free to carve out principalities for themselves further away in the Levant.

The sheer number of the knights and their burning combativeness served to offset their inexperience and, too often, military folly. Their attacks, coupled with those of Alexius's own revived armies, steadily forced the Turks to withdraw from the coastal areas and to reduce their bastion to the central Anatolian plateau. By the time of Alexius's death in 1118, little more than two decades after Peter the Hermit led his motley vanguard to the Bosphorus (and its speedy massacre on the other side), Byzantium had recovered something like onethird of Asia Minor: the coastal strip from Trebizond westwards, all land west of a line from Sinope through Ancyra to the south-western shores on the Aegean and all of the southern coast as far as Antioch. In the next several years further gains were made in the reconquest of Anatolia until about 1140, the high tide of Byzantine territorial recovery.

Thereafter there was continuing erosion, culminating in the Battle of Myriocephalum in 1176, a disaster like that at Manzikert a hundred and five years before. One might describe those two encounters as the first and second corner nails in Byzantium's coffin. The third was to come with the predators of the Fourth Crusade, driving the Greeks from Constantinople, and conducting what may have been the greatest looting of treasure in history. The Great City was later regained only to fall, as the last remaining possession of the Eastern Empire, when the Ottoman Sultan, Mehmet the Conquerer, drove in the fourth and final nail in 1453.[14]

The history of Asia Minor from the time of glory of Basil II until almost our own day has been that of a succession of new and more muscular peoples and systems supplanting societies once virile themselves but grown tired, weakened and torn apart from within. One after another, the Byzantine, Crusader, Seljuk, Mongol and Ottoman mainsprings unwound, each conquering host leaving behind remnants of its successes for later generations to admire and, in the records of its failures, lessons asking to be understood.

Abbreviations and Short Titles of Frequently Cited References

Baynes and Moss: *Byzantium*: *An Introduction to East Roman Civilization*, Norman H. Baynes and H. Dt. L. B. Moss, ed., Oxford, 1948

Byzantion: *Byzantion*: *Revue Internationale des Études Byzantines*, Brussels, 1931 et seq.

CMH: *Cambridge Medieval History*, Vol. IV, *The Byzantine Empire*; Part I, *Byzantium and its Neighbours*, J. M. Hussey, ed., Cambridge, 1966

CSHB: *Corpus Scriptorum Historiae Byzantinae*, Bonn, 1829–97

EB: *Encyclopædia Britannica*, 17th edn

EI1: *Encyclopedia of Islam*, 1st edn, 1913–48, Leiden

EI2: *Encyclopedia of Islam*, 2nd edn, 1954 ff. (in progress), Leiden and London

Setton: *A History of the Crusades*, Vol. 1, Kenneth M. Setton, general editor, University of Wisconsin, 1969

Reference Notes

Introduction

1. R. J. H. Jenkins, *The Byzantine Empire on the Eve of the Crusades* (hereafter cited as *Eve*), London, 1955, p. 3.

1 *The Wolves of the Steppes*

1. Quoted by René Grousset, *The Empire of the Steppes*, 1939–52. translated by Naomi Walford, Rutgers, 1970, p. 559, note 167,
2. *Ibid.*, pp. 74–5.
3. *Ibid.*, pp. 80–1.
4. V. V. Barthold, *Histoire des Turcs d'Asie Centrale* (hereafter *Histoire*), French adaptation by M. Donskis, Paris, 1945, p. 6.
5. Claude Cahen, *Pre-Ottoman Turkey* (hereafter *Pre-Ottoman*), translated by J. Jones-Williams, New York, 1968, p. 3.
6. For more extensive accounts of the early history of the Turkic peoples, see the works cited above by Cahen, Grousset and Barthold, plus Barthold's *Turkestan Down to the Mongol Invasion* (hereafter *Turkestan*), 3rd edn, E. J. W. Gibb Memorial Trust, 1968; Gerard Clausen, *Turkish and Mongolian Studies*, 1962; *EI1*, 'Turkestan' and 'Turkey'; *EI2*, 'Ghuzz'; *EB* 'Turkestan'.
7. Bernard Lewis, *The Emergence of Modern Turkey*, London, 1961, pp. 7–8.
8. *EI2*, 'Ghuzz'.
9. Grousset, p. xxvi.
10. See also Nora K. Chadwick and Victor Zhirmunsky, *Oral Epics of Central Asia*, Cambridge, 1969, *passim*. Their material is of much later times but references to endless celebrations of the horse testify to a continuity from early periods.

11. Grousset, p. XXVI.
12. Owen Lattimore, *Studies in Frontier History*, Oxford, 1962, pp. 420–1, 483, 504–8.
13. Grousset, p. VIII.
14. Lattimore, p. 25.
15. Cahen, *Pre-Ottoman*, pp. 5–6.
16. 'Notes on the Risala of Ibn Fadlan', translated by Robert P. Blake and Richard N. Frye, *Byzantina Metabyzantina*, Vol. I, Part II, New York, 1949. Minor elisions are not indicated. A few unimportant word changes have been made for readier comprehension.
17. Carl Max Kortepeter, 'The Origins and Nature of Turkish Power', *Tarih Araştımalari Dergisi*, Ankara, 1968, p. 272.
18. Lattimore, p. 485.

2 *From Pagan to Moslem*

1. Geoffrey Lewis, Introduction and translation of *The Book of Dede Korkut*, Penguin Books, London, 1974, pp. 56–7.
2. For a useful summary and bibliography, see entry on 'Shamanism' in EB. For a detailed description of shamanism practised as recently as 1930 in a North Manchurian tribe, see Lattimore, pp. 379–92.
3. M. A. Czaplicka, *The Turks of Central Asia in History and at the Present Day*, Oxford, 1918, pp. 32–3.
4. Kortepeter, pp. 163–4.
5. Barthold, *Histoire*, p. 14.
6. Hamilton A. R. Gibb, 'The Caliphate and the Arab States', *A History of the Crusades*, Vol. I, edited by Kenneth M. Setton (hereafter *Setton*), Madison, Wis., 1969, pp. 22–4.
7. Cahen, *Pre-Ottoman*, p. 8; Barthold, *Turkestan*, p. 225.
8. Cahen, 'The Turkish Invasion: The Selchückids', *Setton*, p. 138.
9. Geoffrey Lewis, p. 10.
10. Kortepeter, p. 273.
11. Barthold, *Histoire*, p. 57.
12. Except as otherwise noted, the material in this section to the end of the chapter is taken from Cahen's previously cited works and from his article 'Ghuzz' (i.e. Oghuz) in EI 1.
13. Barthold, *Histoire*, p. 47.
14. *Ibid*, pp. 57–8.
15. Grousset, p. 142.
16. Gibb, *Setton*, p. 93.

3 *The Seljuks*

1. Quoted by Barthold, *Histoire*, p. 57.
2. Ibid., p. 57.
3. Grousset, p. 149.
4. Barthold, *Histoire*, p. 85.
5. Lattimore, *passim.*
6. Grousset, pp. 83–5.
7. Kortepeter, p. 251.
8. Except as otherwise noted, sources are the works of Cahen, already cited; F. Taeschner, 'The Turks and the Byzantine Empire to the End of the Thirteenth Century', *CMH*, pp. 737–8.
9. Quoted in *EI1*, 'Seljuks', p. 208.
10. Edward Gibbon, *The Decline and Fall of the Roman Empire*, 1776–88, Modern Library Edition, New York, Vol. 3, p. 396.
11. Bar Hebraeus, *Chronography*, translated by Ernest A. Wallis Budge, Oxford, 1932, pp. 195–6.
12. Cited by Speros Vryonis, Jr, *The Decline of Medieval Hellenism in Asia Minor and the Process of Islamization from the Eleventh through the Fifteenth Century* (hereafter *Decline*), University of California, 1971, p. 211 and fn.
13. *EI1*, 'Seljuks', p. 208.
14. See Vryonis, *Decline*, fn. p. 81.

4 *From Zenith . . .*

1. Charles Diehl, *Byzance, Grandeur et Décadence*, Paris, 1919.
2. The historical material in this and the following chapter is largely drawn from the works of twentieth-century Byzantinologists, and military writers, notably:
   Peter Charanis, 'The Byzantine Empire in the Eleventh Century', *Setton*.
   J. F. C. Fuller, *The Decisive Battles of the Western World*, Vol. I, London, 1954.
   H. Grégoire, 'The Amorians and Macedonians' (completed by R. J. H. Jenkins), *CMH*.
   J. M. Hussey, 'The Later Macedonians, the Comneni and the Angeli', *CMH*
   R. J. H. Jenkins, *Eve*.
   C. W. C. Oman, *The Byzantine Empire*, London, 1898, and *A History of the Art of War in the Middle Ages* (hereafter *Art of War*), 2nd edn, London, 1924.

George Ostrogorsky, *History of the Byzantine State*, 2nd edn, translated by Joan Hussey, Oxford, 1968.

Steven Runciman, *A History of the Crusades*, Vol. I (hereafter *Crusades*), Cambridge, 1951, and *Byzantine Civilization*, London, 1933.

Speros Vryonis, Jr, *Decline*, and *Byzantium and Europe*.

Material from other sources and statements of judgement and opinion are specifically annotated.

3. W. M. Ramsay, 'The War of Moslem and Christian for Possession of Asia Minor', *Studies in the History of Art in the Eastern Provinces of Asia Minor*, Aberdeen, 1906, p. 293.

4. Runciman, *Byzantine Civilization*, p. 179.

5. Vryonis, *Byzantium and Europe*, pp. 132, 134.

6. Oman, *The Byzantine Empire*, p. 155.

7. Gibbon, Vol. 2, p. 866.

8. Quoted by Sirarpie Der Nersessian, *Armenia and the Byzantine Empire*, Harvard, 1945, p. 29.

9. Oman, *Art of War*, p. 203.

10. Fuller, p. 394.

11. Oman, *The Byzantine Empire*, p. 219.

12. Vryonis, *Decline*, p. 2.

13. J. Laurent, *Byzance et les Turcs Seljoucides*, Paris, 1913, fn. p. 13.

14. Runciman, *Byzantine Civilization*, p. 146.

15. Hans Delbrück, *Geschichte der Kriegskunst in Rahmen der Politischen Geschichte*, Vol. 3, Berlin, 1907, p. 205.

16. Ferdinand Lot, *L'Art Militaire et les Armées*, Paris, 1946, pp. 68–9.

17. *Ibid.*, pp. 67–8.

18. The description of the Byzantine army and its soldiers is largely taken from Oman, *Art of War*, pp. 186–99.

19. Quoted by Oman, *Art of War*, p. 189.

20. Fuller, p. 392.

21. *Ibid.*, p. 295.

22. Oman, *Art of War*, p. 203.

23. *Ibid.*, pp. 201–3.

24. Runciman, *Byzantine Civilization*, p. 43.

25. Gibbon, Vol. 2, p. 897.

26. Jenkins, *CMH*, p. 183.

27. John Geometres, quoted by Grégoire, *CMH*, p. 151.

28. See, for example, Ostrogorsky, p. 289, and Grégoire, *CMH*, pp. 172–5, the latter basing his opinion on Leo the Deacon, Scylitzes and Zonaras.

29. Michael Psellus, *Chronography*, translated by E. R. A. Sewter, London, 1953, p. 25.

30. Jenkins, *CMH*, pp. 190–1.

31. Quoted by Oman, *Art of War*, p. 215.
32. Charanis, *Setton*, pp. 179–80.
33. Fuller, p. 389.

5 . . . *to Nadir*

1. Quoted by Peter Charanis, 'Economic Factors in the Decline of the Byzantine State' (hereafter 'Economic Factors'), *Journal of Economic History*, Vol. 13, No. 4, Fall 1953, Wilmington, Del., p. 416.
2. Quoted by Psellus, p. 23.
3. The thesis is expounded at length by Jenkins, *Eve*, pp. 8–11. See also Wilhelm Ensslin, 'The Emperor and the Imperial Administration' in Norman H. Baynes and H. Dt. L. B. Moss (eds), *Byzantium: An Introduction to East Roman Civilization* (hereafter *Baynes and Moss*), Oxford, 1948.
4. Vryonis, *Decline*, p. 73.
5. The historical material that follows is drawn principally from Grégoire/Jenkins and Hussey, in *CMH*; Ostrogorsky; Vryonis, *Decline*; Charanis, in *Setton* and 'Economic Factors', and Psellus. Vryonis and Charanis ascribe more causality to the civil wars, the others tend to stress the decline of the peasant soldiery.
6. Delbrück, p. 196.
7. Ostrogorsky, pp. 294–5.
8. Jenkins, concluding Grégoire's chapter, *CMH*, p. 183.
9. Fuller, p. 389.
10. Ostrogorsky, p. 323.
11. André Andréadès, *Baynes and Moss*, p. 201.
12. Charanis, *Setton*, p. 201.
13. Ostrogorsky, pp. 231–2.
14. Oman, *Art of War*, pp. 180–1, citing Cedrenus and Zonaras.
15. Lot, p. 70.
16. Psellus, p. 116.
17. *Ibid.*, pp. 131–2.
18. *Ibid.*, p. 125.
19. *Ibid.*, p. 205.
20. So E. R. A. Sewter, in a note to his translation of Psellus's *Chronographia*, citing Cedrenus, p. 304.
21. Runciman, *Crusades*, p. 55.
22. Hussey, *CMH*, p. 207.
23. Vryonis, *Decline*, p. 74
24. Oman, *Byzantine Empire*, p. 250.
25. Attaliates and Cedrenus, quoted by Vryonis, *Decline*, p. 89.

6 *Armenia: Buffer that might have been*

1. Matthew of Edessa, *Chronicles*, French translation from the Armenian by Eduard Dulaurier, Paris, 1858, p. 114.
2. The historical material in this chapter is taken mainly from C. Toumanoff, 'Armenia and Georgia', *CMH*, and his 'Background to Manzikert', *Proceedings of the XIIIth International Conference of Byzantine Studies*, Oxford, 1967; Grégoire/Jenkins and Hussey, *CMH*; M. Canard, 'Byzantium and the Muslim World to the Middle of the Eleventh Century', *CMH*; Vryonis, *Decline*; Der Nersessian, *Armenia*.
3. For further discussion of the strategic importance of the Lake Van area, see Emile Janssens, 'Le Lac de Van et la Strategie Byzantine', *Byzantion*, Vol. 42, 1972, pp. 388–404.
4. M. Canard and Haig Berberian, Introduction to their translation of *History of Armenia*, by Aristakes of Lastivert, Editions de Byzantion, Brussels, 1973, p. XXII.
5. Hussey, *CMH*, p. 204.
6. Runciman, *Crusades*, pp. 34–5.
7. Laurent, fn. pp. 50–2.
8. Cahen, *Pre-Ottoman*, p. 65; see also Andréadès, p. 286.
9. See Laurent, fn. p. 78.
10. Matthew, pp. 152–4.
11. Ramsay, p. 296.
12. Vryonis is persuasive on this point, *Decline*, pp. 210–16.

7 *The Arrows of the Infidels*

1. Matthew, pp. 40–1.
2. Quoted by Edmund Burke, *The History of Archery*, London, 1958, p. 102.
3. Matthew, p. 42.
4. Information about the composition and weapons of the Seljuk armies is drawn principally from Mehmet Altay Köymen, *Alp Arslan Zamanı Selçuklu Askeri Teşkilatı* (Military Organization of the Seljuks at the Time of Alp Arlsan), University of Ankara, 1967; and to a lesser extent from Cahen, *Setton*. Inferences, however, are the author's.
5. Vryonis, 'Seljuk Gulams and the Ottoman Devshirmes', *Der Islam*, Vol. 41, 1965, Berlin, p. 225.
6. Cahen, 'The Turkish Invasion: The Selchükids', *Setton*, p. 158.
7. Köymen, *passim*.
8. Ogier Ghiselin de Busbecq, *The Turkish Letters*, translated by Edward Seymour Forster, Oxford, 1927, pp. 105–8.

9. For a more extensive description, see Ralph Payne-Gallwey, *A Summary of the History, Construction and Effects in Warfare of the Projectile-Throwing Engines of the Ancients, plus a Treatise on the Structure, Power and Management of Turkish and Other Oriental Bows*, London, 1907; Paul E. Klopsteg, *Turkish Archery and the Composite Bow*, Evanston, Illinois, 1934; Burke; Gordon Grimley, *The Book of the Bow*, London, 1958.

10. Grimley, pp. 44–7.

11. Walter Emil Kaegi, Jr, 'The Contribution of Archery to the Turkish Conquest of Anatolia', *Speculum*, January 1964, Cambridge, Mass. p. 98.

12. *Ibid.*, p. 101.

13. Michael Attaleiates, *Histories, CSHB*. Translations of pp. 93–163 by Fr George T. Dennis s j (unpublished ms; pagination that of *CSHB*).

14. *Ibid.*, pp. 32–3, 45.

15. Busbecq, p. 137.

16. Marco Polo, *Travels*, translated by William Marsden, re-edited by Thomas Wright, New York, 1948.

17. They are summarized by R. C. Smail, from whose *Crusading Warfare*, Cambridge, 1956, pp. 75–83, I have taken material for the remainder of this chapter.

18. William of Tyre, *A History of Deeds Done Beyond the Sea*, translated by E. A. Babcock and A. C. Krey, Columbia University, 1943, quoted by Smail, p. 76n.

8 The Seljuk Raids: 1048–69

1. Marius Canard, 'La Campagne Arménienne du Sultan Salguqide et la Prise d'Ani en 1064' (hereafter 'Armenian Campaign'), *Revue des Etudes Armeniennes*, Vol. II, 1965, p. 245.

2. E.g. Ibrahim Kafesoğlu, 'The Battle of Manzikert', *Islam Ansiklopedisi*, Vol. 7, translated by Armağan Tranter (unpublished MS); Yilmas Ortuna, press release, Ankara, 1971; Ali Sevim, 'Malazgirt Meydan Savaşı ve Sonuçları' ('The Battle of Manzikert and its Outcome'), translated by JoAnne Noonan Gümüş (unpublished ms), *Malazgirt Armağani*, Ankara, 1972.

3. Abbas Hamdani, 'A Possible Fatimid Background to the Battle of Manzikert', *Études Byzantines/Byzantine Studies*, Vol. 1, 1974, Pittsburgh, pp. 171, 175.

4. For example, Nejat Kaymaz, 'Malazgirt Savaşi ile Anadolu'nun Fethi ve Türkleşmesine Dair' ('The Battle of Manzikert and the Conquest and Turkization of Anatolia'), translated by JoAnne Noonan Gümüş (unpublished MS), *Malazgirt Armağani*.

5. Claude Cahen, *Pre-Ottoman* and 'La Première Pénétration Turque en Asie-Mineur' (hereafter 'Penetration'), *Byzantion*, Vol. 18, 1938, *passim*.

6. Aristakes, p. xxxi.

7. The account of events in this chapter is taken principally from Cahen's 'Penetration', his *Pre-Ottoman*, and his chapter in *Setton*. I have also drawn on Vryonis, *Decline*; Ostrogorsky; Runciman, *Crusades*; F. Taeschner, 'The Turks and the Byzantine Empire to the End of the Thirteenth Century', *CMH*, as well as contemporary sources.

8. Anna Comnena, *The Alexiad*, translated by E. R. A. Sewter, Penguin Books, London, 1969, Book I, p. vii-viii.

9. Hamdani, p. 171.

10. Aristakes, p. 66.

11. Matthew, p. 74.

12. Aristakes, pp. 83, 89.

13. *Ibid.*, p. 80.

14. See H. R. Ellis Davidson, 'The Secret Weapon of Byzantium', *Byzantinisches Zeitschrift*, Vol. 66, 1973, pp. 61–74, and J. Haddon and M. Byrne, 'A Possible Solution to the Problem of Greek Fire', *Byzantinisches Zeitschrift*, Vol. 70, 1977, pp. 91–9.

15. Matthew, pp. 99–102.

16. Aristakes, p. 83, 89.

17. Busbecq, p. 121.

18. Matthew, pp. 112–13.

19. Laurent, p. 24.

20. Barthold, *Turkestan*, p. 306.

21. Matthew, p. 104; Michael the Syrian, *Chronicles*, French translation by J. B. Chabot, Paris, 1905, p. 170; Aristakes, p. xxxi.

22. Faruk Sümer and Ali Sevim, 'Islam Kaynaklarına Göre Malazgirt Savaşı' ('The Battle of Manzikert according to Islamic Sources'). Translated by Armağan Tranter (unpublished ms).

23. Barthold, *Turkestan*, p. 306.

24. Runciman, *Crusades*, p. 61.

25. The account of the campaign is summarized from Canard's 'Armenian Campaign', an anthology of Arab, Armenian and Greek histories of the episode.

26. Laurent, fn. pp. 57, 74.

27. Matthew, pp. 125–6.

28. Sevim, *Malazkirt Armağani*, p. 220.

29. Attaleiates, pp. 95–6.

30. Vryonis, *Decline*, p. 90.

9 The Feckless Response: 1068-70

1. Scylitzes, *Brevarium Historicum*, *CSHB*, Vol. 35, pp. 659–705. Translated by P. David Kovacs (unpublished MS; pagination that of *CSHB*). This history and that of George Cedrenus are difficult to distinguish and latter portions of them, covering the climactic period discussed in this book, are now believed to have been written by neither but by an unknown continuator. For convenience, however, I have referred to the Scylitzes-Cedrenus material in the *Corpus Scriptorum Historiae Byzantinae* simply as *Scylitzes*.

2. Basic sources of events in this chapter are Scylitzes, pp. 659–87; Attaleiates; Psellus; Bar Hebraeus; Nicephorus Bryennius, *Histoire*, *CSHB*, Vol. 26, translated by Henri Grégoire; *Byzantion*, Vol. 23, 1953, pp. 55–7. Additional material is from Cahen, Vryonis and Laurent and, for Moslem writings, from *EI1* and Sevim.

3. Scylitzes, p. 659.

4. *Ibid.*, pp. 665–6.

5. Attaleiates, p. 99.

6. *Ibid.*, p. 102.

7. Charles Lebeau, *Histoire du Bas-Empire*, Paris, 1833. Vol. 14, pp. 469–70.

8. Scylitzes, p. 672.

9. Attaleiates, p. 113.

10. Psellus, p. 269.

11. Attaleiates, p. 125.

12. Psellus, p. 270.

13. *Ibid.*, p. 270.

14. Scylitzes, p. 688.

15. Cahen, *Pre-Ottoman*, has it both ways: pp. 27 and 71.

16. Cahen, 'La campagne de Manzikert d'après des sources Musselmanes' (hereafter 'Moslem Sources'), *Byzantion*, Vol. 9, 1934, pp. 613–42 (summary on 625).

17. Bar Hebraeus, p. 220.

10 Twilight at Manzikert

1. Köymen, 'The Importance of the Malazgirt Victory with Special Reference to Iran and Turkey', *Journal of the Regional Cultural Institute*, Vol. 5, No. 1, Ankara, 1972, p. 9.

2. Hamdani, p. 178.

3. Gibbon, Vol. 3, p. 401; Laurent, p. 58; Lebeau, p. 489; Runciman, *Crusades*, p. 62; Lot, p. 72; Delbrück, p. 205. Cahen,

'Moslem Sources', cites Ibn al-Adim, Sibt, Qalansi and Matthew, fn. p. 629.

4. Attaleiates, p. 151.
5. Fuller, p. 397.
6. Principal original sources on the events in this chapter are Attaleiates, Scylitzes (himself relying very heavily on Attaleiates), Psellus, Bryennius, Bar Hebraeus, Matthew of Edessa and Aristakes.
7. Psellus, Book VII, p. 9.
8. Attaleiates, p. 146.
9. Scylitzes, pp. 689–90.
10. Attaleiates, pp. 147–8.
11. Matthew, p. 166.
12. Bryennius, Book I, XIII.
13. Ostrogorsky, fn. p. 351.
14. Matthew, pp. 165–6.
15. The episode is summarized by Cahen, 'Moslem Sources', p. 627.
16. Bryennius, Book I, XIV.
17. *Ibid.*, Book I, XIII, p. 511.
18. *Ibid.*, Book I, XIV, p. 514.
19. For example, Oman, *Art of War*, p. 127.
20. Attaleiates, p. 150.
21. *Ibid.*, p. 153.
22. Sümer and Sevim, *passim*.
23. Ibid., quoting Ibn al-Adim, Sibt and Bundari, *passim*.
24. Gibbon outlines such an ancestry, Vol. 3, fn.p. 402.
25. Attaleiates, p. 158.
26. Bryennius, Book I, XIV.
27. For a careful discussion of them and their varying degrees of credibility see Cahen, 'Moslem Sources', and Sümer and Sevim, *passim*.
28. Ramazan Şeşen, 'Alp Arslanın Hayati Ile Ilgili Arapça Kaynaklar' ('Arabic Sources dealing with the Life of Alp Arslan'), translated by Zeyneb Uşakligil, (unpublished MS), *Turkiyat Mecmusi*, Vol. 17, Ankara, 1972, pp. 101–12.
29. Bryennius, Book I, XV, XVII.
30. Attaleiates, p. 154.
31. Bryennius, Book I, XIV.
32. Attaleiates, p. 156.
33. *Ibid.*, pp. 156–7.
34. *Ibid.*, p. 157.
35. Marguerite Mathieu, 'Une Source Negligée de la Bataille de Mantzikert', *Byzantion*, Vol. 20, 1950.
36. Bar Hebraeus, p. 220.

37. Attaleiates, p. 160.
38. Bryennius, Book I, XVI.
39. Oman, *Art of War*, p. 217.
40. Feridun Dirimtekin, 'Selçukluların Anadolu'da Yerleşmelerini ve Gelişmelerini Sağlayan Iki Zafer' ('The Two Victories that Enabled the Seljuks to Settle and Progress in Anatolia'), translated by JoAnne Noonan Gümüs (unpublished MS), *Malazgirt Armağani*, Ankara, 1972, pp. 231–58.
41. Bryennius, Book I, XVII.
42. *Ibid.*, Book I, XVI.
43. *Ibid.*, Book I, XVII.
44. Attaleiates, p. 161.
45. *Ibid.*
46. *Ibid.*, pp. 162–3.
47. Vryonis, quoting Michael the Syrian, *Decline*, p. 103.
48. Psellus, p. 356.
49. *Ibid.*
50. Bryennius, Book I, XVII.

11 *'All They that take the Sword . . .'*

1. Matthew of Edessa, p. 170.
2. Sümer and Sevim, citing Ibn al-Adim, Bundari and Sibt.
3. Scylitzes, p. 700.
4. Gibbon, Vol. 3, p. 403.
5. *Ibid.*, pp. 404–5.
6. Cahen, 'Moslem Sources', p. 636.
7. Sümer and Sevim; Cahen, 'Moslem Sources', *passim*.
8. Cahen, 'Moslem Sources', p. 638.
9. Psellus, Book VII, p. 18.
10. Bryennius, Book I, p. 20.
11. Psellus, Book VII, pp. 18–24.
12. See Sewter's footnote in Psellus, p. 360.
13. Bryennius, Book I, p. 22.
14. Cahen, 'Moslem Sources', pp. 639–40.
15. Bar Hebraeus, p. 223.
16. Scylitzes, p. 703.
17. Psellus, Book VII, p. 32.
18. Scylitzes, p. 704.
19. Psellus, Book VII, pp. 32–3.
20. Scylitzes, pp. 704–5.
21. Ostrogorsky, p. 345.
22. Şeşen, pp. 110–11.
23. Bar Hebraeus, p. 224.

24. Gibbon, Vol. 3, p. 405.
25. Matthew, p. 172.

12 ' . . . and yet I am mine own Executioner'

1. Quoted by Vryonis, 'Nomadization and Islamization in Asia Minor', *Dumbarton Oaks Papers No. 29*, 1975, from Eflaki's anecdotes about the 'Mevlana', founder of the Whirling Dervish order, pp. 70–1.
2. Laurent, p. 92.
3. The historical material of the period 1071 to 1095 in this chapter is taken from standard modern sources, principally Vryonis, *Decline*; Cahen, *Pre-Ottoman* and his chapter in *Setton*; Runciman, *Crusades*; Charanis in *Setton*; Ostrogorsky and Laurent.
4. Laurent, p. 93.
5. Cahen, *Pre-Ottoman*, p. 72.
6. Vryonis provides a lucid and economical account, *Decline*, pp. 103–13.
7. Runciman, *Crusades*, p. 67.
8. Ostrogorsky, p. 345.
9. Vryonis, *Decline*, p. 113.
10. Cahen, *Pre-Ottoman*, p. 76.
11. Anna Comnena, Book VII, p. 11.

13 Contra Paganos

1. Bernold's report on the Council of Piacenza, *Monumenta Germaniae Historica*, ss., Vol. V.
2. Jenkins, *Eve*, p. 3.
3. See Charanis, 'The Byzantine Empire in the Eleventh Century', in *Setton*, p. 213.
4. Carl Erdmann, *Die Entstehung des Kreuzzugsgedankens*, Stuttgart, 1935; English translation by Marshall W. Baldwin and Walter Goffart, *The Origin of the Idea of Crusade*, Princeton, 1977, p. 168.
5. Jenkins, *Eve*, p. 3.
6. Anna Comnena, Book VIII, p. 5.
7. See Frederic Duncalf, 'The Councils of Piacenza and Clermont', in *Setton*, p. 228.
8. Runciman's exposition is to be found in his *Crusades*, pp. 79, 91–2, and his 'The Pilgrimages to Palestine Before 1095', in *Setton*, pp. 73–8.

9. For an account, see Einar Joranson, 'The Great German Pilgrimage of 1064–65', *The Crusades and Other Historical Essays* presented to D. C. Munro, New York, 1928.
10. Runciman, *Crusades*, p. 50.
11. *Ibid.*, p. 37.
12. Gibbon, Vol. 3, p. 420.
13. Duncalf, *Setton*, p. 243.
14. The coffin nail metaphor is that of Professor Andrew S. Ehrenkreutz.

Bibliography

Medieval Sources

CHRISTIAN

Aristakes of Lastivert, *History of Armenia*, French translation from the Armenian by M. Canard and Haïg Berberian, Editions de Byzantion, Brussels, 1973.

Attaleiates, Michael, *Histories, CSHB*, Vol. 50, English translation pp. 93–161 by Fr George T. Dennis sj. (unpublished ms); French translation pp. 151–66 by Emile Janssens, *Anneraire de l'Institute de Philologie et d'Histoire Orientales et Slaves*, Vol. 20, 1968–72.

Bar Hebraeus (Gregory Abù'l Faraj), *Chronography*, translated by Ernest A. Wallis Budge, Oxford, 1932.

Bryennius, Nicephorus, *Histories, CSHB*, Vol. 26, French translation by Henri Grégoire, *Byzantion*, Vol. 23, 1953, pp. 55–7.

Comnena, Anna, *The Alexiad*, Vols 39–40, translated by E. R. A. Sewter, Penguin Books, London, 1969.

Matthew of Edessa, *Chronicles*, French translation by Eduard Dulaurier, Paris, 1858.

Michael the Syrian, *Chronicles*, French translation by J. B. Chabot, Paris, 1905.

Polo, Marco, *Travels*, translated by William Marsden, re-edited by Thomas Wright, New York, 1948.

Psellus, Michael, *Chronography*, translated by E. R. A. Sewter, London, 1935.

Scylitzes, John, *Brevarium Historicum*, English translation by R. David Kovacs (unpublished ms), *CSHB*, Vol. 35, pp. 659–705.

William of Tyre, *A History of Deeds Done Beyond the Sea*, translated by E. A. Babcock and A. C. Krey, New York, 1943.

ISLAMIC

Idrisi (Abu 'Abd Allah Muhammed), *Geography*, French translation by P. Amédée Jaubert, Paris, 1936.

Ibn Fadlan, Ahmad, *The Risala*, translated with notes by Robert P. Blake and Richard N. Frye, *Byzantina Metabyzantina*, Vol. I, Part II, New York, 1949.

Additionally:

Lewis, Geoffrey, *The Book of Dede Korkut*, Introduction and translation, Penguin Books, London, 1974.

Şeşen, Ramazan, 'Alp Arslan' ın Hayatı Ile Ilgili Arapça Kaynaklar' (Arabian Sources dealing with the Life of Alp Arslan; summaries in Turkish translation), *Türkiyat Mecmusi*, Vol. 17, Ankara. English translation by Zeyneb Uşakligil (unpublished ms).

Sumer, Faruk and Sevim, Ali, 'Islam Kaynaklarına Malazgirt Savaşı' (The Battle of Manzikert According to Islamic Sources), Turkish Historical Association, Ankara, 1971. English translation by Armağan Tranter (unpublished ms).

Later works

Andréadès, André, 'Economic Life', *Baynes and Moss*.

Barthold, Vasily V., *Histoire des Turcs d'Asie Centrale* (cited as *Histoire*), French adaptation by M. Donskis, Paris, 1945.

—*Turkestan Down to the Mongol Invasion* (cited as *Turkestan*), 3rd edn E. J. W. Gibb Memorial Trust, 1968.

Baştav, Şerif, 'La Bataille Rangee de Malazgirt et Romain Diogène', Cultura Turcica, Ankara, 1971–3.

Brehier, Louis, *L'Eglise et l'Orient au Moyen Age*, Paris, 1921.

Burke, Edmund, *The History of Archery*, London, 1958.

de Busbecq, Ogier Ghiselin, *The Turkish Letters*, translated by Edward Seymour Forster, Oxford, 1927.

Cahen, Claude, '*La campagne de Manzikert d'après des sources Musselmanes*' (cited as 'Moslem Sources'), *Byzantion*, Vol. 9, 1934.

—'*La Première Pénétration Turque en Asie-Mineur*' (cited as '*Penetration*'), *Byzantion*, Vol. 18, 1948.

—*Pre-Ottoman Turkey* (cited as *Pre-Ottoman*), translated by J. Jones-Williams, New York, 1968.

—'The Turkish Invasion, The Selchükids', *Setton*.

Campbelk, G. A., *The Crusades*, London, 1935.

Canard, Marius, 'Byzantium and the Muslim World to the Middle of the Eleventh Century', *CMH*.

—'*La Campagne Arménienne du Sultan Salguqide Alp Arslan et la*

Prise d'Ani en 1064' (cited as 'Armenian Campaign'), *Revue des Études Arméniennes*, II, Paris, 1965.

Chadwick, Nora K. and Zhirmunsky, Victor, *Oral Epics of Central Asia*, C.U.P., 1969.

Chalandon, Ferdinand, *Histoire de la Première Croisade*, Paris, 1925.

Charanis, Peter, 'Byzantium, the West and the Origin of the First Crusade', *Byzantion*, Vol. 19, 1949.

—'Economic Factors in the Decline of the Byzantine State (cited as 'Economic Factors'), *Journal of Economic History*, Vol. 13, No. 4, Wilmington, Del, 1953.

—'The Byzantine Empire in the Eleventh Century', *Setton*.

Cirac, Estopañan Sebastian, *Skyllitzes Matritensis, Reproductions y Minituras*, Barcelona, 1965.

Clauson, Gerard, *Turkish and Mongolian Studies*, London, 1962.

Czaplicka, M. A., *The Turks of Central Asia in History and at the Present Day*, O.U.P., 1918.

Delbrück, Hans, *Geschichte der Kriegskunst in Rahmen der Politischen Geschichte*, Vol. 3, Berlin, 1907.

Der Nersessian, Sirarpie, *Armenia and the Byzantine Empire* (cited as *Armenia*), Harvard, 1945.

—'Armenia in the Tenth and Eleventh Centuries', *Proceedings of the XIIIth International Conference on Byzantine Studies*, Oxford, 1967.

Dirimtekin, Feridun, 'Selçuklularin Anadolu'da Yerleşmelerini ve Gelişmelerini Sağlayan Iki Zafer' ('The Two Victories that Enabled the Seljuks to Settle and Progress in Anatolia'), translated by JoAnne Noonan Gümüş (unpublished MS), *Malazgirt Armağani*, Ankara, 1972.

Diehl, Charles, *Byzance, Grandeur et Décadence*, Paris, 1919.

Duncalf, Frederic, 'The Councils of Piacenza and Clermont, *Setton*.

Ellis Davidson, H. R. 'The Secret Weapon of Byzantium', *Byzantinisches Zeitschrift*, Vol. 66, 1973, pp. 61–74.

Ensslin, Wilhelm, 'The Emperor and the Imperial Administration', *Baynes and Moss*.

Erdmann, Carl, *Die Entstehung des Kreuzzugsgedankens*, Stuttgart, 1935; English translation, *The Origin of the Idea of Crusade*, by Marshall W. Baldwin and Walter Goffart, Princeton, 1977.

Finlay, George, *A History of Greece: The Byzantine and Greek Empires*, Part II, O.U.P., 1877.

Fuller, J. F. C., *The Decisive Battles of the Western World*, Vol. I. London, 1954.

Gibb, Hamilton A. R., 'The Caliphate and the Arab States', *Setton*.

Gibbon, Edward, *The History of the Decline and Fall of the Roman Empire*, 1776–88, Modern Library Edition, New York, 3 Vols.

Grégoire, H., 'The Amorians and the Macedonians', *CMH*.

Grimley, Gordon, *The Book of the Bow*, London, 1958.

Grousset, René, *The Empire of the Steppes*, 1939–52, translated by Naomi Walford, Rutgers, New Jersey, 1970.

Haddon, J. and Byrne, M., 'A Possible Solution to the Problem of Greek Fire', *Byzantinisches Zeitschrift*, Vol. 70, 1977, pp. 91–9.

Hamadani, Abbas, 'A Possible Fatimid Background to the Battle of Manzikert', *Tarih Araştırmaları Dergisi*, Ankara, 1968.

—'Byzantine-Fatimid Relations Before the Battle of Manzikert', *Byzantine Studies*, Vol. 1, Pittsburgh, 1974.

Hamidullah, M., 'Map of the Battle of Manzikert', *Islamic Culture*, Vol. 19, Hyderabad, 1945.

Hoffmeyer, Ada Bruhn, 'Military Equipment in the Byzantine Manuscript of Scylitzes', *Gladius*, Vol. V, Granada (Spain), 1966.

Honigmann, Ernst, *Die Ostgrenze des Byzantinischen Reiches, corpus Bruxellense Hist. Byz.* III, Brussels, 1935.

Hussey, J. M., 'The Later Macedonians, the Comneni and the Angeli', *CMH*.

Janssens, Emile, 'Le Lac de Van et la Stratégie Byzantine', *Byzantion*, Vol. 42, 1972, pp. 388–404.

Jenkins, R. J. H., *The Byzantine Empire on the Eve of the Crusades* (cited as *Eve*), London 1953.

—'The Amorians and the Macedonians' (completion of chapter), *CMH*.

—*The Imperial Centuries*, London, 1966.

Joranson, Einar, 'The Great German Pilgrimage of 1064–1065', *The Crusades and Other Historical Essays Presented to D. C. Munro*, New York, 1928.

—'The problem of the spurious letter of Emperor Alexius to the Count of Flanders', *American Historical Review*, Vol. IV, No. 4, New York, 1950.

Klopsteg, Paul E., *Turkish Archery and the Composite Bow*, Evanston, Illinois, 1934.

Kaegi, Walter Emil, Jr, 'The Contribution of Archery to the Turkish Conquest of Anatolia', *Speculum*, Cambridge, Mass., January, 1964.

Kafesoglu, Ibrahim, 'The Battle of Manzikert', translated by Armağan Tranter (unpublished MS), *Türk Ansiklopdisi*, Vol. 7, 1955.

Kaymaz, Nejat, 'Malazgirt Savaşı ile Anadolu'nun Fethi ve Türkleşmesine Dair' ('The Battle of Manzikert and Conquest and Turkization of Anatolia'), translated by JoAnne Noonan Gümüş (unpublished MS), *Malazgirt Armağani*, Ankara, 1972.

Kortepeter, Carl Max, 'The Origins and Nature of Turkish Power', *Tarih Araştımaları Dergisi*, Ankara, 1968.

Köymen, Mehmet Altay, *Alp Arslan Zamanı Selçuklu Askeri Teşkilatı* (Military Organization of the Seljuks at the Time of Alp Arslan), translated by Zeyneb Uşakligil (unpublished MS), University of Ankara, 1967.

—'The Importance of the Malazgirt Victory with Special Reference to Iran and Turkey', *Journal of the Regional Cultural Institute*, Vol. 5, No. 1, Ankara, 1972.

—'Selçuklu Devrinin Özellikleri' ('Characteristics of the Seljuk Period'), translated by Zeyneb Uşakligil, (unpublished MS), *Atsız Armağnı*, Istanbul, 1976.

Lattimore, Owen, *Studies in Frontier History*, OUP, 1962.

Laurent, J., *Byzance et les Turcs Seljoucides, dans l'Asie Occidentale jusqu'en 1081*, Paris, 1913.

Lebeau, Charles, *Histoire du Bas-Empire*, Paris, 1833.

Lewis, Bernard, *The Emergence of Modern Turkey*, London, 1961.

Lewis, Raphaela, *Everyday Life in Ottoman Turkey*, London, 1971.

Lot, Ferdinand, *L'Art Militaire et les Armées*, Paris, 1946.

Luttwak, Edward N., *The Grand Strategy of the Roman Empire*, Johns Hopkins, Baltimore, Md., 1976.

Mango, Andrew, *Turkey*, London, 1968.

Mathieu, Margaret, 'Une Source Negligée de la Bataille de Mantzikert', *Byzantion*, Vol. 20, 1950.

McEvedy, Colin, *The Penguin Atlas of Medieval History*, Penguin Books, London, 1961

Munro, D. C., 'Did the Emperor Alexius Ask for Aid at the Council of Piacenza, 1095?', *American Historical Review*, Vol. 27, New York, 1922.

Oman, C. W. C., *The Byzantine Empire*, London, 1898.

—*A History of the Art of War in the Middle Ages*, 2nd edn, London, 1924.

Ostrogorsky, George, *History of the Byzantine State*, translated by Joan Hussey, 2nd edn, 1968, Oxford.

Payne-Gallwey, Ralph, *A Summary of the History, Construction and Effects in Warfare of the Projectile-Throwing Engines of the Ancients, plus a Treatise on the Structure, Power and Management of Turkish and Other Oriental Bows*, London, 1907.

Ramsay, W. M., 'The War of Moslem and Christian for the Possession of Asia Minor', *Studies in the History of Art in the Eastern Provinces of the Asia Minor*, Aberdeen, 1906.

—'Intermixture of Races in Asia Minor', *Proceedings of the British Acadamy*, 1916.

Runciman, Steven, *Byzantine Civilization*, London, 1933.

—*A History of the Crusades*, Vol. 1 (cited as *Crusades*), CUP, 1951.

—'The Pilgrimages to Palestine before 1095', *Setton*.

Sevim, Ali, 'Malazgirt Meydan Savaşı ve Sonuçları' ('The Battle of Manzikert and its Outcome'), translated by JoAnne Noonan Gümüş (unpublished MS), *Malazgirt Armağani*, Ankara, 1972.

Smail, R. C., *Crusading Warfare*, C.U.P., 1956.

Stark, Freya, *Rome on the Euphrates*, London, 1960.

Sümer, Faruk, 'The Turks in Eastern Asia Minor', *Proceedings of the XIIIth International Conference on Byzantine Studies*, Oxford, 1967.

Taeschner, F., 'The Turks and the Byzantine Empire to the End of the Thirteenth Century', *CMH*.

Toumanoff, C., 'Armenia and Georgia', *CMH*.

—'Background to Manzikert', *Proceedings of the XIIIth International Conference on Byzantine Studies*, Oxford, 1967.

Vyronis, Spyros, Jr, *Byzantium and Europe*, London, 1967.

—*The Decline of Medieval Hellenism in Asia Minor and the Process of Islamization from the Seventh through the Fifteenth Century* (cited as *Decline*), University of California, Los Angeles, 1971.

—'Nomadization and Islamization in Asia Minor', *Dumbarton Oaks Papers*, No. 29, 1975.

Walker, Warren S. and Uysal, Ahmet E., *Tales Alive in Turkey*, Harvard, 1966.

Wittek, Paul, 'Deux Chapitres de l'Histoire des Turcs de Roum', *Byzantion*, Vol. 11, 1936.

Index